BREAKS

IN THE

AIR

THE   BIRTH   OF

DUKE UNIVERSITY PRESS

BREAKS IN

RAP   RADIO   IN

DURHAM + LONDON

THE AIR

NEW   YORK   CITY

2022

JOHN KLAESS

© 2022 DUKE UNIVERSITY PRESS
All rights reserved
Printed in the United States of
America on acid-free paper ∞
Project editor: Lisa Lawley
Designed by Matthew Tauch
Typeset in Untitled Serif and ITC
Officina Sans by Westchester
Publishing Services

Library of Congress Cataloging-in-
Publication Data
Names: Klaess, John, [date] author.
Title: Breaks in the air : the birth of rap
radio in New York City / John Klaess.
Description: Durham : Duke University
Press, 2022. | Includes bibliographical
references and index.
Identifiers: LCCN 2021059695 (print)
LCCN 2021059696 (ebook)
ISBN 9781478016236 (hardcover)
ISBN 9781478018872 (paperback)
ISBN 9781478023500 (ebook)
Subjects: LCSH: Rap (Music)—New
York (State)—New York—History
and criticism. | African American radio
stations—New York (State)—New
York. | Radio stations—New York
(State)—New York—History. | Radio
broadcasting—Deregulation—New York
(State)—New York. | Radio in popular
culture—New York (State)—New York. |
BISAC: MUSIC / Genres & Styles / Rap
& Hip Hop | SOCIAL SCIENCE / Ethnic
Studies / American / African American
& Black Studies
Classification: LCC ML3531 .K613
2022 (print) | LCC ML3531 (ebook) |
DDC 782.42164909747/275—dc23/
eng/20220627
LC record available at https://lccn.loc.
gov/2021059695
LC ebook record available at https://lccn.
loc.gov/2021059696

Cover art: DJ Mr. Magic (left) and
Marley Marl on air at WBLS-FM
107.5, October 21, 1983, New York.
Photo by Michael Ochs Archive/
Getty Images.

FOR

ANN + RICHARD

CONTENTS

I wrote most of this book while listening to the radio. Public radio has been a constant companion, a sober voice in our increasingly insane times. And the dial—yes, it's still a dial—in my car was reliably tuned to Hot 97, a way of keeping up with hip-hop radio in the present as I plunged deeper into its past. But I wasn't always listening to radio in the sense we tend to imagine it. Just as often it was MP3s of historical broadcasts of rap radio, downloaded or ripped from the internet or acquired from tape collectors generous enough to share their quarry. Other times it was live web streams from the outskirts and undergrounds of New York or London or Los Angeles or Manchester or any of the burgeoning world capitals of dance music, uncanny in the resemblance they bear to the underground programs of the 1980s. It's been a long time since radio was limited to the canonical form it takes in our imagination, if it ever was just that. Still, one thing connects these disparate broadcasts: they all express their time and place in sound, inimitably.

This book is the story of one such time and one such place, New York City in the 1980s. It's about how a group of DJs, entrepreneurs, and fans took an art form rooted in vinyl, aerosol, and the body and converted it into FM waves. All historians think their time period is exceptional, and I'm no exception. Few places have hosted a convergence of so many of their era's defining themes as New York in the last quarter of the twentieth century. Individuals and institutions; policy and politics; race and space; class and status; sound and subjectivity—it's all there. Historians have variously described the 1980s as a period of "fracture" and as a period of "synthesis." The history of rap radio shows that both characterizations are true.

Listening to the history of rap radio can show us how, for better and for worse, popular culture and politics collided in 1980s America.

What I want to demonstrate by examining radio is something that, on the surface, seems obvious: that rap didn't enter the recording studio a fully formed genre. Its success was never predestined and, as intrinsically appealing as rap can be, its audiences were constructed over time, not present from the jump. The argument that I make throughout this book is that radio played an instrumental role in the aesthetic, social, and commercial development of hip-hop. It helped make the genre what it is. The horizon of this argument might be expressed simply: no radio, no rap. In practical terms, unpacking a formulation as nebulous as "rap radio" means looking outside and around both rap and radio. Radio, like few other mediums, is impacted by the tides of the times. National politics matter. Radio is heavily regulated by the federal government, meaning that who can access radio and what can be broadcast is limited by rules the FCC and legislators establish during any given administration. Further, radio is a cutthroat industry, and audience demand for particular kinds of music and types of information determines what goes on the air. A station's life and death can be determined by how well its management and programming staff understand the tastes and desires of those on the other end of the receiver. And radio is public in ways that few mediums are. For the last century, radio has been one of the most widely used communications mediums in the world, found in the homes and automobiles of the richest and poorest in America alike, in the largest cities to the most remote outposts. Which is all to say that writing a history of radio—no less rap radio—means cueing in to how all of these forces bore on those sending breakbeats through the air.

What does this mean in practice? It means that the history of rap radio isn't just one of DJs and MCs in the studio—though most of this book is devoted to following them into the studio and to listening closely to their broadcasts. It's also a history of Reagan-era regulatory policy. It's a history of post–civil rights activism. It's a history of the music industry and the deep historical will to commodify Black sound and Black expressive labor. It's a history of individuals finding a public source for self-expression in the fecund ruins of postindustrial New York City.

I want to take this time set the stage for the stories that follow for two reasons. First, one of my goals has been to expand what histories of radio and histories of hip-hop can be. This book would not be complete without attending to the unique mix of social, musical, technological, political, commercial, and individual histories all converging on the radio studio. I want this history to be a model of the kinds of stories that are available when we place the medium at the center. The second reason is to set expectations. This book is about hip-hop in the 1980s. That's why we're all here. But in order to tell the story I wanted to tell, I had to take the time to outline the social and political stakes of the era. So, while a chapter-length treatment of, say, broadcast deregulation might not seem relevant, to leave it out would be to ignore a force that inarguably shaped hip-hop (it also seemed particularly appropriate to our current moment to linger on the incipient merger of information and entertainment in American mass media). Same goes for the passages detailing radio ratings methodologies and advances in broadcast marketing strategy. It's obvious to the point of meaninglessness to say music never exists in a vacuum, but it bears repeating.

I also need to acknowledge that this history is not "complete." Old school hip-hop heads and information fiends will notice some glaring omissions: the World's Famous Supreme Team doesn't get nearly enough attention; Hank Love and DNA are in the background, but never the fore; the students who broadcast hip-hop at New York University's WNYU-FM, as well as students at Columbia University's WKCR-FM, Hofstra University's WRHU-FM, and Fordham University's WFUV-FM, and the rest of the students who brought their energy and talent to putting rap music on college radio are conspicuously absent; the underground post-punk and downtown mix shows that incorporated rap barely missed the temporal cutoff point; I only gesture at the fact that Public Enemy, among many other artists, got their start in radio at Adelphi University's WBAU-FM, and the group's Bomb Squad credit radio as an inspiration for their production strategies. No doubt readers and fans will find others. And this is just where radio hosts are concerned. When you start expanding the field of omissions out to the station workers, the friends, the mothers, and everyone else who played midwife to hip-hop, the field of possible histories expands infinitely. Not to mention that this history played out differently in cities across the United States and across the world. At an early stage in writing, I was drawn to this project as one of "completing" hip-hop history, of adding new voices and individuals to the mix, only later to realize how naïve that was. Still, histories of rap have privileged recording artists and gravitated toward a few highly public figureheads. Those without lengthy discographies or cultivated public personas didn't always receive as much credit as they deserved—all in all a different kind of historical distortion. In one of our first conversations, DJ Chuck Chillout told me that he would consent to an interview because "a lot of guys are getting left out." He's right. Rap has a pantheon and a canon. I hope this history has broadened, if only a little, the kinds of stories that constitute hip-hop and radio history.

No rap radio show was complete without shout-outs. Fittingly, I have a few of my own:

I want to first thank all of those who shared their time and stories with me. Shout-out to Chuck Chillout, Teddy Tedd, Special K, Daddy-O, Kool Keith, Wanda Ramos, Jay Dixon, and Dutch. These interviews are the core of this history, and I hope you all recognize your experiences in the text. I want to give special thanks to DJ Chuck Chillout, who granted an interview to a clueless graduate student in the winter of 2014, and whose generosity propelled this project forward at a crucial crossroads, and to Teddy Tedd, who provided insight, constructive criticism, and conversation about the project over a period of several years.

A round of gratitude is due to all of the folk historians and tape collectors who've worked so tirelessly to preserve this history. Thank you for documenting it. Thank you for your generosity in sharing it. Thank you for continuing to fight against loss. Your labors haven't gone unnoticed or unappreciated.

Marissa Glynias and Kirill Zikanov each provided detailed and insightful commentary on a number of chapters at multiple stages. The final document is immeasurably better for their care. Thank you to those who commented and started conversations following presentations of this work at meetings of the Society for Ethnomusicology; American Musicological Society; AMS-New England; and the AMS Popular Music Special Interest Group, for helping me see the project from fresh angles.

Gundula Kreuzer deserves special thanks for her assiduous readings and generous suggestions.

Shout-out to the Sound Studies working group. Thank you for helping me hear media history and auditory culture more capaciously.

Shout-out to the Black Sound and the Archive Working Group. To say this group has helped me think through the crucial themes of this book would be an understatement. BSAW has felt like a long-sought intellectual home, and I'm constantly impressed by the intelligence and creativity in that space. A special thanks to Daphne Brooks and Brian Kane for making it happen.

New Haven Regular Singers: thank you for your voices and community.

A warm shout-out to Mark Rodgers, Peter Selinsky, George Overton, and Evan Henry for their conversation and support.

Thank you to the Music Department softball team, for reminding me what it means to win (even as we lose consistently, badly).

A big thank you to Michael Veal, who has been in dialogue with this project since its inception. Thank you for your engagement, your encouragement, and your direction. For reminding me why we write, and who we write for. And to Brian Kane and Michael Denning, who read most of this manuscript and provided invaluable feedback.

Shout out to Ken Wissoker and everyone who contributed to this book at Duke University Press. The published book is much, much better than the manuscript I first submitted, and it's only so because of their work, expertise, and professionalism.

To all my family, extended and immediate.

To Ariana Hackenburg, for her friendship, support, and patience.

Finally, to Ann and Richard Klaess, without whom none of this would be possible. Thank you.

Introduction
Breaks in the Air

June 1982—2 AM, and receivers tuned to 105.9-FM anywhere in the greater New York metropolitan area return a low, steady hum of static. The previous hour's program of Jamaican roots reggae and dub versions has ceased transmission, and the next broadcasters have yet to populate the airwaves. White noise: signal in the form of absence laden with possibility. Radio silence: an intermission potent with the desire for presence, communication.

Moments pass, and the static abides. From within this tensing anticipation, a voice comes over the airwaves, stumbling before finding its cadence:

"It's world . . . this is the *World's Famous Supreme Team Show*! My name is Just Allah the Super Star here with my main man. . . ."

"And y'all know who I am. It's Se'Divine the Mastermind. And that's right, you get up *right now* and wake up everybody you know. Even if you don't know them, still wake them up! Knock on everything, because we got something we got to tell you all tonight so be . . . up. . . ."

Anyone listening closely to this broadcast may have heard a slight "click" coinciding with Se'Divine's enunciation of "tonight." Just as well, most probably missed it. As the DJ urges his listeners to rouse their households and relations, he sets a cassette in motion.

The tape dispenses a heavy groove, and the transmission comes alive, pulsates along with the kick drum and low-string vibrato. In form, the Supreme Team could be at any park or club jam in New York, exhorting an audience into action over a disco arrangement repeated back onto itself. In delivery, however, their address is tailored to radio, implicitly commanding their audience to listen across space. The groove lingers, and Just Allah continues with an enthusiasm at odds with the late hour:

"So everybody get up and let the world know that the World's Famous Supreme Team is on the air!"

Se'Divine adds, "If you are incarcerated at this time, don't you forget that we are still thinking about you! So send us some letters in here at 80 Riverside Drive. . . ."

"And get your tape recorders ready because the Supreme Team is going to rock the house tonight, for you!"

Animated by the insistent beat and the imagined presence of an audience tuned in from bedrooms, backrooms, and in-between spaces across New York, the duo continues their introductory remarks. Shout-out "to all of the Gods and Earths." All you artists out there, keep sending your tapes because "four or five studios" are monitoring the broadcast. And if you're tuned in "only to find fault," "you ain't going to find nothing."

"How about some World's Famous enlightenment?" Se'Divine asks, and the mix show begins in earnest with the first cut of the evening, an original sung-rapped setting of the 5-Percenter credo "The Enlightener" to a mid-tempo disco groove à la "Rapper's Delight."

"Welcome to the *World's Famous Supreme Team Show* on WHBI 105.9-FM. . . . We are officially on the air."[1]

Sign-On

At the time of this 1982 broadcast, Se'Divine the Mastermind and Just Allah the Superstar of the World's Famous Supreme Team counted among a small cohort of DJs and independent radio hosts who adapted live hip-hop to the sound medium. Leasing one to two hours each week on New York's open-format WHBI-FM, DJs like the Supreme Team brought the street to the studio, so to speak, converting the full range of hip-hop's musical, verbal, and social stylings into broadcast programming.

Yet the DJs and hosts on WHBI were hardly the only broadcasters captivated by the ways rap music and hip-hop culture might be adapted to radio. Between 1979 and 1987, an unlikely assembly of individuals sought to present rap and hip-hop within the strictures of broadcast sound. These individuals came from divergent positions in life (from vaunted civil rights activists to investment bankers to hip-hop crews from the Bronx River Houses to kids from the Jersey suburbs); they maintained contrasting relationships to the broadcasting industry (from station owner to DJ to program director to independent broadcaster); and they upheld distinct, often incommensurable attachments to the music and culture that proved the source of so much energy and investment during 1980s. Despite these differences, these individuals shared visions of prosperity in which the broadcast of rap music represented both a means and an end. Their efforts turned the radio studio into a space of possibility and conflict, a site for community representation and zone of encounter across difference. Their reimagination of hip-hop through broadcast media fractured the bedrock of popular music and created new possibilities for African American cultural and political expression in the late twentieth century.

This book is a history of the broadcast of rap music in New York between 1979 and 1987, the period spanning the release of the first commercial single to feature rapping to the advent of what historians and fans alike refer to as the "golden era" of hip-hop, though the narrative necessarily extends back into the 1970s and forward toward the 1990s.[2] It's helpful to think of this period as rap's nascent commercial era, the aperture through which the expressive cultures of Black and Latinx teens intersected the music and media industries to explosive effect. During this interval, a few important things happened. For one, rap music emerged as a recognizable musical genre. Prior to the early 1980s, hip-hop was a live, embodied practice. When the first hip-hop artists went into the studios, there were no scripts for what a rap record should sound like. Though the genre remained unwieldy by mid-decade, it didn't take long before trade publications, record labels, and the listening public understood rap as a coherent musical-cultural force. Not least because of these records, round about the mid-1980s rap became a viable commodity within the global music and culture industries, complete with a new wave of corporate sponsors and branding opportunities. Still, it's one thing to press records and another thing to sell them. Across the 1980s labels and entrepreneurs proved you could do both. After years of experimentation and adolescent exuberance, by 1987 rap music had gained such commercial and creative momentum that the years that followed mark a coming of age. By the close of the 1980s, rap had reached a period of commercial, musical, and institutional maturity.

But this maturation didn't occur suddenly, and it was by no means inevitable. This stretch of hip-hop history is instructive in part because so much was up for grabs. A network of fine cracks crazed the surface of American culture. As Daniel Rodgers has aptly described, it seemed as if the social fabric and time were simultaneously "fragmenting and accelerating."[3] Foregrounding these competing forces of dissolution and quickening helps us key into the contingency at work here. For example, multiple strains of hip-hop competed for a limited number of record deals and scant access to airplay, even as the long-term commercial prospects for the music remained uncertain. If we look outside hip-hop toward broader trends in telecommunications, profound transformations set in motion by deregulation destabilized a previously steadfast broadcasting industry. These transformations in the industry were themselves paralleled by neoliberal social and economic reforms that imperiled minority communities in new and pernicious ways, spurring the demonization of those same communities across a range of popular media (think, for example, of Reagan's "welfare queen," or the difference in crack vs. powder cocaine sentencing). At no point was it certain that this minority youth music would gain popular acceptance on its own sonic merits (unless, of course, you're a proponent of the argument that America will cannibalize any and all Black culture, that hip-hop was always already doomed to be the United States' most valuable twentieth-century export).[4] Nor was it at any point certain what such a music would sound like. Radio, sitting at the nexus where these strains join, gives us a way of dramatizing the connections between the social, the sonic, and the technological. In short, radio provides a lens through which to reconsider the intertwined histories of sounds, institutions, communities, and legal formations converging in the post–civil rights conjuncture.

But what can radio tell us about this period that the canonical histories of hip-hop have not?[5] While historians have helped us understand radio as a broad force in rap's commercialization, most histories simply take radio for granted in the same way that we take the medium for granted in our daily lives; it's both everywhere and nowhere, and thus not worth paying a lot of attention to. The practices, technologies, and institutions that supported every broadcast remain far from attention. What might happen if we place them in the center? Putting pressure on the medium itself allows us to tell new stories about this period in both musical and African American history. But finding these stories demands first that we listen. What opportunities did musicians and cultural brokers like the Supreme Team see in community radio? Similarly, what about rap music appealed to the owners and managers of New York commercial radio institutions WBLS-FM and WRKS-FM? And what can we learn from the decisions they made, from the sounds and perspectives they privileged in their broadcasts?

The key here is to think of radio as more than a channel for the dissemination of rap records. Uncovering the significance of radio to early hip-hop necessitates attention to the set of musical, social, and economic adjustments stations and broadcasters made to convert the live performance culture of hip-hop into broadcast programming. To remain attuned to this process, I focus on how individuals adapted hip-hop to broadcast media rather than simply on rap radio—though, as a disclaimer, I use *rap radio* as shorthand throughout. This emphasis on process allows us to attend to agency and creative choices instead of getting stuck in the ontological morass; it allows us to cue into change over time instead of fixing a static object. Scholars have recently gone so far as to question whether radio is, in fact, a single, unified medium. Instead, they offer the terms *assemblage*, *constellation*, *site*, and *field*, a vocabulary that emphasizes the ad hoc and unsettled, a language tailored to the ways in which aspects of radio can be either durable or malleable across contexts, connected to or discrete from other technologies and practices. Daniel Fisher and Lucas Bessire are exemplary when they remind us that "radio's boundaries . . . cannot easily be assumed *a priori*; its objectness is always potentially unsettled by shifting social practices, institutions, and technological innovations and by broader domains in which it finds shape, meaning, and power."[6] In foregrounding the process of adaptation in this book, I mean to query how broadcasters selected music for broadcast; how they altered it; what technologies aided and limited them; how they addressed the audience; the extent and type of audience participation; the vicissitudes of reception; what the public broadcast of this music and culture meant to young people of color in New York; and the tension between community and institutional aesthetic priorities. The histories entailed by these questions offer new perspectives on youth culture during the Reagan years, and provide an opportunity to revisit the timing and mechanics of rap's transition from a community-based art form into a global commercial phenomenon.

Perhaps the clearest consequence of the emphasis on adaption is that we hear the evolution of rap music with fresh ears. For one, radio forces us to attend to what listeners actually heard every week. When we listen to tapes of broadcasts from the 1980s, we hear recent rap releases, sure. But we also hear classic breakbeats and deep cuts from personal archives, snippets of live shows from tapes, amateur submissions, and the full range of community patter by all of the friends, girlfriends, fans, and family that nurtured this art form at a critical moment. Amid the social richness of broadcasts, radio allows us to evade the trap of discographic historiography and recuperate a shadow playlist lost to time— made as much of flesh and voice and magnetic tape as vinyl—forgotten in favor of a few tracks solidified in the amber of historical memory. Crucially, however, radio lets us hear the records DJs selected, as they played them. As the DJs I've spoken with repeated over and over, radio isn't like the club. You don't have to work a dance floor. On the radio, you can tinker. You can invent. What this means in practice is that radio DJs availed themselves of radio's unique technological and social affordances to experiment with sound. Mixing techniques, virtuosic turntablism, novel combinations of recorded sound, the progression of moods and tracks over time—DJs treated the radio studio as a sonic laboratory. There was no shortage of experimental parameters to tweak each week. Radio lets us hear the evolution of hip-hop in real time, changing imperceptibly but indelibly week to week.

Similarly, radio inflected the commercial trajectory of rap music in ways that are hard to account for and harder to quantify. Nevertheless, the harder you look, the closer radio is to the center of rap's economies. As labels signed more acts and pressed more records, they all turned to the hip-hop DJs with access to radio to promote their product. For an artist early in their career, getting a tape or a record on air was a sure way to get work. But to stop here would be to stop at the discographic. When it comes to rap's commercialization, radio helps us excavate the thousands of small enterprises that give birth to a genre. For hosts at WHBI, who funded their own programs, radio meant record pools, selling their audience to sponsors, and dozens of other hustles to keep their show on the air. Radio turns our attention to the inextricable link between the club and the airwaves, to the lines and connections that make a scene. And because radio in New York is big business, we see the pressures that any media organization faces start to bear on musical aesthetics. In short, radio lets us see all of the commercial activity that makes a musical economy, not just a record industry.

At its most basic level, radio is a communications technology. For as long as the medium has existed, folks have sent signals across the electromagnetic spectrum with or without hopes of reaching an auditor. Focusing on adaptation allows us to hear just how central radio audiences were to the evolution of rap music. While many histories of radio assume that broadcasts are unidirectional, proceeding from an active host to passive listeners, recent research in radio has worked outward from the assumption that audiences are never passive, and that communication in broadcasting flows both ways. Elena Razlogova has observed that the earliest network radio programs "unfolded as if in intimate conversation with their audiences," imbuing each program with the mark of the "listener's voice."[7] For anthropologists Daniel Fisher and Lucas Bessire it is an axiom that radio presents "a channel for two-way dialogues."[8] But we need not look to radio in other contexts to understand the ways in which radio in 1980s New York facilitated, even depended upon, dialogue between broadcaster and audience. We need only listen more carefully to the *World's Famous Supreme Team Show*. In the brief excerpt with which I opened this introduction, the Supreme Team suffuse their address with calls to action. The Supreme Team do not just ask their audience to listen, they ask them to record the program. They do not just shout-out their incarcerated fans, they also acknowledge their humanity and ask them to write letters. Throughout the broadcast, the Supreme Team implore listeners to call the station with their requests and dedications. They advertise an upcoming live performance, thus mobilizing populations across space, and remind fans that record labels are listening, providing an extra incentive to any artist with a demo tape to mail it to the station. Though comical in its overstatement, the Supreme Team's opening incitement that all listeners do what they can to wake New York and spread the word is indicative of how all parties to the broadcast understood the relationship between listener and broadcaster. Listeners were integral to the Supreme Team's broadcast programming and to the construction of the *World's Famous Supreme Team Show* as a social forum. Lines of communication were fluid, emanating from the studio, returning to it, and escaping, as it were, into the ether. As a site for the broadcast of a community-made and -based dance music, as a mode of spreading information, and as a space for performing and reaffirming social bonds that existed prior to and beyond the moment of broadcast, rap radio might best be thought of as a collaboration between broadcaster and listeners, as a community aesthetic project.

If the Supreme Team's opening gambit figures rap radio as a joint community undertaking, then how might we learn to locate this community within the sound of their transmissions? And what can we learn about the emergence and experience of rap music by emphasizing the participatory, social aspects of broadcasts? Just like the FM signal that carried their broadcasts, the Supreme Team were ambitious with regard to the audience they hoped to reach, and indifferent to the physical and social barriers that segregated populations across New York's urban geography. Had we listened deeper into their broadcast, we would have heard the Supreme Team's listeners shout-out their neighborhoods and their relations. We would have found ourselves interpellated by their address, and drawn into their performances of affiliation as they rattled off dedications to Herbie Herb ("We don't have time to play your tape this week, but we will soon"), Chocolate City, and hip-hop notables Butchie Butch, Jazzy Jay, Davy D, and the All Mighty Fly MCs. We would have heard them plug, on behalf of one listener, a party at Harlem's PS 154 Harriet Tubman. Their dedications continued for nearly ten minutes, and as they wound down, Se'Devine let callers deliver their own shout-outs on the air. First Tanya from Mount Vernon, then Sonya in Bed-Stuy. Listener Nefertiti gave a shout to "the Nation," Tre sent a message to all the "Gods out in the Bronx," and a caller who forgets to identify himself as he's rushed by the hosts gave peace to his crew, the "Killer Four Connection," listening in Brownsville, Brooklyn. Tuning in to the dispersion of these listeners across space, a phenomenon Alex Russo calls the "human geograph[ies] of radio reception," warrants nothing short of a reconfiguration of the architectural and affective terrain of New York.[9]

Shout-outs demonstrate that radio has the power to remake space.[10] The performance of shout-outs testifies to the ways listeners in New York used radio to load place names with emergent personal and community value, and to write and rewrite their communities into the urban landscape. But radio does not operate under the same logic as terrestrial communications. Within its broadcast range, radio blankets and penetrates built environments. Electromagnetic signals reside between and reflect off of the architectural spaces of urban environs, traversing with ease social and physical boundaries that inhibit human mobility. Radio, in a sense, is both omnipresent and nowhere. Though bound to the time of the broadcast, these signals are available to anyone willing to tune in to their frequencies. From this perspective, there is no center, and there are no margins, no metropole or periphery. There are instead spectral landscapes, layered atmospheres haunted by presences and absences that remap the city in ways that can upend hierarchies of spatialization and power.[11] Starting from the dispersed, ethereal geographies of radio signals saturating the rubble and wreckage that begins so many histories of hip-hop offers a new way of narrating New York. Communities come into being, effervesce, and dissolve nightly, serialized in the manner of weekly broadcasts. If window-shattering sound systems and graffiti provide important perspectives onto early hip-hop's politics of visibility (and audibility), so too does the use of broadcast media to re-sound and reimagine minority communities in the postindustrial city.

With this emphasis on audibility comes an important question: How can we move beyond metaphor and actually hear hip-hop's early communities? Christine Ehrick expresses a common sense of historiographical longing when she writes, "Those of us interested in radio's sound qualities often face the dilemma of analyzing and discussing voices that we may never get to hear. . . . We grope for ways to use words to tap the reader's aural imagination."[12] Despite a lack of institutional archives, the history of rap radio is an exception to this silence. Thanks to the efforts of fans, collectors, and artists over time, the history of rap radio in New York is exceptionally well represented by extant recordings of broadcasts. A quick internet search can return dozens of examples of the voices of Mr. Magic, Special K, or Afrika Islam. Anyone can enjoy hours of broadcasts by Chuck Chillout and Red Alert with a few clicks. Across the 1980s, listeners actively recorded transmissions of rap radio programs to cassette tapes. Many recorded these tapes as a means of always having the most recent music available to them, either taping full programs or creating mix tapes out of recordings of their favorite segments from several different programs. Others taped broadcasts of live performances in order to duplicate and sell the recordings, or to mail them to kin located outside of New York. Still others recorded programs in order to capture a shout-out they delivered over the air, to hear their name registered in another's shout-out, or to save an advertisement or event announcement for later reference. Over time, many fans kept their cassette recordings, with some amassing large, thorough collections, recalling Andrea Bohlman and Peter McMurray's observation that tape is, first and foremost, a storage medium, and cassettes themselves "things to keep."[13] Among collectors, these tapes became important aesthetic and economic objects, sold and traded within niche markets operating on their own logics and protocols for valuation, scarcity, and exchange.[14]

With the advent of file sharing and internet archiving technology in the late 1990s, many collectors and fans converted their cassettes into digital MP3 files and uploaded them to the Web. For almost twenty years, collectors have stored and exchanged recordings of rap radio over the internet, and several large-scale repositories of tapes have been born and died since 2013, when I began collecting tapes myself. At the time of writing, significant collections of MP3 recordings of rap radio still reside in the less-trafficked corners of the internet. As Jonathan Sterne notes,

MP3s appear to be the perfect medium for "'end-to-end' networks like the internet," a format designed for the storage and movement of audio files from user to user across a frictionless infrastructure.[15] The internet itself, in this view, is understood as a stable, timeless space in which files, once uploaded, remain. Still, the same mechanisms that make the internet such an ideal space for uploading and sharing also make it prone to loss and ephemerality.[16] Sites go up and down, files are lost, and entire collections disappear, daily. Many of the sites I had turned to for rare tapes were gone upon later search; there were always new ones in their places. Further, the MP3 format often masks what Sterne calls its mediality, or "the complex ways in which communications technologies refer to one another in form or content."[17] In facilitating access to new files, and in hiding the many *re*mediations—from vinyl to 8-track to reel-to-reel to electromagnetic wave to cassette and back, to name one particularly tortuous path—MP3s falsely promise to give us access to the content of a recording.[18] They hide the dense webs of practice and sociality that were part and parcel of 1980s cassette culture. With cassettes of hip-hop programs, the picture is complicated further by competing archival practices. Some collectors act on a preservationist impulse, sourcing, storing, and cataloging anything they can get their hands on, and sharing their tapes freely. Others are less ready to share and stricter about what enters the archive. For these collectors, controlling access to tapes represents a means of giving credit where they believe credit is due. Restricting trade to an inner circle is their way of policing boundaries between the committed and the tourists. When evaluating the tapes that are available to listeners and historians in the present, we'd do well to remember Regina Kunzel's observation that archives are "less depositories of documents than themselves historical agents, organized around unwritten logics of inclusion and exclusion."[19]

In order to treat recordings of early hip-hop with the sensitivity and sophistication they deserve, I propose thinking of each cassette recording and its MP3 doubles as an archive in and of itself. Any work with them must find a way to reconcile a given recording's individual histories of production and transmission through time and space with its status as dehistoricized content stored and circulated through the internet; writing about tapes must acknowledge the material world in which a recording was made, valued, and disseminated while understanding the transhistorical resonance of the events to which it attests. To accomplish this, I ask that we listen to the numerous, imbricated histories present in each recording, to the ways in which these tapes are themselves repositories of past action as well as present sites of intentional remembering. First, I treat each recording as an inscription of an event, replete with all of the lived-ness and liveness implicit in any performance. These tapes tell us something about what was performed, what was heard, and what it may have meant to those involved. By this I mean to think of these recordings as an archive in the sense that performance theorist Diana Taylor understands it, as embodied performances sounding the "lived and the scripted and the citational practices that exist in both."[20] Second, as inscriptions of events, these tapes are also suitable to exegesis as texts. Although I attempt to be sensitive to the fact that no source provides a conduit to an "unalloyed view of historical reality," many of the chapters of this book attempt to develop a hermeneutics for reading community, labor, and aesthetic codes from these recordings.[21] The readings I offer in these chapters move between material world and recording, attentive to the unexpected and surprising ways that life gives meaning to sound. Finally, these recordings had and continue to have lively social existences. Though their precise routes of transmission and alteration are unknowable, they came to us after long histories of valuation, trade, discard, and remediation. They each bear the trace of those who have encountered them, be it in direct ways such as the editing and splicing of a tape or subtle ways like the adding of a single tick to the number of downloads tallied in digital metadata. When possible, I have attempted to make the social and material histories of tapes central to my treatment of them. When not possible, I at least acknowledge the fullness and messiness of the worlds in which they participate. As archives, each of these tapes are partial, unruly, idiosyncratic assemblages of bodies, sounds, material, and affect.

Listening to the ways these communities adapted their musical and cultural practice to radio thus provides a means of narrating the development of a musical form, the hopes and aspirations of a community, and a pivotal moment for a city. And it is with these interwoven strands in mind that I call this history one of "breaks in the air." In a literal sense, the history of rap radio is one of breakbeats transduced and transmitted across the electromagnetic spectrum: of breaks cut, as it were, through the air. Yet I also invoke "the breaks" in the sense that MC Kurtis Blow did on his landmark record of the same name. Throughout his rhymes, Blow puns on the word "breaks," deftly moving between homophones ("brakes on a bus, brakes on a car") and toast-style exclamations ("break it up, break it up, break it up!") as he spins his tale.[22] But the crux of his rap revolves around tough breaks, situations of low luck, disadvantage, and

11

poor circumstance. We might think of the period covered in this history as one of exceptionally tough breaks for New York and its minority communities, characterized as it often is by budget crises, community disintegration and displacement, the deterioration of the physical environment, real estate speculation, and the tandem rise of the HIV and crack epidemics. Like Blow, I try see these breaks as a generator of novel forms of expression and affiliation, the blasted landscapes of the Bronx as a source of creativity and fecundity rather than unmitigated despair. The final sense in which I invoke breaks signifies something perhaps less obvious. Theorists and historians of African American history have riffed and troped on the many meaning of the *break* or *breaks* in order to better understand the vagaries of Blackness in the United States. For these writers, the breaks are grooves and cuts capaciously defined, those places and subjectivities that, much like a broadcast signal, are present yet obscured, invisible or subterranean, always slightly behind the beat but nevertheless in anticipation of it.[23] I offer this period in hip-hop history as an extended break, one resisting the teleological gravity of the golden era and its distorting allures in order to hear the history of hip-hop as it was and as it might have been. Throughout this book I ask what we can learn by listening to these forms of life carried on errant frequencies. To hear these breaks, we need only tune our receivers.

Chapter Overview

Writing a history of radio presents some unique challenges. There are more characters, events, and broadcasts than could possibly be accounted for. Further, the sources I have to work with make telling a strictly chronological story tricky. Some time periods at certain stations are exceptionally well represented, while others are characterized by silent archival gaps. In order to overcome this, I've organized this history of rap on the radio in New York around portraits of three radio stations with distinct sonic and business profiles: WBLS-FM 107.5, WRKS-FM 98.7, and WHBI-FM 105.9. I chose these stations to organize the narrative for several reasons. First and foremost, these stations were the first to air rap music, and offered programming by hip-hop DJs for the better part of the 1980s. Just as important, however, these stations were owned, operated, and programmed by three organizations with radically different operating models and media philosophies. Yet it is precisely these differences that help us understand just why so many actors in the media industry were drawn to rap music at this moment.

For one, WBLS was owned and operated by a consortium of New York's Black elite. Headed by Manhattan borough president Percy E. Sutton and funded by a who's-who of African American professionals under the banner of the Inner City Broadcasting Corporation, WBLS was the crown jewel in a portfolio of media properties acquired in the service of building a national Black media network. Sutton and his associates sought to reimage Black life and call Black folk across the world into a new political consciousness, and mass media was the tool of the times. They were also the first commercial station to program a rap radio show. It's impossible to understand the first rap radio programs in New York without seeing them within this context. In contrast, WRKS was a commercial media property par excellence. Operated as part of the national RKO network of broadcast properties, the station was run and programmed by a team of radio professionals—the highest achievers in their domain. This group came to rap through musical savvy, a close connection to club culture, and a small fortune's worth of market research. Contrasting how these two powerhouse FMs approached rap, and how they positioned rap after identifying each other as competitors, helps us understand what broadcasters and DJs stood to gain, and just how high the stakes were for this new music.

Situated between the dial from these two juggernauts was WHBI. The Big "H," as listeners affectionately referred to it, differed substantially from WBLS and WRKS in one important way. Broadcasters on WHBI paid for their own airtime. For most hours of the week, WHBI specialized in multilingual and community programming. This was evident as early as December 1984, when the *New York Times* reported that, thanks to WHBI, "nearly everybody in the Greek-American neighborhood of Astoria, Queens knows [radio host] Tina Santorineou . . . everybody's sister, mother, or sweetheart." The same was said of Gilda Miros and Puerto Ricans in the South Bronx, Art Raymond and the Jewish enclaves of Borough Park and Flatbush, and Bob Law and Bed-Stuy's Black community. In 1987, *Radio and Records* magazine boasted of "WNWK's Tower of Babel: 35 Languages Broadcast Weekly."[24] What this meant in practice, however, was that enterprising DJs could buy airtime each week and play whatever they wanted, without any of the politics, financial considerations, or jockeying for position that came with a show on commercial radio. As a result, shows on WHBI gives us a closer look at how aspiring hip-hop icons wanted to present their culture and their music. Through the broadcasts of the *Zulu Beat, The Awesome 2 Show*, and the *World's Famous Supreme Team Show*, we can hear how those closest to hip-hop selected and mixed elements of their culture for a listening audience.

Broadly, the chapters in this book track these stations over time, moving from the large-scale and structural to the intimate. Chapter 1 sets the stage for 1980s radio by reviewing the deregulation of the broadcast industry. This, more than any other force, transformed broadcasting at the moment rap became a commercial music. During the 1970s, widespread sentiment in favor of broadcast deregulation swept through the radio industry. In part, this "deregulation fever" was a response to perceived Federal Communications Commission (FCC) overreach. Career broadcasters in the 1970s rejected what they felt were onerous and inconsistently enforced licensing requirements and railed against limitations on programming that could only have been written by bureaucrats. Support of deregulation was also the product of a more general, society-wide naturalization of neoliberal ideologies that saw unregulated markets and self-sufficient individuals as the engines and ends of economic activity. By the 1980s, a broad coalition had organized with the aim of reducing and simplifying the regulatory framework that structured all aspects of broadcasting. United in this coalition were Republicans and Democrats, some minorities and the white majority, broadcasters and legislators alike. The power they exerted collectively emboldened ongoing legal and administrative efforts to alter broadcast regulation at fundamental level. Referred to as *deregulation*, the consequences of this reauthoring of broadcast industry regulation were manifold and difficult to quantify. An important result, however, was an infusion of capital into radio, and a subsequent explosion in the industry's profit potential. The new regulatory regime created a corporate-legal climate in which investments and revenues in radio skyrocketed, and barriers to corporate consolidation diminished, if not disappeared outright. At the time when rap emerged as a radio-ready music, the industry became more competitive than at any point in its history, with broadcast property values increasing each year across the 1980s, and total advertising revenues increasing, in some markets, tenfold across the decade. In a media market like New York City, rap's controversies were therefore not simply aesthetic or racial. They had profound economic implications as well.

The next chapters shift attention to WBLS. If deregulation altered the broadcast landscape at the highest level, parallel developments in American racial politics also impinged on the broadcast of rap. Specifically, rap became a public music during a vexed moment in the history of the reception of Black music. In the early 1980s, African American musical genres counted among the most popular and profitable in the world while African Americans themselves witnessed the previous generations' civil rights gains erode before their eyes. Accompanying a slate of regressive policies—including but not limited to school resegregation, mandatory minimum sentencing, and the decimation of social services—were pathologized representations of Black sounds and bodies in popular media. R&B, neo soul, funk, electro, post-Motown, and other African American musics topped charts and enjoyed unprecedented "crossover" success. Yet the representations that fleshed out perceptions of African American artists were often fabrications rooted in stereotypes. In disco's wake—the widespread 1979 disavowal of which is itself a study in the mechanics of the appropriation and cannibalization of African American and queer culture—a new radio format surfaced to account for the widespread appeal of Black music and the continuing reticence to engage racialized cultural production as such on high-stakes popular media. Called "urban contemporary" (UC), stations espousing this format adopted a style rooted in a politics of respectability and a rhetoric consonant with incipient 1980s multiculturalism. Where stations like WBLS had, as recently as 1979, suffused their broadcasts and marketing with signifiers of African American culture, UC radio preferred to couch its decidedly Black cultural production in a language of color-neutral universality. Hip-hop, a quintessential African American music, found itself introduced to a media market that both demanded and refused Black cultural production. This chapter situates the first broadcasts of rap within a station committed to, on the one hand, a nationwide project of Black political awaking through mass media and, on the other, a new Black youth music that chafed against its founders' self-image.

Rap's ascendance to radio was, as one might guess, a rocky path, and one made all the rockier by the station owners' and managers' disdain for rap music. Still, WBLS programmed hip-hop shows for the better part of the 1980s. Chapter 3 provides a close reading of a number of broadcasts of *Rap Attack with Mr. Magic*, arguing that the resources WBLS provided to host Mr. Magic and his DJ Marley Marl, along with the imperative to create mixes specifically for consumption by radio, changed, in subtle but indelible ways, the aesthetic trajectory of hip-hop. WBLS's studio enabled Marley Marl to experiment with new and different styles of mixing, offering the outfitting necessary to combine recorded sound in previously unimaginable ways as well as the opportunity to do so.

Foregrounding the importance of listener attention and sonic detail, I argue that radio did as much to influence the sound of the genre as did studio record production, and that the two existed in a deeply responsive feedback loop.

Stations never broadcast in isolation, however. In a media market like New York, wherever there's money to be made, there's competition. Chapter 4 shifts the focus across town to WBLS's main UC competitor WRKS. Not long after completing their transition to the UC format, WRKS unveiled a marketing campaign that equated their music with the "sound of the streets." For years, KISS-FM pursued a strategy that cast the station's brand as the sound of New York. In this chapter, I put pressure on this messaging to narrate the pains the programmers, DJs, and management at WRKS took to live up to their own hype. Despite their location within a corporate broadcasting giant, the staff at KISS-FM did a remarkable job localizing their programming and targeting their offering to a young, opinionated New York audience. By looking at how different individuals at WRKS found, selected, prepared, and mixed music for broadcast, I look at the ways in KISS-FM sounded the streets of New York.

The next chapters turn away from commercial radio. Instead, I give extended accounts of two shows on WHBI: the *Zulu Beat* with DJ Afrika Islam, and *The Awesome 2 Show*. Chapter 5 narrates the broadcast run of the *Zulu Beat* from the perspective of community. Drawing on theories of broadcast publics, I show how rap radio programs offered listeners a means of affirming communities that existed in the world and built new, serialized communities that emerged from the act of collective listening. Here, I am interested in how listeners interacted with the *Zulu Beat*, provided content for each broadcast, and used the one-to-many structure of broadcasting to send messages, perform kinship, and overlay different locales with affiliation and affect in a manner not possible through other modes of communication. In this regard, shout-outs become an important practice, and I use this chapter as an opportunity to query the work they do in the world.

The final chapter draws on a series of long, detailed interviews and exchanges I had with DJ and radio duo the Awesome 2 between the winters of 2016 and 2018. I approach this chapter from the perspective of work and labor. The Awesome 2, like many DJs at the time, paid for their airtime. Doing so required them to hustle, and, in their recollections, they were as much entrepreneurs as they were radio hosts. In describing how they funded and programmed their show, I shed light on the transformation of hip-hop's economies, marking the shift from the largely informal networks of production and exchange into the tightly controlled formal economies of the music industry. I do so to push back against histories of rap's commercialization that ascribe too much agency to record labels, and against rags-to-riches narratives that rely on a telos of wealth and fame. Instead, I ask what we might learn from an account of early hip-hop that eschews success as an organizing principle and instead focuses on the uncertain.

ONE

Deregulating Radio

In a September 1979 issue of *Broadcast Programming and Production,* not two weeks before the first broadcast of "Rapper's Delight," columnist Clarence McKee urged readers "not to count their regulatory chickens before they hatch."[1] McKee had just returned from the annual conference of the National Association of Broadcasters, where he observed that attendees were "ecstatic," swept into a frenzy of speculation by the FCC's recent proposal to revisit the purpose and implementation of broadcast regulation. Though preliminary, the proposal outlined the commission's intent to severely deregulate the radio industry. The language of the proposal was clear, and its calculated understatement belied the scope of its ambitions: "[To] initiat[e] a proceeding looking toward the substantial deregulation of commercial broadcast radio." In McKee's reading, the FCC had found sufficient evidence to suggest that "it might now be possible to rely on competitive radio market forces to assure the same public interest benefits formerly sought to be achieved by the current rules and regulations." Reflecting changes in the logic of regulatory oversight a decade in the making, the FCC declared the current regulatory framework unfit to assure that radio served the "public interest" in the face of rationalizing market forces.[2]

Between 1979 and 1987, the FCC removed, revised, or reduced many of the substantive regulations governing the commercial radio industry. These changes have come to be known as "deregulation," both colloquially and in industry discourse. By the time the FCC released its "Notice of Inquiry" in 1979, broadcasters of all sizes and political persuasions had voiced support for deregulation. The totalizing language of the notice echoed the rhetoric of bipartisan campaigns rehearsed over half a decade. As early as the fall of 1977, politicians sought to rally broadcasters behind their cause, with Democratic congressman Lionel Van Deerlin confessing to a room of radio veterans, "I see the prospect for virtually the total deregulation of radio."[3] The deregulatory message came at a moment when broadcasters were primed to listen. In addition to the usual complaints—onerous reams of paperwork, short license terms, unclear requirements for community service—economic hardships roiled the communications industry across the 1970s, and a series of perceived FCC missteps into broadcast content regulation won the unlovable bureaucracy no affection.[4] As a result, broadcasters found themselves allied with lawmakers from both sides of the aisle in a "surprisingly heterogeneous coalition against continued regulation."[5] In the span of a few short years, the banal realm of broadcast regulation became the stuff of gossip. The theme of the 1978 National Radio Broadcasters Association convention was, fittingly, "Deregulation," and over three thousand attendees reportedly joined together in chants of "Deregulation now!"[6]

Policy proposals were quick to follow. In June 1978, Deerlin's House Subcommittee on Communications proposed a complete rewriting of the 1934 Communications Act—the bedrock of modern communications policy—to result in the complete abolition of the broadcast division of the FCC.[7] The bill was as part of a larger effort to solidify antitrust legislation in telecommunications, and it proposed to do so by recourse to a broad notion of the public. "It's not for the sake of deregulation, or to make life pleasanter to you," Deerlin told broadcasters as he lobbied for his bill, "but it makes sense for the American Public."[8] In March 1979, Republican Senator Barry Goldwater introduced a bill to the Senate floor proposing similar amendments to the 1934 Communications Act, "prescrib[ing] regulations to result . . . in marketplace competition and in deregulation of the provision of telecommunications services," ultimately prohibiting the FCC from requiring stations to provide news, public affairs, or locally produced programming.[9] Goldwater's was one of several similar bills introduced that year. Despite the irreconcilable politics of these politicians, their legislative efforts are consonant with Daniel T. Rodgers's observation that, at the close of the 1970s, "the market" emerged as the focal point of discourse on public life. The market, so defined, represented "a way of thinking about society with a myriad of self-generated actions for its engine and optimization as its natural and spontaneous outcome."[10] Though both pieces of legislation failed to pass, their language captures the precise aspects of regulation that would come under scrutiny in the early 1980s. Both questioned whether the "public interest" would be better served by the vagaries of supply and demand.

Regulating the Public Interest

It was this short phrase, the "public interest," that catalyzed much of the debate around deregulation. The "public interest" principle became a cornerstone of the broadcast licensing procedure with the ratification of the Radio Act of 1927. Beginning with its predecessor, the Radio Act of 1912, the US government classified the electromagnetic spectrum as part of the public trust, mandating that all radio operators broadcasting on any portion of the spectrum hold a license to do so. As part of the public trust, no citizen or corporation is permitted to own the frequency on which they broadcast. They instead lease rights to a frequency for a limited term. Accordingly, radio broadcasters exercise their trade as trustees of the public. Under the auspices of the US Department of Commerce and Labor, the 1912 act gave the federal government the power to control who broadcast over which frequencies, alleviating the "chaos" of unregulated transmission.

21

In the first decades of radio, the federal government understood the medium as a tool for communicating and disseminating information. They paid little mind to radio's potential to entertain or to lubricate commerce. By the 1920s, neither regulators nor advertisers could ignore radio's emerging function as an entertainment medium. In order to address the need for supervision of the spectrum and to centralize the review of license applications, the 1927 act created the Federal Radio Commission (FRC), an agency charged with overseeing and enforcing the licensing procedure as well as use of the spectrum. In exchange for the right to broadcast over the spectrum, licensees were required to serve the public, from whom they "rented" the airwaves. The 1927 act stipulated that licenses be granted based on a station's capacity to "serve the public interest, convenience, and necessity." For the Hoover administration, the public interest carried a distinct protectionist bent. In 1924, Hoover himself argued that "[radio] is not to be considered as merely a business carried on for private gain, for private advertisement, or for entertainment of the curious. It is a public concern impressed with the public trust and is to be considered primarily from the standpoint of public interest to the same extent and upon the basis of the same general principles as our public utilities."[11] Though, in the official language, the word *interest* is ambiguous enough to allow for its reinterpretation with the vicissitudes of the economy or developments in technology, its thrust is clear enough: insofar as the electromagnetic spectrum belongs the public trust, its mandate is to serve the interests of that public.

From its earliest years, radio regulation maintained a tortured relationship to the medium's capacity to attract advertising dollars. Michele Hilmes has argued that early radio legislation and organizations defined the "public interest . . . as commercial interest as early as the 1920s."[12] Her discussion of the public interest in early radio uncannily presages the debates of the 1970s and 1980s: "In displacing outright state definitions of national priorities and values onto a presumably transparent system of commercial entertainment driven by advertising dollars, American radio created an extraordinarily effective way of masking its public function behind the discourse of private choice."[13] A little over half a century following its initial regulation, *de*regulation operated by a similar feat of sleight of hand, locating the public interest in the consonance between the public's desire for certain programming and a broadcast market's ability to provide it.

If the 1927 act skirted the issue of radio's commercial applications, the Communications Act of 1934 addressed them directly. The 1934 act birthed the Federal Communications Commission (FCC), consolidating the numerous organs and agencies responsible for telecommunications regulation and expanding the purview and powers of the former FRC. Citing its importance in the facilitation of interstate commerce, the Roosevelt administration classified broadcast media as part of the economic infrastructure of the United States. Like numerous other New Deal agencies, the FCC was tasked with monitoring prices, promoting competition by preventing monopolies, and drafting and enforcing technical operating standards. Yet, unlike railroads, trucking, or other industries essential to interstate commerce, radio developed a distinct entertainment function. Within radio, the debates leading to the passage of the 1934 act revolved around the appropriate balance of commerce, entertainment, and information. Surely too much advertising was predatory, the argument went. And surely too much entertainment was decadent. Regulation in the decade following the 1934 act sought to address what percentage of available frequencies should be reserved for noncommercial programming, limitations on direct advertising in the content of broadcasts, and the extent to which the medium should remain a source of public information, in addition to the more mundane tasks of license review and the revision of regulation to keep pace with technological development. These debates, and the shifting conception of the role the FCC should play in guiding their solutions (e.g., consumer protection, cartel management, content guidelines), would define radio regulation across the twentieth century.

Policy measures designed to protect the public interest were gradually added to the books, but several exercised a decisive influence on the shape and function of the radio industry. These requirements included limitations on ownership, license terms, and content guidelines, specifying what could be broadcast, to whom, and for how long. To accommodate the rapid postwar growth of the commercial radio industry, limits on station ownership were set at five television stations, seven AM stations, and seven FM stations, provisioning the ownership of no more than one of each property in a given market and reaching no more than 25 percent of the total US population.[14] This rule became known as the 5–7-7 rule. In 1953, 5–7-7 was expanded to 7-7-7 and remained unchanged until 1984. The term of each license was set to three years, after which stations were required to file for a renewal of their application. Further, an "anti-trafficking" law prohibited stations from reselling any commercial property or license before the first three-year licensing term had expired. This rule ostensibly encouraged commitment to the enterprise of broadcasting by preventing owners from rapidly buying and offloading properties. This law held until 1983, when the minimum license term was lowered from three years to a single year, radically diminishing the period an owner must hold a property before reselling.

With regard to broadcast content, the public interest specified several specific measures. True to the conception of the medium as one essential to the healthy exchange of information, the "public interest" clause held that a certain percentage of all broadcast time be devoted to news and public service content. An additional "fairness doctrine" required that stations allot equal time to speakers representing multiple perspectives on issues of pressing public importance, preventing a station from operating as a mouthpiece for any single ideology. Direct advertisement was permitted to exceed no more than 6 percent of broadcast time each hour. Less clear in application, but no less clear in intent, was the requirement that each station serve the local community to whom they broadcast. As defined by convention and law, the "public interest" clause stipulated that a station must serve the communities located in its immediate environs. Yet the "ascertainment" of local service, the process by which the FCC determined whether or not a station had adequately served its market, was, like the "public interest" itself, notoriously vague. In large, diverse markets like New York, this task proved particularly difficult. In practice, local service designated anything from providing local news to featuring interviews with regional notables or political figures to allowing local or amateur broadcasters access to a station's resources. However imprecisely defined or inconsistently enforced, stations were required to document their local service, and a station could be audited at any time to demonstrate their commitment to their local audience.

The policies of the FCC were contested throughout the middle of the century. Nevertheless, the authority and scope of the institution expanded throughout the twentieth century. The commission continued the largely unremarkable work of enforcing and revising communications policy with little threat of a major upheaval. Revolution arrived, however, with policymakers' fetishization of the market in the mid-1970s.

The Fowler Commission

Though the Ferris commission of the late 1970s proved instrumental in recasting the rhetoric of regulatory reform in terms of atomistic and self-propagating market forces, with the effect of subtly altering the rationale of regulation from legal and technological grounds to economic ones, it largely failed to progress its agenda. Appointed to the position of chairman of the FCC in 1981 by President Ronald Reagan, Canadian lawyer and former radio broadcaster Mark Fowler achieved considerably more success. Fowler benefited from the pervasive influence of neoliberal economic and social thought, a program whose "centerpiece is invariably a call for commercial media and communication markets to be deregulated," and from the support of the Reagan administration, whose platform espoused precisely those reforms.[15] The telecommunications industry was one of many industries deregulated in the 1980s, starting with the reform of the airline industry, followed by the trucking, railroad, and oil industries, and concluded finally by the incipient deregulation of the financial sector.[16] And while, as Jennifer Holt argues, the deregulation of media industries writ large was inconsistent and contradictory in practice, the deregulation of the radio industry was thorough and decisive.[17] The deregulation of the commercial radio industry was predicated on a reinterpretation of the "public interest" clause—a reinterpretation supported by the language of the 1934 Radio Act—equating the public interest with the health of the industry rather than public well-being.

Fowler famously viewed the FCC as a "New Deal Dinosaur," a creature imaginatively rendered "with a head too small for its body, a body too big for its environment, and a tail that just goes on and on."[18] In an attempt to decapitate the misshapen beast, Fowler introduced a packet of reforms, passed by the FCC with little delay or debate. In lobbying broadcasters to support his platform, he couched his reforms in a language of absolute freedom, stating, "I mean that you, the broadcaster, should be as free from regulation as the newspaper. . . . No renewal filings, no ascertainment exercises, no content regulation, no ownership restrictions beyond those that apply to media generally, free resale of properties, no petitions to deny, no Brownie-points for doing right, no finger wagging for doing wrong."[19] Fowler was fast to make good on his word. The initial reforms eliminated the requirement for formal ascertainment, instead compelling stations to demonstrate their community service only upon a challenge to their license. With ascertainment went program log-keeping requirements, limitations on the airtime allotted to direct advertising, first raising the maximum to 8 percent before eliminating it entirely along with all nonentertainment program guidelines. By 1982, led by Senator Bob Packwood, Congress passed an amendment to the 1934 Communications Act to increase the station license term from three to seven years. After the initial wave of reforms in 1981 and 1982, Fowler's commission attacked the remaining regulations. In 1984, the 12–12–12 rule replaced the 7–7–7 rule, nearly doubling the number of AM, FM, and TV stations a single person or corporation could own. In 1987, the FCC abolished the fairness doctrine, no longer mandating equal airtime to be afforded to opposing viewpoints. Later that year, the number of properties a person or company was allowed to own and operate within a single market expanded to allow a single entity to own two AM, two FM, and one TV stations. To some observers, Fowler's zeal for deregulation more closely resembled "unregulation."

Recourse to the market in the domain of content regulation meant that the "public interest" quite literally indexed the desires of the public as those desires were channeled through the market. Beneath these reforms lie a logic of generative circularity that Fowler pithily summarized when he told the *New York Times* that "the 'Public Interest' [will] be determined by the Publics' interests."[20] Because many different demands exist in the population, the argument went, a diverse range of stations should arise to satisfy those demands. If a type of content were demanded by the public, the market would produce a program or service to meet it. Any program not satisfying an existing demand or producing a new one would be naturally culled from the marketplace. The competition inherent to such unregulated markets would result in a productive equilibrium, an efficient industry tied to those it served in ever tightening cycles of responsive recursion. This is a standard interpretation of neoliberal approaches to market economics, and of competition in capitalism more generally. But as an interpretation of the "public interest" it was radical, diverging substantially from previous commissions and equating the public well-being with that of the industries serving them.

The industry that resulted from these regulatory reforms was one primed to maximize growth and liquidity. The elimination of the antitrafficking law allowed outside investors to turn over properties at a much faster rate, and the increase in license terms allowed owners to retain successful properties with fewer modes of contestation available to competitors. Decoupled from content regulation and public service requirements, programmers and owners were theoretically free to pursue a creative or business direction suited to their vision of a station. Yet the competition deregulation spawned encouraged the opposite. Rather than naturally diversifying, markets paradoxically fragmented and homogenized, with larger stations copying the tactics of their more successful competitors while others targeted niche audiences, hedging their success on their ability to monopolize the attention of smaller constituencies.

Black media-owners began to voice fears that an industry both tightening and growing would leave little room for minority-owned media, which often lacked the resources and access to capital of its network and white-owned counterparts. The FCC responded to these fears, passing additional regulations to increase the number of minority owners in the broadcast industry. In 1978, even as the FCC shifted toward a regulatory framework undergirded by neoliberal, free market ideology, it implemented a series of rulings designed to increase the number of stations owned by minorities. These measures provided financial incentives to minority owners ranging from tax breaks and short-term, low-interest federal loans to early purchasing access to distressed properties. These measures helped savvy broadcasters expand their holdings. Within a year of their passage, Percy Sutton's Inner City Broadcasting Corporation acquired seven new stations in major markets around the country. By 1981, over a hundred new Black-owned stations had begun operations.[21] But the initial successes of the efforts would be overshadowed by the precipitous decrease in minority owners across the 1980s, reaching its nadir at the close of the decade.

National Association of Black Broadcasters executive director James Winston's prescient 1976 observation that "the industry is consolidating rapidly [and] small owners—particularly [Black owners]—are being squeezed out of the business by duopolies and superduopolies" was realized scarcely a decade later.[22] Others worried that they would have to generalize their format to stay in business, abandoning their core African American constituency to stay on the air.[23] Despite the clamor of minority broadcasters, the American legal apparatus lagged behind the concerns of those in the industry. When the Supreme Court ruled on *Metro Broadcasting Inc. v. FCC,* Justice Sandra Day O'Connor captured what many had feared when, in her dissenting opinion, she wrote, "The market shapes programming to a tremendous extent. Members of minority groups who own licenses might be thought, like other owners, to seek broadcast programs that will attract and retain audiences, rather than programs that will reflect the owner's tastes and preferences."[24]

In 1985, writing in the past tense, a *Mother Jones* staff writer echoed a common perspective when he reflected that "the Specter of Monopoly was obvious."[25] Yet commercial broadcasters seemed largely to echo Fowler's assertion that "bigness is not necessarily badness. Sometimes it is goodness."[26] Many broadcasters were vehement in their support of deregulation, agreeing that less time spent appeasing a bloated government bureaucracy was more time that could be spent doing what they loved: making radio. Industry notable Jim Duncan felt that "the FCC . . . made life easier for broadcasters," with "fewer regulations, fewer forms to fill out, less interference in programming, and less restrictive ownership limitations."[27] In the second edition of the 1984 textbook *The Radio Station*, radio veterans Michael Keith and Joseph Krause informed students of the industry that "the government . . . is no longer perceived as the fearsome, omnipresent Big Brother it once was. Today's broadcasters more fully enjoy the fruits of a laissez-faire system of economy."[28]

Shrewd managers, programmers, and investors were able to realize profit in the industry on a scale previously inconceivable in commercial radio. Between 1976 and 1986, the average price of a station in New York increased tenfold. In 1978, after only four years of operation under the ownership of Inner City Broadcasting Corporation, the price of WBLS increased from $1.35 million to $18 million.[29] The first sale of a New York property to exceed $10 million transacted in 1980 with the sale of classical format station WHN for $14 million. By 1985, the average price of an FM radio station in New York hovered around $10 million with the highest sale of 1985 reaching $49 million. In 1986, WNEW-FM sold for $52 million, despite the station having never exceeded 3.3 percent of total market share in any ratings category. WNEW-FM's price tag was a recognition of the frequency's potential rather than the station's performance, which was lackluster by most ratings and revenue metrics. In step with station prices, total radio industry revenues in New York nearly doubled between 1976 and 1986. In 1976, total revenue in the New York market capped out at $88.6 million. After climbing steadily throughout the decade, revenues in 1986 exceeded $226.5 million. The increased liquidity of broadcast properties, combined with an ingress of parties looking to diversify their holdings in radio, greatly increased the volume of transactions. In 1976, 413 stations were sold nationally at an average price of $437,440 for a total of $180 million. By 1985, that number grew to 1,500 sales at an average price of $1 million for a total of $1.4 billion.[30] In the first half of 1986, transactions were estimated to exceed $2.25 billion.[31]

The deregulation of the commercial radio industry encouraged a closer relationship between radio and investment communities. The precipitous increase in station prices and property transactions can be partially accounted for by Wall Street's increased interest in financing radio properties. With the capacity to realize higher returns on investment, and with a regulatory framework that allowed for both rapid acquisition and divestment, investors increasingly entered into business relationships with radio personnel, strengthening ties to an industry whose intensive management requirements and thin profit margins previously made for unappealing investments. Multiplied by the 1981 capital gains tax reduction, the changes in ownership limitations and the influx of investment capital amplified the scarcity of radio properties, driving prices higher. A greater number of broadcast companies traded on public markets or were purchased by private equity firms, including future behemoth Clear Channel. Radio commentators remarked on the new and creative methods of financing applied to broadcast industry. "If you've got valuable broadcasting assets and no cash, you're the perfect investment banking client," one investment executive wrote.[32] Jim Duncan noted that the 1980s witnessed seemingly "unlimited sources of financing" become available to radio, "mak[ing] the biggest deals possible."[33]

If, in the 1970s, loans could only be obtained for small operational ex-
penses or for minor buyouts, the 1980s saw the rise of an "increasingly
sophisticated matrix of financing alternatives."[34]

This explosion of money in radio represented sea change in the industry. Yet, despite entering a period of overall prosperity, the radio
industry often remained hostile to minority owners. There were efforts, both superficial and substantive, to expand minority ownership
throughout the 1980s. In the fall of 1985, the FCC reviewed a proposal to
broaden its distress sale policy, making stations available at a reduced
rate even as they underwent license hearings. The measure ultimately
failed to pass. As William Barlow observes, the removal of public service
requirements made distress sales unnecessary, with the last recorded
distress sale transacting in 1986.[35] In October 1985, Black media owners
and attorneys convened at a symposium in Washington, DC, to discuss
the issue with legislators and policymakers, foremost among whom was
Mark Fowler. At the end of the symposium, Fowler summarized the pro-
ceedings by acknowledging that there were "unacceptably low" levels
of minority ownership. "The FCC should continue its distress sale, tax
certificate, and EEO procedures," he conceded, "but the real solution
to boosting minority ownership is connecting minorities with brokers,
bankers, and dealmakers."[36] For Fowler, minority ownership was not to
be encouraged by incentive-based policies or a regulatory framework
amenable to service-oriented stations, but through better access to the
financial resources now commonplace in commercial radio.

Minority owners' skepticism that new financing alternatives represented a solution to disparities in ownership did not stem from a distrust
of Fowler or the FCC. Rather, Fowler's suggestion that African American owners place their faith in lending institutions ignored historical
and enduring patterns of racism in the availability of loans. Black media
owners criticized throughout the 1980s the continuing racism of lenders, who often refused to finance Black appeal stations or stations owned
by African Americans. Unable to secure full financing from a conven-
tional bank, for example, Percy Sutton purchased WLIB for $1.7 million
in 1971 and WBLS for $1.35 million in 1974 in part with investments from
group of fifty-eight prominent members of Harlem's Black community in
the name of the Inner City Broadcasting Corporation. Sutton repeatedly
maintained that he viewed WLIB, the preeminent source of news, political commentary analysis, and special interest programming for New
York's Black communities, as the ideological and operational core of his
endeavors in media. Though ICBC lost money on WLIB some years of its

operation, they earned enough from "cash cow" WBLS and their other ventures to cover their losses, expand their radio and newspaper holdings, purchase the Apollo Theater, and acquire new properties in cable and unrelated industries.

These biases against minority owners extended further than lending practices. They also manifested in a station's ability to attract advertisers, the financial lifeblood of a commercial radio station. In 1986, nine Black stations ranked first in their market, yet none led their markets in revenue, with some ranking as low as fifth. Amos Brown speculates that the birth of the urban format, a revision of traditional full-service Black radio, was partially a response to advertisers' unwillingness to do business with Black owners or stations with a perceived Black audience, a decision predicated on the myth that Black listeners "don't buy products, goods, or services."[37] Percy Sutton expressed exasperation with advertisers, the failure of ratings services to adequately sample Black listening habits, and the entrenched discrimination facing Black media in an interview with *Black Enterprise*: "We're not an ethnic station, we're a people station. We want to be in the mainstream of radio. Some of the ad agencies would like to label WBLS as a black or ethnic station to lessen the quality of our station and its audience. We may have better ratings than our competitors, but the agencies tell us ours are black ratings. The problem is that they don't think black folks buy anything."[38]

The abiding discrimination of advertisers and lending institutions notwithstanding, WBLS thrived in the 1980s, remaining lockstep with competitor WRKS for the first and second positions every year between 1980 and 1987—this in an era where minority ownership dwindled and barriers to entry only grew steeper. As the FCC dismantled the regulatory scaffolding of the commercial broadcast industry, owners and managers nonetheless chased their visions of prosperity. For Percy Sutton, this meant ownership of a full battery of media outlets, owned and controlled by the community they served. Power, to Sutton, lay in the management of the flow of information. For Mayo, too, prosperity entailed ownership of radio stations to empower his Black constituents by providing them with "information and knowledge."[39] In the early 1980s he took his first steps toward the assembly of a large and profitable network of radio stations spanning the nation. By mid-decade, he had built a portfolio of media properties by heeding the winds of regulatory reform. "When the FCC began allowing companies to own two FM properties in the same market," Mayo remarked of his purchase of a second station in the Chicago market, "I did the research to find out what the biggest hole here was that would allow us to maximize ratings without hurting [partner station] v103. That's how we came up with the hip-hop format."[40] The financial and creative pressures endemic to the new radio industry pervaded the collaborations between DJ and manager and fueled the competition between stations. The tensions singular to this constellation of forces wended their way into the studio, inflecting how, when, and why stations broadcast rap music, forming what Alejandra Bronfman calls the "infrastructures, both material and political, that created the possibility of content."[41] It is against this backdrop, of an industry in turmoil, of a nation rediscovering its fascination with Black cultural production, of multiplying lines toward prosperity and failure in broadcast media, that rap sounded over the radio.

Sounding Black Progress in the Post–Civil Rights Era

"Oh, my God, I think I'm having a rap attack!" Upon hearing this message, listeners tuned to 107.5-FM on a Saturday night knew to ready their tape decks and nudge up the volume on their stereos. Mr. Magic's *Rap Attack*, coming at you live from WBLS, "In a Class by Itself." No defibrillators necessary, as rap trio Whodini joked on their 1983 single, "Magic's Wand," an ode to the host of the first program dedicated to rap music on commercial radio.[1] With the wave of his wand, so it went, Mr. Magic performed a strange alchemy. In casting sound over the airwaves, he transformed vinyl into precious metal. "The moment he went on the air," MC Jalil rapped, "It was plain to see a new phase was here." The culture of live hip-hop, "DJs jammin' in the street, MCs rappin' to the beat," gave way to the "triple platinum . . . smash" of "Rapper's Delight," as well as the major-label ambitions that followed in the single's wake. First from hole-in-the-wall WHBI-FM, and then from WBLS's state-of-the-art studios, Magic's tenure on the radio spanned 1979–89, coinciding with rap's emergence as a global commercial juggernaut. Behind the mic, fingers draped over a platter, Magic divined New York's musical desires before they passed to consciousness.

Though not alone in his efforts to broadcast rap to the masses, Mr. Magic occupies a vaunted position among artists and listeners who came of age in the 1980s. *Rap Attack* straddled the worlds of the street and the commercial radio studio, conferring legitimacy to hip-hop even as the music remained too controversial to penetrate daytime rotation beyond the occasional single. Supported by the imprimatur that accompanied a slot on New York's number-one-rated radio station, the first broadcasts of *Rap Attack* put the music of the Treacherous Three, LL Cool J, and Run-DMC in the company of Reagan-era Black-radio staples such as the O'Jays, Donna Summer, Teddy Pendergrass, Grace Jones, and MFSB. Long-form Grandmaster Flash and the Furious Five mixes resounded from the same point on the dial as Frankie Crocker's far-ranging funk and soul sets. Magic and his "Engineer All-Star Marley Marl" introduced audiences to Roxanne Shanté, Big Daddy Kane, Salt-N-Pepa, Kool G Rap, and Eric B. and Rakim, among many others. For artists who debuted in the 1980s, to have a single played on *Rap Attack* was to open a gateway to the highest planes of achievement in the music industry. For those whose music reached listeners through *The Stretch Armstrong and Bobbito Show* in the 1990s, who came of age during the *Rap Attack*'s heyday, ears glued to their radios, Mr. Magic stands out as a symbol of a hip-hop culture unique to New York, an icon of a moment characterized by exhilaration and cohesion, populated by its own values, mythologies, styles, and interborough beefs.

For WBLS's owners and management, however, *Rap Attack* presented a dilemma. Its music did not fit naturally into WBLS's playlists—rapping was still too inscrutable for the station's core demographic of older listeners—nor did it correspond to the station's carefully crafted image. WBLS was founded by Percy Sutton, a civil rights activist turned attorney of Malcolm X turned Manhattan borough president, and financed by a consortium of Black investors. In sound, service, and image, WBLS espoused a politics of respectability. Sutton and his cohort operated WBLS as part of a post–civil rights era political program that saw mass media as the key to progress in the long freedom struggle. More than just providing a channel for the dissemination of information and a platform for mobilizing direct political action, WBLS's owners envisioned the station as a means of reimagining Black life, in sound. Speaking of the station's commitment to countering the stereotypes of African Americans rampant in film, television, and advertising, an early WBLS programming manager remarked, "Our idea is to create an image, and to destroy an image that has been created."[2] Note, in that formulation, the passive voice, a subtle nod to centuries of representation of Black life made without recourse to Black folk. To this end, the station projected an urbane, urban, upwardly mobile African American listener through programming that presented, as one WBLS DJ put it, "sophistication, something for the adults."[3] To those in management roles, the new music coming from New York's Black youth seemed to run counter to the station's mission of racial uplift through music, news, and information. Although MCs' raps increasingly addressed the same issues that so concerned WBLS's investors, they found little common ground on which to unite their common politics.

The conflict between management and rap music was, at its core, a generational and class conflict, and it was one whose battles were waged in the domain of radiophonic sound. Mr. Magic remarked as much as he prepared to leave the station in the late 1980s, placing hip-hop in a deep-historical lineage of African American popular musics. "It was really a problem of generations," he said. "It was basically very similar to the situation in the '50s with rock and roll—it was the music of one particular generation, a music which their parents just couldn't understand."[4] When each side refused to cede, WBLS's studio became a site of generational conflict over strategies of representation, gain, and progress. Despite its apparent intractability, this impasse proved generative. DJs, hosts, and WBLS's management ultimately marshaled the station's resources toward the prosperity of both WBLS and rap music. Unwittingly, each side provided a set of novel resources to the other. WBLS afforded Magic and Marley Marl a massive audience brought together in the simultaneity of broadcast; the station's cutting-edge technological resources furnished a laboratory for the two DJs to experiment with new sounds and modes of distribution while bringing rap music deeper into the fold of New York's musical economies, and eventually to listeners around the world. *Rap Attack*, in turn, attracted a large swath of young listeners to WBLS's late-night and daytime broadcasts, allowing the station to retain its ratings, and thus its profitability, through the 1980s. As Magic, Marley Marl, and the ownership of WBLS pursued their visions of prosperity, the projects of Black-owned media and rap music each thrived throughout the 1980s.

Percy Sutton and the Promise of Mass Media

"The Chairman," the borough president, CEO, activist, entrepreneur. "The Wizard of Ooze," the mellifluous and exhorting voice of Black progress.[5] Wherever he spoke, commentators took note of Percy Sutton's voice—his precise diction delivered with a minister's cadence, the sharp alternation between intensity and ease, the slight tenor drawl at the end of a phrase. They wrote of its charms and power.

Long before Percy Ellis Sutton presided over a communications empire, he dreamed of sending that voice across the frequencies of his own radio station. Hours spent listening to the invisible medium stoked the imagination of a young Sutton. From his family's farm in Prairie View, Texas, he trawled the airwaves for far-flung transmissions. During idle hours, he walked the grounds with the tones of radio announcers' declamations resounding in his head and a corncob pipe hanging from his mouth, addressing everyone and no one, "Hello, ladies and gentlemen, this is Percy Sutton coming to you from high in the clouds over the Smith-Young Tower."[6] Though he would never fulfill his dream of hosting his own radio program, he would go one further. At the crest of a distinguished career in civil rights activism, law, and politics, Sutton turned his acumen toward the ownership of mass media outlets. Those enterprises, in turn, reshaped the place of minority ownership in the communications industry and rerouted the trajectory of Black music in the final quarter of the twentieth century.

Born the youngest of fifteen children in November 1920, Sutton grew up amid the "absolute segregation" of the Deep South outside of San Antonio, Texas.[7] In the face of Jim Crow's violent reminders of the place of Blackness in America, the Sutton household proclaimed commitments to education and uplift. Sutton's father, Samuel James, just old enough to have experienced the transition from slavery to emancipation, made education, business, and community service his life's work. His mother, Lillian, taught in San Antonio schools while raising the family's children.

A frequently cited anecdote suggests that Sutton was not long for Texas.[8] At the age of twelve, so the story goes, he boarded a New York–bound passenger train without a ticket or arrangements. Sutton found board with a family northwest of Harlem on 155th Street, and work doing odd jobs in the area surrounding the Apollo Theater. Though he returned to Texas just a few weeks after arriving in New York, his brief experience in the city remained with him, and he would return to New York periodically through his teens and as a young adult. The singular culture of 125th Street beckoned. In Harlem, Sutton glimpsed a Black community otherwise.

Sutton fought restless as a young man. After short stints at Prairie View A&M, Tuskegee University, and Hampton University, he dropped out to chase a childhood dream of becoming a pilot. When America entered World War II, he enlisted, serving as an intelligence officer for the

Tuskegee Airmen. The war had a transformative effect on Sutton, instilling a sense of direction in a young man prone to wander, and, when the war ended, he wasted no time in resuming his education. Upon finishing his bachelor's degree, he relocated to New York, where he enrolled in Columbia University's School of Law. The cost of living in New York and the pace of study at Columbia, however, exacted a toll. Despite assistance from the GI Bill, Sutton juggled three jobs to support his schooling. When Columbia proved unwilling to accommodate Sutton's schedule, he transferred to Brooklyn Law School, finishing the remainder of his degree over the next four years.

In 1952, Sutton passed the bar exam, and a year later he opened a legal practice with his brother, Oliver, in Harlem. The young lawyer came of age professionally just as the civil rights movement intensified throughout the country. Sutton threw himself headlong into the struggle for equality. The firebrand activist organized freedom rides and protests, championed boycotts of products and businesses that discriminated against Blacks, and encouraged others in the North to travel south. When hundreds were arrested in the course of demonstrations, Sutton offered his legal services, often refusing compensation from those he helped.[9]

Sutton's record of service supported his quick rise to leadership positions in New York's National Association for the Advancement of Colored People (NAACP), and into the inner circle of New York's Black political and business elite.[10] His father's lessons found new resonance in the rarified world of Gotham politics. "We believed that Blacks in New York would advance through the political process," Sutton described of his cohort's philosophy. "[We] discovered that political power and economic power went hand in hand. These were the people who would play a role in running the city and the state. They used their clout to develop economic opportunities for Blacks."[11] As Sutton made his first forays into elected office, he did so with the conviction that the concentration of capital and electoral representation in the Black community would return the greatest economic—and therefore political—gains.[12]

His first bid for office spanned eleven years and eleven losses. Voters consistently denied him the offices of city council, state assembly, and state senate. In a 1974 profile in *New York Magazine*, Sutton opined that the losses were an education in the "Byzantine" world of New York City politics. Each loss yielded trial-and-error lessons in the ephemerality of power, the closed-door alliances that tipped elections, and the importance of controlling one's public image.[13]

The turning point in Sutton's electoral career came in 1963, when the candidate became the personal attorney of minister Malcolm X. The way Sutton tells it, the two had been long acquainted through their mutual involvement in the civil rights movement, but not close, nor particularly amiable toward one another. After a debate on New York's WOR-AM, pitting each guests' perspectives on the tactics and timing of the movement against one another, Malcolm X confessed an admiration for Sutton's work, but demurred that Sutton would not take on a client as controversial as he. Sutton replied that, indeed, he would, and in the following weeks Sutton signed on as the personal legal representative of Malcolm X and Betty Shabazz. Many, including Sutton, credit his first electoral success in 1964 to an endorsement by Malcolm X. But Sutton wondered if this endorsement alone was sufficient to account for his success. Privately, Sutton considered the effects his access to radio time may have had on his performance at the polls.

In the weeks leading up to the 1964 election, Sutton had given several further appearances on WOR-AM and, notably, WLIB-AM, a news and current events station with interspersed hours of gospel, R&B, and blues serving New York's disparate Black communities. During his appearances, Sutton spoke directly to his prospective constituents, fielded phone calls from listeners, and responded to host Harold Jackson's questions about the candidate's positions on crime, housing, employment, and transportation. At other times, he debated his opponents live in the radio station. A key appearance came during the 1964 Harlem riots, ignited by the shooting of an African American student from the Bronx by a white police officer. As protests intensified over the course of six days, Sutton took to the airwaves of WLIB-AM, imploring the rioters to seek peaceful solutions. He empathized with the protesters' frustrations, echoing their rage while arguing that any destruction they wrought would ultimately be upon themselves.[14] While protesters found Mayor Wagner's similar pleas to be "browbeating" and "colorless," if "standard for any public official in a moment of crisis," Sutton's address had a more sympathetic reception.[15] While under no pretense that Sutton had quelled the riots, WLIB owner Harry Novik was struck by the politician's performance. In the hours following the broadcast, Novik, laden by perpetual debt and a rancorous labor dispute with his employees, confided in Sutton that he was considering leaving the radio business. Should Sutton be interested, Novik continued, he would extend to him the first option to buy the station. In the months that followed, the idea of owning a radio station echoed in the back of Sutton's mind.

Sutton considered Novik's offer at a time when Black intellectuals turned to mass media as a new front in the battle for civil rights. With increasing ferocity across the 1960s, a wave of activists positioned radio and television as instruments for seeding a new political consciousness and molding the psychology of a nation. Calling attention to the changing terrain of racial discourse in post–civil rights era, Charles Hamilton argued, "If we would understand the nature of The Modern Political Struggle we would understand that its essence lies not in traditional debates among ourselves. . . . We would quickly resolve those differences and move to a new level. . . . The mass media is a new variable. How are we going to use it? To continue to debate and blast each other—to the entertainment of white people? Or to carefully politicize masses of Black people?"[16] At the close of the 1960s, critic Harold Cruse posited mass communications as the key to consolidating political power in America. For Cruse, mass media's power derived from the breadth of its reach, and from its ability to funnel all facets of modern life through its distorting machinery.

> Mass cultural communications is a basic industry, as basic as oil, steel, and transportation in its own way. Developing along with it, supporting it, and subservient to it, is an organized network of functions that are creative, administrative, propagandistic, educational, recreational, political, artistic, economic and cultural. Taken as a whole, this enterprise involves . . . the *cultural apparatus*. Only the blind cannot see that whoever controls the cultural apparatus—whatever class, power group, faction, or political combine—also controls the destiny of the United States and everything in it.[17]

Sutton emerged from his eleven-year electoral trial intrigued by the power of mass media to shape public opinion and influence political outcomes. After his election to the office of Manhattan borough president in 1966, he proposed the prospective acquisition of WLIB-AM to prominent Black politicians and businessmen around New York. For the next five years, Sutton lobbied prominent Black New Yorkers, seeking investment and advocacy. Convinced he had the support needed to broker a deal, in 1970, Sutton formed the Inner City Broadcasting Corporation (ICBC) and, with assistance from small business and minority development loans and substantial community investment, ICBC purchased WLIB. In interviews, Sutton disclosed the logic behind ICBC's prospective acquisition, noting that "we wish to see communications media be used as an instrument for black social advancement." More telling may have been his response to criticism that, along with his 1971 purchase of a controlling share in New York's *Amsterdam News*, he was amassing a media machine. "I'm not building a media machine—machines are out of date," he retorted. "I think I now know how the system really works. It is the image-making potential of communications that attracts me."[18]

Inner City Broadcasting

WLIB was a logical first acquisition for ICBC. Novik had built the station into a beacon of goodwill in New York by prioritizing programming that "create[d] a dialogue across the ghetto walls" and faithfully administered to the community he served.[19] With its studios located in the Theresa Hotel on the corner of 126th Street and Lenox Avenue, WLIB broadcast from the beating heart of Harlem. In this community-oriented AM, ICBC found a station that matched its aspirations.

ICBC's vision for WLIB was twofold and simple. Radio should educate, and it should empower. Sutton seized on the idea of Black-owned, Black-operated, Black-oriented radio as an opportunity to counter what he perceived to be damaging representations of African American culture in mass media, with a broadcast philosophy rooted in his generation's inflection of respectability politics. Owning a radio station meant he could staff the station with voices and personalities that reflected a refined image of Black life in New York. Owning a radio station meant that he could program the station's transmissions to cultivate solidarity among the peoples of the African diaspora. And owning a radio station meant that he could employ talented young people from New York, keeping the profits within the community and offering job training to ambitious individuals. The station, for Sutton, would re-sound African American life in the minds of listeners and serve as a springboard for talented Black broadcasters and journalists.

For the strength of ICBC's vision and the collective clout they brought to media, the sale came dangerously close to imploding. In the end, it was important only that funding did come through. For Sutton and his milieu, WLIB's importance extended far beyond its symbolic value. To be effective, ICBC's image-making mission required a national network of Black-owned radio, newspaper, and television properties. Calls for minority media ownership surged in the early 1970s. Previous debates about equality in Black radio had focused largely on programming and employment issues, relegating ownership disparities to the background. Revelations of just how deep ownership disparities ran, however, reshuffled priorities. A study reported by the *New York Times* in the summer of 1970 found that of the 310 Black format stations licensed by the FCC, only eight were Black-owned. At the beginning of the decade, .002 percent of American radio stations were Black-owned.[20] Spearheaded by "an informal network of new African American media advocacy groups," Black broadcasters organized formal and informal alliances to press new "affirmative action" proposals to increase minority ownership. ICBC's media-savvy partners positioned themselves on this vanguard of Black media.[21]

ICBC's lofty aims for WLIB were not met with universal applause. Critics raised doubts about the honesty of the new management's intentions. They questioned whether a marriage of political power with the communications infrastructure would indeed serve the Black community's best interests. Judge and Harlem civic leader Livingston L. Wingate was among the earliest and most fervent detractors of the acquisition. Shortly after the finalization of the sale, Wingate argued, "I am completely in favor of black ownership of the media that serve Harlem and the black community, but I am completely opposed to any situation in which the media merge with the political apparatus. The politicians will end up using the media to tell the people only what the politicians want them to know. This is unhealthy. The community will be hurt."[22] Other critics doubted the sincerity of the ICBC's rhetoric, seeing the open invocation of race as a publicity strategy. Nation of Islam minister Elijah Muhammad gibed that "they're trying to look more black than they really are."[23]

Criticism aside, by the winter of 1972 ICBC had installed new staff and air personalities at WLIB. Operations at the station went well enough that Sutton and company considered something that a year prior would have been extreme for the cash-strapped upstart: acting on a clause in their initial contract with Novik conferring to them the option to purchase WLIB's sister FM within a year. Behind the scenes, the principal investors of ICBC scrambled to raise the money to act on the option. President of ICBC H. Carl McCall explained to the press that Inner City's leadership envisioned WLIB-FM's orientation toward entertainment as a counterbalance to the heavy community service programming of WLIB-AM. He explained, "We can only compete favorably in the New York Market if we can offer our listeners the variety and range of programs and services that an AM/FM operation allows."[24] When the sale lagged and the FCC forced WLIB-FM to change its call letters—a measure necessary when two stations are owned by different entities—ICBC saw an opportunity. Rumor spread that the newly minted WBLS-FM stood for the "Black Liberation Station," a sly nod to the previous call sign and a statement of continuity across the transition.

As the sale of WBLS solidified in the fall of 1973, McCall summarized the ICBC's second acquisition with candor: "Raising the money was a difficult task, but we had to struggle to do it because communications is of chief importance to Blacks in America and we absolutely must control a part of the media."[25] Though the FCC approved the sale of WBLS to Inner City on July 25, 1974, wavering support from investors imperiled the sale.[26] ICBC encountered continued skepticism from lenders for a loan totaling near 40 percent of WBLS's $1.35 million price. Yet the outlook of Inner City's executives may have been bleaker than the situation warranted. In the interim, Inner City's base of support had swelled to fifty-eight investors.[27] After several unpropitious meetings with lenders, ICBC secured the funding necessary to purchase WBLS. With an eye toward 1975, Pierre [Pepe] Sutton, son of Percy, vice president of ICBC, and newly appointed president of WBLS, announced that the group had arranged funding with banks "without giving any equity to outsiders."[28]

41

"The Total Black Experience in Sound"

ICBC assumed control over WBLS at an auspicious moment. In the period spanning ICBC's decision to act on the purchase option to the FCC's approval of the sale, 107.5 had earned a reputation as a tastemaker. ICBC's executive team favored a hands-off approach in the early years of WBLS, entrusting two proven figures in New York radio to realize their vision. ICBC brought on Dorothy Brunson to oversee the station's operations and gave the current programming manager, Frankie Crocker, the latitude to mold the station to his hearing.

If there was ever a manager in radio well suited to the job at WBLS, it was Dorothy Brunson. She began working for ICBC in 1971 as manager of WLIB-AM, a position she came to with a long list of accolades earned climbing the ranks of the broadcast industry. Brunson started her career as an accountant, moved on to become the operating manager at New York's iconic R&B format station WWRL, and found herself at WLIB after a short-lived but highly successful tenure as the founder and manager of America's first Black-owned advertising agency.[29] The Suttons' mission was one that clearly resonated with her: Brunson counted herself among the earliest investors in ICBC. She was a shrewd broadcast manager, combining a knack for reading audiences' desires with a grounded outlook suited to the radio business. When prompted, she candidly admitted that her greatest personal motivation was a desire to be rich.

Given her qualifications and desire to work in media, the decision to transfer to WLIB should have been an easy one. Yet she noted that she accepted the position at WLIB reluctantly and only "after . . . much prayer," citing a sexist line of questioning in her interview with Pierre Sutton and the absolute disarray of the station's finances, the reality of which stood at a remove from the grandiose posturing of ICBC's leaders. "The previous owners took all of their advertising with them the day the station was sold," Brunson would recall. "Before we bought the station it had $1.5 million worth of sales. The day we bought it, it had $186,000. There was nothing there. No money to pay the bank, the bills, or the employees."[30] Though she remained ambivalent toward the Suttons— "While the Suttons were doing political parties, no one got paid"—her assessment of the project of Black-owned media remained high, if shot through with a resigned pragmatism: "In the 1970s, [the Suttons and their friends] represented political power in New York. Anything that benefitted the black community went through them." Brunson quickly turned the station around—a messy task she summarized as "getting rid of the union" and "fir[ing] all the uncles and cousins and nieces and nephews."[31] On the strength of her performance at WLIB-AM, ICBC offered to add WBLS to her managerial duties.

Crocker joined WLIB-FM in 1971 with a larger-than-life persona, emboldened by his successes as a DJ and programming manager. Before arriving at WLIB, Crocker spent nine years apprenticing and DJing at New York's WMCA and WWRL. During that time, he figures, he performed every job in a radio station, working his way up the Top Forty and soul radio ranks. He describes his tenures at WMCA and WWRL as replete with hardships endured for his love of radio, as the period when he paid his dues, which, in Crocker's telling, did not come cheap. "I still remember living in the 135th Street YMCA," Crocker told a reporter from the *Amsterdam News*, reflecting on his start in radio. "I lived in the Y in Brooklyn, Pittsburgh and in the back of my car in Queens when I worked at WWRL. There was no money in radio then . . . I worked for free. . . . I wanted to be in radio so I did what I had to do."[32] After hours, Crocker made the rounds at New York's clubs. Crocker was a careful student of the behind-the-scenes calculations that informed station programs and relished any access to airtime. Over the years, he honed the tones and rhythms of his distinctive broadcast address, and by the dawn of the 1970s, his was New York's iconic radio voice.

When he caught his break, Crocker wasted little time adopting the trappings of a successful soul DJ. Crocker cultivated what journalists interpreted to be an uncanny correspondence between his on-air stylings and off-air lifestyle. On the air, Crocker the "Chief Rocker" was slick and boastful, able to spin virtuosic figures of speech in his sonorous baritone with ease. "Aren't you glad you live in a town where you can hear the Frankie Crocker sound when the sun goes down?" he asked listeners in the space between cuts. "Tall, tan, young, and fly . . . anytime you want me baby, reach out for me, I'm your guy." Off the air, he garnered attention for his material excesses, a fashion sense that trafficked in the ostentatious, and his considerable, much-publicized sexual appetites.[33]

To those who knew him, however, there was a disjuncture between his façade as the "Eighth Wonder of the World" and his private demeanor. Wanda Ramos, an administrative assistant turned music director and early employee at WBLS, recalls Crocker as unfailingly warm, if aloof at times.[34] To Ramos and others, Crocker was a deeply serious person— serious about music, serious about radio, and serious about the ameliorative role both might play in the conflict-riven landscape of contemporary America. To be sure, the arrogance and flamboyance that received so much media attention were a crucial part of the Crocker persona.[35] But Crocker grew resentful as he felt journalists reduced his public image to a caricature of his on-air style. "Frankie liked to live well—his home, his cars, his clothes," Ramos observed. "But he didn't mess around—didn't party, no alcohol, no nasty drugs. Nothing that would dull his senses, cloud his mind."[36] In addition to his widespread popularity and unassailable skills as a DJ, it was this seriousness, this commitment to music and its social engagements, that ICBC's leadership saw in Crocker. When the new management took control of WBLS, they permitted Crocker the leeway to recast the sound and image of the station.

After hiring new air and programming staff, Crocker changed WBLS's programming strategy from a model that accorded autonomy to the station's DJs to a more regimented, formatted playlist.[37] The results were immediate.[38] Under Crocker, WBLS joined a small cadre of stations with a "progressive Black" format. According to a feature in *Broadcasting,* these stations, "born of a new black consciousness and geared specifically to that portion of the black community for which soul music is not enough, combine all aspects of the black experience." Progressive Black stations slowed the pace of their broadcasts and programmed a

43

more "professional" sound. Such a sound featured jingles and logos with higher production values. Commercials, drained of obtrusive sound effects and delivered through the improved clarity of FM signal, eschewed the characteristic "ethnic" sound that so rankled critics. DJs programmed a wider variety of music and adopted a manner of speaking that self-consciously departed from the announcers on soul radio. They measured the pace of their on-air speech, reduced the amount of slang in their address, and spoke with standardized diction, leading some to laud their "professional" sound and others to wonder where the Black announcers had gone. For one station manager, this change in sound reflected the expectations of northern, urban Black audiences. Rejecting the fast-paced, jive-talking address of previous generations of radio personalities, he remarked, "In the early days, there was a need for identity, to say: 'O.K., he's black so he sounds like he's from down home.' I'm 38, my parents were born in the ghetto and so was I, and I really don't relate to that." Sophistication and polish were the new industry buzzwords. Progressive Black stations broadcast a sonic portrait of one segment of modern, urban Black life.[39]

WBLS amplified the unifying mission behind its progressive Black format with the tag line "The Total Black Experience in Sound." Its playlist expanded from predominately jazz with occasional blues, R&B, and gospel to include more popular music. In 1973, Crocker commented on the rationale underlying the transition in the station's programming with his characteristic bravado: "We choose records by feeling. Sure, we look at the charts, but we're usually so far ahead of the trades that it takes time for them to catch up."[40] Programming records by feeling, however, required Crocker to trust his DJs. Crocker was a savvy hiring manager, assessing prospective DJs with the same combination of instinct and experience that drove his programming choices. As his first hires in 1972, Crocker welcomed two women to WBLS as DJs and air personalities, Vy Higginsen and Lamarr Renee. Higginsen broadcast from noon to 4 PM, while Renee went on the air from 8 PM to midnight. Higginsen remembers her surprise when Crocker hired her. Though she had graduated from a broadcasting trade school—the only woman in her class—and worked in print and radio at *Ebony* and other publications as a writer and reporter on fashion and cosmetology, she had no experience as a DJ. During her interview at WBLS, she pitched Crocker an idea for a fashion and beauty show directed at WBLS's female audience. On the spot, Crocker offered her a position as a DJ. Some critics interpreted Crocker's surrounding of his afternoon drive-time slot with two women as the radiophonic extension of his playboy persona: always one woman on each arm. Higginsen offers that it was a progressive move on Crocker's part. He knew the sound he wanted for WBLS, he knew the attitude he wanted from his DJs, and he knew the impression it would make to have two educated, musically cosmopolitan women in WBLS's lineup.[41]

WBLS's DJs often improvised their mixes in the way the best live DJs might. As one song played, it might inspire an idea for a follow-up. Other times, the frequency of phone calls to the station or listener requests guided their selections. With WBLS's exhaustive record library, DJs were able to pursue a given mood or theme in their sets, or to follow the wordless dictates of intuition across their broadcast slot. On the strength of Crocker and his DJs' mixes, WBLS gained a reputation for musical range and eclecticism. Observers noted the station programmed the classic Black genres—blues, jazz, gospel, R&B, soul—but had branched into African and Caribbean music, deep cuts from classic albums, sides from artists lost to history, crossover hits from white musicians, and cuts from politically forward funk outfits. Mixes came to reflect the personalities of the DJs and diversity of the audience. "Those four hours were magic," Higginsen recalled, "because you could create."[42] Yet the musical programming of WBLS seemed to exceed eclecticism and communicate a deeper philosophy about the relationship between sounds and people. Recounting the artists she might program in a given hour, Higginsen remarked that her programming selections sought to express something essential about Black life through sound. "We had our format—the top end, quarter hour, etc.—but included a variety of music," she said. "Gospel, something old, something new, jazz as a part of the history, Esther Philips, instrumentals, Stanley Turrentine, Oscar Grover Jr. . . . Anything that captured the spirit . . . how the beat worked for us."[43]

Crocker shared a conviction with the Suttons: commanding an audience's attention entailed an obligation to educate. There was a practical component to educating the listener, in Crocker's view, allowing the station to cultivate and retain the desired audience. Crocker told a reporter from *Broadcasting*, "You don't want to stick your head right into the noose right away. You stick your toe in the water first and get a little bit wet. That way you don't lose your audience. That's the education process."[44] Yet music also formed the basis for a mode of subtle social education. Music, in the right mix, could cultivate empathy and understanding in listeners. Perhaps idealistically, it could close the fissures separating Black and white and ease tensions within the Black community. "We have a license to serve a community that happens to be black," Crocker noted. "It's obviously an audience oriented toward black music and when you play James Brown back-to-back with John Coltrane it shows the James Brown fan something he may not have heard before, and the cat who likes John Coltrane gets to hear the James Brown he himself wouldn't put on the record player. I've always felt this would work because it's all one music. You can educate under the guise of entertainment."[45] Selections were as much about retaining and growing listenership as they were exposing the station's listeners to one another through the chemistry of the mix. Musical unity aspired toward social unity; expanded taste might yield an expanded mind. At WBLS, the mix served as a metaphor for their programming and their audience.

The sound of WBLS, however, was not reducible to its musical programming. If *Broadcasting*'s reporters were quick to notice the new sound of Black Progressive radio, air staff and management were quick to put that new sound into words. When I asked Wanda Ramos what she listened for in records during her time at WBLS, she noted that she and the programming staff were unusually attuned to the production quality of records: "It has to sound *good*. It has to sound right. You know within thirty seconds if it's right for the station."[46] ICBC executive Hal Jackson reiterated the importance that features such as commercials reflect the image of the station. Barred were predatory lenders, advertisements couched in pernicious stereotypes, and products that pandered or sounded too good to be true. No screaming wines, no credit companies. For one commentator, the effect was shocking, writing, "WBLS's sound is as highly produced and polished as WWAT(AM) New York, an R&B station. But the pace is starkly different. The jingles are, to the ear accustomed to AM production, painfully slow. The disk jockeys speak hardly louder than a whisper, and all contrast in pace and coloring is achieved with music and logos, never with the on-air voice."[47] All the sounds and features that framed WBLS's musical programming conditioned the way audiences received it. They suggested a set of images and associations to attend the sound. The perspectives of WBLS's air personalities and the sonic profile of the station acted as an auditory paratext, supplementing the music by suggesting an attitude with which a listener might encounter it, and a set of dispositions and images that might accompany it.

None of the DJs at WBLS entertained the notion that, because they broadcast to a predominately Black audience, they were broadcasting to an exclusively Black audience. In their 1973 profile of Black Progressive formats, *Broadcasting*'s reporters insinuated what ratings services would confirm in the following years: a large number of white audience members listening across the color line bolstered the mass market success of Black-format stations like WBLS. The executives at Inner City welcomed a crossover audience and understood that the political mission of stations like WBLS and WLIB stood to improve with the support of sympathetic white listeners. Brunson, with her keen entrepreneurial eye, viewed the white audience as something more than a felicitous consequence of the appeal of Black music: they represented a business opportunity. "When I looked at our audience, I found it to be very sophisticated and it had a strong component of gay white males," Brunson recalled of her market research. "They loved us and they had money, so we started cultivating them and other whites whose profiles mirrored that of the affluent blacks we also wanted to reach."[48] Higginsen felt that voyeurism was in no small part responsible WBLS's substantial white audience. She offered her explanation for the station's cross-racial appeal when she noted, "People listened to the station because it gave them an opportunity to sneak into the Black community, almost peeping and enjoying simultaneously."[49] For those at WBLS, the popularity of Black music in the mid-1970s, the station's urbane image, and the deep-historical pull of cross-racial fascination all contributed to its appeal among white listeners.

By the time ICBC took over the station in the fall of 1974, WBLS had risen to the fifth-highest-rated station in the entire New York market.[50] When ICBC took control of WBLS, the new management announced that there would be no personnel changes, nor would they tamper with the station's format. Regarding the transition, an Inner City spokesperson stated simply, "We've got a winner."[51] Questioning the group's commitment to their broadcast community, critics of Inner City alleged that the group had only followed through with the purchase after the station's recent reversal of fortune. Satisfied by Inner City's luck, Carl McCall retorted, "We always intended to buy from the beginning, and the new, good ratings don't really enter into it. It does make it all the better, though."[52]

Rating the Value of Education and Entertainment, 1975–1978

WBLS grew its audience into 1975. With more listeners came increased scrutiny of the station's format. Outlets around the country adopted elements of WBLS's sound, or copied its format wholesale, and reporters familiar with WBLS began to refer to "Black Progressive" as the "Crocker

Format," as much a sign of WBLS's idiosyncratic style as a testament to the music press's fascination with the station's signature DJ.[53] The scale and pace of listeners' positive response to the new tones of Black radio surprised even those who brought it to fruition. "We were selling ourselves, the station, and FM simultaneously," recalled Higginsen, incredulous of the immediacy of WBLS's turnaround. As listeners tuned in to WBLS in greater numbers, the station began to register in the accounting of several national radio ratings surveys. These ratings, as imperfect as they were, provided a quantitative measure of WBLS's growing listenership; they made the station visible to the radio community on a national stage and opened the door to new planes of profitability. As staff at WBLS relished their position near the top of the charts, the station's profits chafed against its politics.

The first indications that WBLS could compete favorably against New York's highest-rated stations came in December 1974, when ratings services released their trend reports for the summer and fall of that year. According to *Pulse*, the dominant ratings service of the early and mid-1970s, WBLS finished the fall–winter 1974 ratings period ranked eighth overall in the New York market, when accounting for the entire broadcast day. Yet, between the hours of 7 PM and 12 AM, WBLS accrued the greatest number of listeners from the categories of men and women ages eighteen to thirty-four, surpassing New York's highest-rated station, WABC-AM.[54] WBLS trailed WABC, a Top Forty format station headed by radio heavyweight and format architect Rick Sklar, only in the number of teens who tuned in. WBLS's victory in those demographics, though marginal, was no mean feat. That, less than two years into the implementation of its new format, WBLS boasted of audiences totaling just over 4 percent of all radio listened to in New York indicated the timeliness of the "Total Black Experience in Sound."

WBLS's first ratings breakthrough came in the summer of 1975. According to *Pulse*, WBLS had raced to the front of the pack, claiming the highest ratings of all stations among adults between 3 PM and 7 PM. Referred to as the "afternoon drive time," this daypart commanded the highest prices from advertisers, eager to target captive commuters as they transitioned out of their workday. Stations accordingly clamored for the attention of listeners during this block. To those in the know, WBLS's dominance during this daypart was no surprise. Frankie Crocker strategically timed his personal broadcast slot to greet listeners as they left work and settled into their evenings. Ratings data confirmed what impressionistic data could only suggest: WBLS's core constituency was, in fact, a coalition of disparate demographics and affinity groups, drawing Black and white, young and old, soul fan and hard rocker, queer and straight, together in a community tuned to 107.5 FM. Pierre Sutton, then station manager of WBLS and vice president of ICBC, seized the occasion to comment on WBLS's momentous achievement, telling the *Amsterdam News*, "This marks the first time that a Black owned radio station has made a universal appeal while maintaining the integrity of its identity."[55] For ICBC, WBLS had achieved dominance without compromising its audience or its image. The station had not sold out.

As WBLS garnered national attention, the station's management and air staff seized the occasion to rehearse the station's political commitments. Pepe (Pierre) Sutton spoke frankly about WBLS's financial windfall, but reiterated Inner City's position on mass media ownership as a vehicle for African American progress. "We didn't come in with the notion of making piles of money," he said. "We came in because Black communications is essential to Black development."[56] Yet, as Sutton continued, he broached a tension made unavoidable to the board at Inner City. Black-oriented news and public affairs format radio was far from lucrative. Not all listeners, it seemed, were ready—or wanted—to be moved to action. "We began to program WLIB-AM very heavily towards public service because we wanted to move the community to do things," Sutton said, "but we found out painfully that radio is basically an entertainment device. You can put out all the messages you want but if you don't have people listening to you then you don't have any impact."[57] If ICBC embarked on their experiment in minority media ownership with grand plans for uplift and progress, with WBLS they confronted a dialectic that would define their tenure in radio ownership: that between entertainment and education.

By the summer of 1978, WBLS raised its ratings to a 7.9 share in the New York market, closing in on WABC's 8.1. The station's rise to prominence caused ICBC to revisit how they voiced their mission to the public. As WBLS enjoyed mass market success, the stations' spokespersons shied away from the revolutionary rhetoric that had characterized its publicity in its early years. Early on, ICBC stressed the potential of WBLS and WLIB to open minds and instigate organized action. In a particularly evocative example, Pepe Sutton told the *Amsterdam News*, "Communication is essential to organization, and organization is essential to progress. . . . In Haiti, slaves were allowed to have drums . . . and revolution

49

was effected."[58] By 1978, however, ICBC representatives opted for messaging of a different tack, shifting away from revolution toward the legitimacy of their stations and audiences. In the spring and summer of 1978, Hal Jackson expressed a sentiment now central to WBLS's messaging when he told *Billboard*, "We are black owned and we serve the black community. But we are a people station. We feel we are New York."[59] Months later, as WBLS closed in on the number-one-rated in the New York market, Jackson spun the same message in slightly different terms: "We're not the number one black station. We're not the number one FM station. We're number one."[60]

The change in messaging was a rebuttal of claims that in any way qualified the station's ascent. To call WBLS the "best Black station" was to reprise the separate-but-equal, segregationist logic that ICBC existed to combat. Yet there were also practical concerns that fueled the station's rhetorical turn. The change in messaging stemmed in part from ICBC's recognition that WBLS's appeal extended far beyond the Black community. Push the revolutionary message too hard, and they risked alienating the casual listener so important to their elevated ratings. The change was made more pressing, however, by the discrepancy between WBLS's ratings and its advertising revenue. Though WBLS maintained its position in the top-five-rated stations in New York for nearly three years, its quarterly revenues were not commensurate with its ratings. By 1978, as WBLS broached the title of highest-rated station in America, the station had not entered the top five highest-earning stations in New York. The change in rhetoric, emphasizing WBLS as a "people" station that served that Black community, was as much about avoiding being pigeonholed as a Black or ethnic station by advertisers as it was broadening its appeal to listeners. Even market-topping ratings could only do so much to move advertiser budgets from "Top Forty" to "Black." According to Sutton, the burden fell on WBLS to prove the value of Black consumers to accounts that still believed that "Blacks don't buy toothpaste or fly on airplanes."[61] Caught between a desire to educate and entertain their audience, to ensure the station's integrity and while keeping it commercially viable, WBLS articulated a position that sought to move beyond the strictures of race even as it invoked race as its reason for being. WBLS's rivalry with WABC marked the beginning of this tense period of self-definition. It would come to a head in the following years, first with the advent of disco radio, and then with the emergence of the urban contemporary format in its wake.

The Disco Wars

On a Sunday evening in July 1978, tiring of his station's "mellow" sound, programmer Eddie Cossman broke from WKTU-FM's format. For the previous five years, WKTU's blend of soft rock and adult contemporary was met by listeners with a lukewarm reception. Characterized by *Billboard* as "a rock station for people who don't like rock," WKTU finished the May–June ratings period with a 1.2 share, stagnating against the ratings bedrock, while WBLS and WABC earned 8.6 and 8.0 shares, respectively.[62] The way he tells it, Cossman called programming consultant Ken Burkhart that evening and asked him to prepare a disco format. The format was to be ready to air the next day. Equivocation wasn't an option. "I've been in radio too long to accept that argument, 'Let's wait for one more [ratings] book,'" he told *Billboard*.[63] Cossman's decision, though abrupt, mobilized months of careful observation. "I looked at other stations which were doing disco, but were not totally disco," he told *Billboard*. "I looked at WBLS-FM New York, which was doing disco, but is black-oriented. I realized that we could reach beyond just a black audience."[64] Without publicity or notice, WKTU implemented a disco format, airing on Monday, June 24, at 6 PM.

Cossman's target audience spanned the advertiser's gamut and then some. Latino, Jewish, white, Black, gay, straight—what mattered was that they partied in the city's thriving clubs and bought disco records soon after they arrived on shelves. By all measures, Burkhart's new format succeeded in attracting this demographic admixture and more to WKTU. Far from a stroke of luck, Burkhart had prepared his disco format from half a year of assiduous research. During that period, he surveyed more than five hundred owners of discotheques, DJs, promoters, and record store owners. He distilled their preferences into a 150-track playlist and used that playlist to program the newly branded "Disco 92."[65] WKTU's all-in approach to disco aimed to capture the zeitgeist.

When the first books came in, they showed an immediate spike in ratings, and WKTU's numbers continued to improve through the end of 1978. When Arbitron released their survey in late December, the numbers they published surpassed WKTU's most optimistic forecasts. The station had garnered an 18.4 share of men and women ages eighteen to thirty-four, and a 14.4 for all adults. The biggest surprise to analysts came in the firm's measurement of teen listeners. Following the change in format, WKTU accounted for 31.5 percent of teen listening in New

York, bringing the station's total market share to a dominant 15.8. Dethroned, WABC receded to second place with an 8.0 share. WBLS fared far worse. By December 1978, WBLS's ratings fell from 7.7 to 3.1.[66] Ratings were only one indication of WKTU's success. For Burkhart, a walk through Central Park convinced him of WKTU's dominance in New York. As he strolled the greens, each radio he passed was tuned to Disco 92.

The meteoric rise of disco radio reflected national demand for the music. Growing out of a mix of soul, rock, and R&B records that found favor in New York's discotheques, "disco" emerged first as a local dance music among the city's queer, Black, immigrant, and all-of-the-above communities. Early disco is notoriously difficult to define. Tim Lawrence offers perhaps the best definition when he writes, "Disco music . . . simply referred to music that worked well in discotheques, whether it was funk or soul or something else."[67] By mid-decade, several distinct strains had risen to prominence. One form—epitomized by Philadelphia International Records—married the percussive rhythm guitar and syncopated bass of funk with the rich arrangements of Motown over midtempo, four-on-the-floor beats. Records in this camp include MFSB's "Love Is the Message," The O'Jays' "Back Stabbers," and Three Degrees' "Dirty Ol' Man," as well as the more straightforward funk of People's Choice's "Do It Any Way You Wanna." Another strain, perhaps reaching its apotheosis in the long-form, synth-and-sex dance anthems of Giorgio Moroder and Donna Summer, offered dancers long plays of android rhythms. The popularity of these styles increased steadily through the mid-1970s. Established acts like Harold Melvin and the Blue Notes and Stevie Wonder, among many others, adapted the sound to their repertoire, and new acts expanded the style. What dancers and trade magazines referred to as "disco music" was the soundtrack to a mid-decade America increasingly obsessed with social dancing. New dance clubs specializing in the genre opened in cities across the country.[68]

Though WBLS had consistently incorporated disco into its programming since its inception, pressure from WKTU forced WBLS to rebrand the station to emphasize their affiliation with the music. WBLS's "Total Black Experience in Sound," as well as its less formal logos "The World's Best-Looking Sound" and "The World's Most Beautiful Sound," fell into disuse as management instituted the tag line "Disco and More."[69] The new logo was a clever compromise. In practice, WBLS could stave off any major adjustments to their playlists while aligning themselves with the era's most popular music. The station's minor rebranding yielded outsized results. By the spring of 1979, WBLS's ratings showed signs of a rebound.[70] Journalists were quick to label the competition between the two stations New York's "disco wars," a description that only intensified the competition between the two outfits.

The station's ratings turnaround gave way to a full recovery when Frankie Crocker returned to the station in the summer of 1979. While the DJ had pled guilty to charges of tax evasion, a US court of appeals overturned his conviction on charges of having accepted payola and perjury, leaving Crocker both humbled and defiant in the wake of the verdict.[71] If he appeared contrite in interviews with the *Amsterdam News*, admitting that the ordeal had prompted some soul-searching, his actions portrayed the opposite. He announced his symbolic return to the center of New York society by riding into Studio 54 wearing a tail-coat, seated atop a white stallion.[72] "The knight who comes to save everybody rides a white horse," Crocker told a reporter of the event. Indeed, despite his new inclination toward introspection, Crocker's swagger outlasted the scandal. Crocker adopted McFadden and Whitehead's extended disco paean to optimism "Ain't No Stopping Us Now" as WBLS's unofficial anthem.[73] Atop the cinematic strings, handclaps, and melismatic incantations of McFadden and Whitehead's groove, Crocker heralded his personal comeback and WBLS's return to prominence. By August, New York's disco format stations were deadlocked.

Disco's significance for WBLS exceeded the yearlong disco wars. The rebrand to "Disco and More" marked the station's most significant capitulation to market forces yet. It demonstrated to WBLS the ephemerality of listeners' attention, and the importance of keeping the station's image as current as its playlist. That WBLS's greatest competition came from disco, an ostensibly Black dance music, seemed to articulate something deeper about the challenges facing of Black-owned, Black-operated, Black-oriented radio stations, cutting to the heart of nationwide debates over the place of race in the culture industries. If certain corners of the music and radio industry cheered disco's ascendance, it was met with skepticism and cynicism in others. Published in December 1978, *Radio and Records* ran a three-part series entitled "Disco's Challenge for Black Radio."[74] In this segment, columnist Bill Speed interviewed radio programmers, label execs, and A&R reps to assess disco's impact on Black-oriented radio. Speed asked "if disco radio, by appealing to black listeners and also to the growing number of white disco followers, poses a threat to black formatted stations."[75] While Speed's interlocutors almost universally agreed that, yes, disco did pose a threat to Black radio, the reasons they offered tended to focus more on the racial problems inherent to disco than the stations that programmed it. Many contended that the label "disco" itself had an insidious deracinating effect. After *Saturday Night Fever*, they argued, audiences knew disco as a chic, white music, now unmoored from the Black communities who had fostered it and continued to enjoy it (as well as eliding the contributions of queer and queer-of-color clubs). The more the music industry naturalized disco as popular music, the more this deracinating effect became injurious. One programming manager of a Black format station summarized the tension succinctly: "[Disco is] our music in Sheep's clothing," he stated, directing his response toward the economic logic of the disco format. "If disco comes along offering advertisers and record companies substantial white audience penetration as well as black, why, in the future, should anyone want to stick to traditional black formats?"[76] Black format stations were vulnerable to loss of listeners because they balanced entertainment with service to their broadcasting community. Within Black radio circles, disco raised concerns over the symbolic ownership of cultural production as much as it did questions about the social necessity of the Black format or financial inequalities in broadcasting.

Despite the attention it garnered, the disco format was short lived. In December 1979, just in time for the new decade, an influential research firm released a report predicting a collapse in disco sales. The report alleged that disco's health was far less robust than the previous year's record sales or club attendance indicated. As disco penetrated further into the mainstream, the report continued, young trendsetting audiences were abandoning it in search of the next big thing. For Wanda Ramos, who left WBLS in 1979 to work as a consultant for disco format architect Ken Burkhart, it was disco's redefinition as an effete, queer music that soured popular audiences on the genre.[77] As for others, radio and record labels had underestimated the extent to which pop culture had been oversaturated with disco. People were tired of it. Among fans of hard rock, "Disco sucks" became a countercultural rallying cry, only thinly veiling the racism and homophobia that raised disco as a call to arms against the mainstream. At the core of disco's abrupt demise, though, were a series of industry miscalculations. Analysts had mistaken an active audience—an audience that buys records and attends clubs—for a large audience. When ardent disco fans stopped supporting the genre, there was no broad base to maintain sales.

Reading the writing on the wall, radio stations in New York severed their connections with the genre. WBLS dropped their tagline "Disco and More" for the forward-looking logo "The Sound of the 80s." WKTU took more drastic measures. The station replaced all of its on-air talent, removed all mentions of disco from their broadcasts and publicity, and changed over 50 percent of its existing playlist, shortening the average track, introducing more R&B, and slowing the tempo to include more ballads.[78] Conceding that WKTU still "had a strong disco sound," program director Paul Zarcone titled the station's new format "progressive urban contemporary." By the arrival of 1980, New York stations formerly employing a disco format broadcast a range of music by predominately Black artists, hoping to retain the attention of disco's diverse community of reception. Beginning with WKTU's "progressive urban contemporary," the moniker "urban" spread rapidly throughout radio circles.

Not all broadcasters, however, felt compelled to distance themselves from disco. In 1979, a disco DJ whose mixes attracted a zealous fan base rented airtime on WHBI-FM 105.9, Newark, a time-brokered, foreign-language station with studios in the basement of a hotel on lower Riverside Drive. Industry trends and consulting reports were irrelevant to the DJ, and WHBI appears on no ratings reports for the period. What mattered was that dancers still responded to disco cuts. In April 1979, *Mr. Magic's Disco Showcase* aired for the first time. For the next three years, Mr. Magic would greet his listeners on Saturday nights to the sounds of Grover Washington Jr.'s track of the same title, intoning over Eric Gale's slip-sliding double-stops, "Good evening, and welcome to the finest music in the Apple. I welcome you and yours to the *Disco Showcase*."

During its brief, but intense, moment of popularity, disco signaled the vexed status of race in the culture industries. It presaged the troubles WBLS would face in the 1980s as it unfurled its urban contemporary format, earned and maintained the number-one-rated position, and debuted the first program dedicated to rap music on commercial radio.

. . . .

In 1977, after eleven years as Manhattan borough president, Percy Sutton stepped down from his post to pursue the office of mayor of New York. His campaign lasted just over a year and ended in a narrow defeat. At the end of the race, Sutton conceded to fellow Democrat Ed Koch, who would hold the office of mayor for four terms.[79]

Tired but undeterred, Sutton returned to his law practice in Harlem. If his bid for borough president had suggested the potential of mass media, his loss in the mayoral race provided confirmation.[80] In the wake of his most recent electoral defeat, Sutton attributed his disappointing performance in the polls to partial and infrequent media coverage of his campaign. In 1975, Sutton sold his shares of the *Amsterdam News*, claiming the paper had become a "political liability," with detractors operating under the "mistaken belief" that he, personally, controlled the content of the paper. And throughout the 1977 race Sutton complained that New York's media failed to cover his campaign adequately.[81] He went so far as to file a lawsuit against the FCC alleging that, in violation of the fairness doctrine, he was denied the airtime he was entitled to.[82]

After a three-month trip across Africa, where Sutton worked to finance and encourage entrepreneurs from a number of sub-Saharan and southern African nations, he returned to New York to resume his legal practice. Yet he soon found himself beset by a familiar restlessness. Years earlier, just after closing ICBC's purchase of WLIB-AM, Sutton had speculated as to how he would continue his work after leaving electoral politics. He told a reporter from *New York Magazine*, "When I leave this office, which I'm going to do, I'm going to travel the length and breadth of this country trying to convince every black person who will listen to me that they ought to get into business. Communications is where blacks are going to make their greatest strides in the coming decades."[83] Following the concession of the mayoral race, he devoted himself to just that. At the request of his son Pierre, then-president of WBLS, Sutton refused several lucrative offers for partnerships at New York law firms to manage his assets in radio full time.[84] What followed was a wave of acquisitions across the spectrum of media. In 1979, ICBC purchased five new radio stations: KBLX and KVTO in San Francisco, KGFJ and KUTE in Los Angeles, and WLBS in Detroit. With a strong track record in the management of media properties, Sutton found himself more easily able to acquire financing, and his financial position at the turn of the 1980s was improved by the successes of his previous ventures. Much of ICBC's capital now came from the earnings of "cash cow" WBLS—then valued at $18 million, a far cry from the $1.35 million purchase price—or was borrowed against the equity of the corporation's current holdings, which were estimated to top $60 million.[85] Without the baggage and surveillance that attends political office, ICBC made their first acquisition of a print outlet in the purchase of *Unique Magazines*, a company specializing in lifestyle glossies. In the following years, Inner City acquired Amistad Electronics, a computer parts manufacturer, and obtained a 50 percent stake in the Sheridan Broadcasting Network, a national Black news network with over one hundred affiliate stations.[86] Inner City's next major initiative was the purchase of the deteriorating Apollo Theater for $250,000, with plans of syndicating a monthly broadcast of performances at the iconic Harlem venue. Emboldened by their expansion, rumors spread that ICBC had acquired a station in Indianapolis for the sole reason of taking it off the air: when conditions were right, this midwestern station interfered with WBLS's signal. Underpinning the corporation's wave of expansion was a plan, still in its infant stage, to install and manage the infrastructure of cable television in New York's outer boroughs. By 1981, Inner City's holdings in radio alone were valued at over $78 million.[87]

At the dawn of the 1980s, Sutton set his sights not on two radio stations, but on an empire.

WBLS and the Urban Contemporary Format

Like so much in the history of radio, the origin of the term *urban contemporary* is unverifiable. Frankie Crocker claims to have invented it to describe WBLS's format in the mid-1970s, and this story is widely repeated as truth. It may well be. Program manager Barry Mayo of New York's WRKS claims that his boss, Lee Simonson, coined the term, while others have attributed it disco format pioneer Ken Burkhart, who himself believes it came out of the sales department at one of his stations.[88] The term does not appear in print before WKTU's 1979 switch to a "progressive urban contemporary" format. Irrespective of its origins, the new format represented more than just an elision of disco. Urban contemporary (UC) came to stand in for a host of anxieties about the place of race in the broadcasting and culture industries.

By the 1970s, Black music had once again become America's popular music. Radios and clubs across the country resounded with soul, R&B, funk, and disco. For historian Daniel Rodgers, the production and reception of Black music cut to the heart of the racial tensions of the post–civil rights era. Amid reports of unraveling cities, bureaucratic and popular resistance to affirmative action, and reprisals of the Black Power movement's calls for a "nation within a nation," the racial makeup of the entertainment industries shifted. Along with increased presence on television and in professional sports, "from Motown to Michael Jackson's mega-successes of the mid-1980s," Rodgers writes, "the popular music industry turned into a showcase of black talent."[89] In the post–disco era it was easy to hear the echoes of tropes dating back to minstrelsy: Blackness, once again, was both pathology and entertainment on the nation's largest stages. Demand for racialized cultural production multiplied, and the music industry restructured to profit from that demand, amounting to a "corporate annexation of black music," to borrow Mark Anthony Neal's apposite phrase.[90] By the time radio stations touted the label *urban contemporary*, the meanings of race in America seemed as uncertain as ever. Born of pressure exerted equally by a sales-hungry record industry, newly constituted radio audiences, and a radio industry freshly structured for profit, the term *urban contemporary* encapsulated the paradoxes of race in the post–civil rights era.

For how much ink trade periodicals devoted to the urban format, there was little agreement about what exactly it was. For the first months of 1980, the answer was some variation of "Urban contemporary is what WBLS and WKTU program," with each station's sound made to stand as its own definition. But the format spread rapidly, and stations across the country adopted it in name and content. An October 1980 roundtable discussion about the urban format demonstrates the range of criteria broadcasters invoked in their definitions. Sonny Joe White of Boston's WXKS rooted his description in broadcast geography, emphasizing the composition of the audience and their desires. "Urban Contemporary comes from inner-city listeners," he argued. "It gets a different style of listener. . . . People who listen to black radio don't like to hear just black music. That want to hear about everything from Africa to Iran to Washington." For another broadcaster, implementing a UC format presented an opportunity to capitalize on the crossover success of many Black artists, attracting the largest and most diverse audience, and thus the highest ratings and the most advertising dollars. Dollars, the panelists agreed, that had previously eluded any station labeled "ethnic" or "Black." The conversation intensified as the participants broached whether UC shared the imperative of Black format stations to inform and support their broadcast community. Amos Brown, station manager at Indianapolis's WLTC, warned that "Urban Contemporary is black without the black. There's no commitment to the audience. . . . It's heavy on the lifestyle information," without informing the Black community "what's going on." To summarize, *Billboard*'s event reporter tried to cut through the euphemism, calling the format "a code word for an R&B, jazz, and soft rock mix."[91]

A definitive answer proved elusive. Urban radio was at once a broadcast geography, a type of listener, a code word for listeners who wanted to hear both Black music and current affairs, a device for selling Black music to white audiences and for selling Black stations to advertisers, a capitulation of Black radio's imperative to serve its broadcast community to the allure of gain, and a formula for mixing music. Not ones to let a good controversy go to waste, the trades continued to interrogate the new format: What is UC? How do we account for its success? And who does it benefit?[92] In June 1982, *Billboard* ran a series of articles covering the format nationally, querying the managers and program directors of urban outlets about their station's broadcast content, constituents, and programing philosophies.[93] For Scotty Andrews of V103 Atlanta, the urban format was simply a form of branding. He expressed a much-echoed viewpoint when he told *Billboard*'s reporter, "We're a black station that goes under the Urban Contemporary banner to try and have mass appeal." Others lamented the urban format's tendency to mask the race of the musicians it featured. In an article entitled "Radio Downplays Blackness," *Billboard*'s reporter conveyed this perspective with a sense of resignation, stating, "Whether you call it 'black' or 'disco' or 'dance music' or 'urban,' it is a format that is winning large shares in many diverse markets, including some that lack a large black population."[94]

In sound, these new urban formats followed the model established by WBLS in the mid-1970s. The rhetoric station managers adopted in the early 1980s bore surprising resemblance to *Broadcasting*'s survey of "progressive Black" formats nearly a decade prior. By 1983, commenters noted that the sound of Black format radio changed as their audiences drifted toward UC stations. Jerry Boulding of WJZZ Detroit noted that more Black stations had a "bright sound, jingles . . . and Black air personalities with good diction." Donnie Simpson of WKYS Washington echoed this viewpoint: "We can all see much more professionalism from our [on-air] people than we did ten years ago, and have really gotten away from that old-fashioned approach of jive talkin' and saying nothing." One broadcaster echoed WBLS in rhetoric and mission, remarking that his station's transition away from "barbeque" radio toward a "professional" sound was an attempt to "be an educator. To elevate our audience to a higher plane."[95] In practice, this entailed a cleaner sound, conspicuously "educated" voices, and a mix of, say, 85 percent Black artists to 15 percent white artists, with crossover acts including David Bowie, Men at Work, Boz Scaggs, Hall and Oates, and Kraftwerk, with a heavy dose of local news and current affairs interspersed.

Programming UC stations proved an exercise in mapping sound to racial identity, of catering to musical tastes at the level of race and ethnicity. At heart, there was an obvious truth here that could not have been less obvious at the time: some Black folk liked white music, some white folk liked Black music, and most au courant young people in New York liked disco. Race was a crude proxy for musical preference, more reflective of blunt radio research methodologies than the complexities of taste. Even shrewd programmers struggled to reconcile disparities between listeners' outward physical appearances and their personal musical tastes. Barry Mayo of WRKS remarked of this programming challenge, "The key is to play white records that black people like and black music that appeals to whites. But I'm dealing [in New York] with three ethnic groups [including Latino] that like to hear records programmed three different ways. The trick is to find music that's hip enough for Blacks but hit-oriented enough for Whites."[96] Jeff Harrison of KDIA San Francisco also spoke of programing as a balancing act. He told *Billboard*, "When I think of what urban radio should sound like, I think of crossover music that each race will feel comfortable with. The music should be universal, combining as wide a range of moods and feelings as possible."[97]

Though little sonic distance separated the urban contemporary format from disco, race emerged as the operative category for interpreting urban radio. If broadcasters diverged in their definitions of the format, taken together, their efforts cast the pressures facing Black radio in sharp relief. Above all, Black broadcasters felt constrained by the expectation that their stations must first and foremost serve their broadcast communities. Even as the profit potential of radio soared in the early 1980s, many broadcasters faced a dilemma. On the one hand, broadcasters debated how to realize the profits Black music and Black-appeal radio had demonstrated it was capable of generating. On the other, they wondered how to continue with their obligation to inform and empower, to bring their people with them, so to speak. Mayo summarized the tension between Black and urban stations pointedly, telling *Billboard*, "Most Urban outlets don't have the same community thrust as Black stations because of their attempt to 'image' for the general market. The distinction exists, and most black radio programmers are pissed about it. After years of community involvement in such activities as voter registration drives, sickle cell telethons, and 'shoes for kids' they felt ripped off, and I can understand it."[98]

Crosstown Traffic: Rivalry on Commercial Radio

While broadcasters debated the identity and merit of the Urban format, WBLS and WKTU vied for the rank of most-listened-station in New York. WBLS eked ahead of the competition for most of 1980 and 1981, and by 1982 the stations' formats began to diverge.[99] With the addition of WRKS to the UC fray, competition between stations tighter than ever, and the potential profits still on the upswing, stations elected to target ever-more-specific demographics rather than contend for the same listeners. WBLS, true to its desire to present an image of sophisticated adult life, sought to attract older listeners by programming more "Black gold," memorable tracks from the late 1950s and 1960s.[100] WKTU, instead, programmed a higher percentage of club hits in hopes of securing teenage listeners, staking its success on an appeal to growing appetites for "street music."[101] In early 1983, warning signs that UC might go the way of disco appeared in the trade press.[102] Each station scrambled to recover its faltering ratings. WKTU doubled down on their appeals to younger listeners, as did WRKS. Management at WBLS, more successful than ever with older demographics, decided that they needed more teenage listeners.

By 1983, the goodwill WBLS enjoyed with their listener base faltered. Not two years after he returned to WBLS, exonerated from his payola scandal, Crocker found himself in another spat with the record industry.[103] In 1981, independent Black music labels spearheaded a boycott against WBLS, alleging that Crocker refused to play product by Black-owned labels. Sutton responded by drawing attention to the net good WBLS had done for Black musicians, labels, producers, and audiences, redoubling his support of Crocker while asserting that WBLS's viability depended on the station's ability to control all aspects of its format.[104] Suspicions of managerial misconduct intensified in the following years when, in 1983, the American Federation of Television and Radio Actors filed suit against Inner City, alleging the wrongful termination of several employees and accusing the corporation of refusing to negotiate with the union in good faith.[105] Another boycott followed shortly after AFTRA announced the suit. To those in WBLS's studios and executive offices, the station's "distinct image [of] polished, partying, Black Urbanity" groaned under the pressures to gain and grow.[106]

UC brought the newly treacherous topography of the media industries into sharp relief. WBLS's reputation as the "Black liberation station" reached new lows as the station saw new highs in profits. As the owners and programmers of UC stations conceded radio's ability to mobilize political action and service African American communities without recourse to the profit motive, we see the mechanics of the process by which deliberative politics shifted from the electoral and business arenas into the cultural. Political scientist Richard Iton argues that, at the cusp of hip-hop ascendance, "official politics [were] pulled into vernacular spaces and . . . de facto decisions [were] made in that realm regarding issues of clear political significance."[107] In these vernacular spaces, musical artists and other cultural representatives proffered strategies for urban revitalization, visions of masculine and feminine identities and relationships between the sexes, and affective dispositions (namely, rage and urgency)—that filtered upward and inflected formal political discourse. Against this history—of a station in turmoil, a service mission faltering under the pressure of market forces, the advent of UC, and a station looking to attract younger listeners—the programming staff at WBLS cut a deal to bring a popular underground DJ to experiment with a rap radio program.

THREE

Commercializing Rap with Mr. Magic's *Rap Attack*

In the spring of 1988, around the time he finalized his plans to leave WBLS-FM 107.5, Mr. Magic reflected on his tenure at the urban contemporary (UC) station. At the time of Magic's departure, his name was synonymous with rap music, with hip-hop culture, and, in some circles, with New York City itself. Yet his recollections betray the trouble roiling beneath the cool exterior he presented during his broadcasts. "The problem wasn't that the show wasn't commercial," he told a reporter from UK-based fanzine *Soul Underground*. "It was simply that the people at the top in WBLS didn't accept rap."[1] Though *Rap Attack* topped weekly ratings and attracted youth-oriented advertising accounts, program managers at WBLS only hesitantly incorporated rap music into its schedule. The situation hardly improved over the near-decade Magic spent at New York's flagship UC station. Upon leaving WBLS, Magic asked a question that historians have grappled with since: Why did broadcast outlets positioned to gain from rap's success so virulently oppose it? To this, I add a few questions of my own: What were the sources of programmers' and audiences' anxieties? Why, despite the increasing overlap between the sound of rap and the sound of drive-time UC radio, did the music elude rotation? And what creative avenues did radio open for rap despite executives' ambivalence?

To be sure, the reasons why management passed over rap music were many. Rapping was an untried and, for some, impenetrable mode of vocalization. Early rap records had different production priorities, and often worse production values than the major-label releases that were the station's standard fare. And, perhaps most important, the image of the young, dark-skinned man rapping from the rubble of the Bronx, an image quickly becoming inseparable from the sounds of hip-hop, grated against WBLS's carefully maintained projection of Black middle-class respectability. In the early 1980s, broadcasters opposed to rap could argue against style, sound, or image with equal verve.

But these justifications crash against Magic's observation that *it wasn't that the show wasn't commercial*. In fact, it's this precise tension that supplies the friction necessary to narrate how DJs negotiated the conflicting sonic priorities of recorded rap music and commercial radio presentation. *Commercial*, here, merits some unpacking. When Magic referred to *Rap Attack* as commercial, he made an aesthetic claim. He indicated that his show conformed to WBLS's guidelines for style, production, and address—that it sounded like other WBLS segments. But *commercial* also suggests the profit potential of the show. Let's tune in to the bass frequencies of that word *commercial*. On the surface, Magic is suggesting that rap music fit WBLS's format in sound and style. It just took slick mixing and a little savvy. But, if we listen low, he's arguing for the legitimacy of his audience, who, despite popular perception, were consumers of products and services. In short, rap could be made to sound and sell just like any of the other music featured on WBLS. To understand how Magic facilitated this commercialization, as it were, of rap, we need to turn to the tapes of *Rap Attack*, and to the kinds of mixing, programming, and composing that he and Marley Marl pursued in the studio. We need listen to the paratextual logic of format, to the ways that a station presents music frames and conditions how listener hear it. In mixing rap to conform to the guidelines of both commercial broadcasting and WBLS's politics of respectability, they helped to legitimize rap even as its detractors contorted the music into a symbol of Black pathology and racial menace.

Mr. Magic Comes to WBLS

Before coming to WBLS, Magic had developed a cult following across New York through his WHBI *Disco Showcase*, appealing as much to his Juice Crew as it did to elementary school students listening surreptitiously in their bedrooms. By day, Magic worked at an electronics store in downtown Manhattan, where he built, repaired, and sold speakers. Magic directed DJs from across the city to come to the store if they ever needed work done on their sound system, turning the small Manhattan electronics store into a citywide hub for DJs. By night, Magic DJ'd events at dance clubs in Manhattan and Brooklyn. Though popular on the club circuit, Magic's real ambition was to DJ on the radio. After hearing about WHBI from a classmate at New York's School of Announcing and Speech, Magic returned to the electronics store with a proposition for his manager: if the store paid WHBI's hourly lease fee, Magic would advertise the business during his broadcasts. Magic's manager agreed to the DJ's terms and, in the spring of 1979, S&H Electronics became the first sponsor of *Mr. Magic's Disco Showcase*.[2]

When Magic's word-of-mouth audiences proved a boon for S&H, the owners extended Magic the money to lease a second hour of airtime. Magic courted additional sponsors, starting with businesses near the electronics store, and extending out to clubs, record labels, and anyone interested in airing product or purchasing advertising time. By 1980, a long list of sponsors, including famed Bronx nightclub Disco Fever, earned the DJ a modest profit on top of WHBI's lease fee. Soon, Magic's *Disco Showcase* spun the soundtrack to late-night New York. Magic invited his MC and DJ friends to the studio to do interviews or to rap on air and broadcast tapes of breakbeats recorded at parties around the city. Gradually, the sounds, personalities, and stylings of New York's blossoming hip-hop culture saturated the *Disco Showcase*. By late 1981, listeners began to tune in to Magic's show specifically for his hip-hop programming. "It was underground. There wasn't no real record pools back in those days or nuthin'," Magic recalls of the *Disco Showcase's* transition toward rap music. "If you had a record, I'd just hook up with you. I'd tell Kurtis [Blow] to come down after he left the [Disco] Fever and he'd just come through and be rockin' the mic!"[3] When, over time, the *Disco Showcase* featured less disco than hip-hop, Magic rebranded the show as *Rap Attack*.

Meanwhile, Frankie Crocker had set to the task of finding a DJ to host a weekly hip-hop mix show on WBLS. Though he and the other managers at the UC station were open about their disdain for the music, WBLS's ratings continued to suffer with younger listeners in the face of competition from WKTU and WRKS. In a gambit to win back these listeners, Crocker and his team decided to feature the music those young people wanted: rap.

The story of how Magic came to be Crocker's DJ of choice is worth recounting. As it goes, Crocker heard about Magic from fellow WBLS programming manager Mae James. James, at the time, was frustrated. No matter her interventions, her daughter defied her bedtime to listen to the 2 AM broadcast of Magic's *Disco Showcase*. When James questioned her daughter as to what she could possibly be listening to in the middle of the night, she learned of Magic and his sway over young listeners in New York. When the spot for a new DJ at WBLS opened up, James floated Magic's name to Crocker.[4]

In the spring of 1982, Crocker reached out to Mr. Magic, to inquire if the DJ was willing to transfer his show to a commercial station. Magic accepted Crocker's proposition with a coolness that betrayed his excitement. "When I was a kid I looked up to [Crocker]," Magic reflected, "in the same way young people today admire Dr. J [Julius Irving]."[5] Transitioning to WBLS seemed an obvious move; WBLS offered the DJ better pay, better hours, and better exposure than WHBI. Crocker, in turn, brought New York's most-listened-to underground radio DJ to WBLS's lineup. As Dan Charnas points out, furnishing Magic his with own show had further benefits for WBLS. If rap could be contained to late nights, the music could be kept from general rotation, leaving WBLS free to serve its highest-value demographics the highest-veneer tracks while still boosting its ratings with young listeners during a less fraught daypart. At 12 AM on Friday, July 23, 1982, Magic broadcast his first shows from WBLS's studios.[6]

Magic maintained his informal attitude and easy demeanor through the first broadcasts of *Rap Attack*. The DJ had studied Crocker's style and address and incorporated elements of each into his persona. Magic, like Crocker, rendered the world in superlatives. He spoke graciously to his "super listeners" with the confidence of a personality who believes his musical offerings are the finest to be heard anywhere. Where Crocker was prone to drawn-out vernacular raps, so, too, did Magic weave long stretches of monologue, though his mic breaks and interactions with the audience were often brief and to the point. Off the air, that same inclination toward confidence and exaggeration—described affectionately by New York producer DJ Premier as a "direct and sarcastic" demeanor—earned Magic a reputation for arrogance.[7]

Shortly after joining the roster at WBLS, Magic adjusted his persona to match his new environment. The smooth-talking Mr. Magic of WHBI's *Disco Showcase* gave way to the harder-edged, beef-propagating Sir Juice—*Juice* here being Magic's preferred term for clout—of the

Rap Attack. During this period, Magic relished in controversy. In some ways, the change in Magic's air personality paralleled a new trajectory in rap music. As the excitement of the post–"Rapper's Delight" moment birthed a scattershot catalogue of avant-electro, postdisco, collage-style breakbeat odysseys, R&B/rap hybrids, and routine rap, a new wave of artists cultivated a tougher image for hip-hop. Substituting disco breaks for hard-rock beats, adding distorted guitars to soundscapes previously dominated by Moog and Fairlight synthesizers, Run-DMC, LL Cool J, and UTFO loaded their self-consciously street-smart rhymes with boasts. These MCs worked the competitive spirit of live rap battles into their recorded work. As the complexity of MCs' flows and lyrics multiplied in the early era of rap recordings, so did their insistence on the superiority of their rhyming abilities. If MCs like Melle Mel, Kurtis Blow, and Spoonie Gee penned rhymes that couched their braggadocio in vulnerability or the enthusiastic call-and-response patter of early hip-hop parties, this new wave of MCs upped the bluster. They made no secret of their desire to conquer stereos all over the world.

Within weeks, *Rap Attack*'s ratings soared, assuaging Magic's misgivings about WBLS's commitment to rap music. Despite Crocker's reputation as a dictator in the halls of WBLS, Magic felt welcome and respected in his early months at the station. "Frankie [Crocker] was wise enough to go back to the streets," Magic told *Billboard*. "He just told me to be the same as I was at HBI, which means learning to blend into his format."[8]

Engineer All-Star Marley Marl

Rap Attack quickly gained a reputation as the home for hip-hop radio in New York. But the way tracks folded and unfolded into one another across a set was as important to the program's appeal as the musical stylings of any given track. Behind the scenes, mixing *Rap Attack*'s three-hour broadcasts into cohesive, unfurling musical journeys was young turntable wunderkind Marlon Williams, better known to super listeners as the "Engineer All-Star Marley Marl."

Hailing from Queensbridge, Queens, Marley Marl learned to DJ on his older brother's turntable equipment. He recalls being drawn to the console precisely because he was prohibited from touching it. At a time when most hip-hop DJs concerned themselves with scratching and cutting vinyl, Marley Marl emulated the styles of radio DJs Ted Currier and

Crocker, preferring understated blends to jagged embellishments. By age fifteen, Marley Marl held a weekly gig at Pegasus, a Manhattan disco club in the East Sixties. An inveterate tinkerer, the young DJ acquired an extensive home sound system through his experiments building and modifying audio equipment that, before long, opened doors to a practical education in production and studio work. "Now I'm noticing keyboard players come to my house, bass players come to my house because I had the equipment," he recalled of the social benefits of his experiments in audio technology. "All of a sudden we're in the house, they're jamming in my house, I'm learning how to EQ the bass. I'm learning how to make everything sound better. That was my training to become an engineer. Right there . . . on the job training."[9]

In addition to informal apprenticeships with hip-hop and funk producers, Marley Marl applied for and received an internship at WBLS, where his responsibilities ranged from the menial to the technical. In addition to running errands, Marley Marl created extended cuts and remixes for host Pat Prescott's noon exercise program. At other times, he would ride along with WBLS's promotional buses, blasting music exclusive to the station across the five boroughs. When Marley Marl and Magic were deployed on the same bus route, the young DJ's stylings caught Magic's ear.

According to Marley Marl, Magic approached the young DJ and asked if he could have a copy of whatever mix the van was playing to program on his radio show. Marley Marl refused. For the young DJ, to give Magic a copy to play on the radio would have been to lose his proprietary style, risking the audiences he drew to his club dates. Unflapped, Magic continued to greet the young DJ in the halls of WBLS, on occasion asking if he had given any more thought to having his music played on the radio. Over time, Magic applied more pressure. Marley Marl would remember Magic approaching him at a WBLS function, explaining with his characteristic confidence, "Yeah, you got those mixes, man. I'm on the radio, I got like a million people listening."[10] Defenses worn, the proposition soon struck Marley Marl as too good to pass up. Marley Marl brought Magic two mixes to play on an upcoming broadcast of *Rap Attack*.

The decisive moment in the two DJs' relationship, however, came as Marley Marl demonstrated a mix for Magic in WBLS's studios. As one record came to an end, Magic selected the next record from the station's crates. Marley Marl rebuked Magic. The two records, in the young DJ's mind, made no sense next to one another. As Marley Marl tells it, "So I went through the records. 'Oh!' Pulled out a record, put it on the turntable, queued it up and got it in time with the pitch. The mix was going off and I mixed it seamlessly, smooth. His head was still bobbing."[11] Magic was impressed—so impressed that he offered Marley Marl twice what the young DJ was making at his club gig to join him in the studio every Saturday.

Marley Marl accepted, but felt torn over the opportunity. He considered himself, first and foremost, a DJ, not a radio engineer. Working with Magic meant submitting to his playlists and sacrificing a degree of autonomy over his sets. The arrangement was further clouded by Marley Marl's lukewarm enthusiasm for recorded hip-hop. Reflecting on that period, Marley Marl remarked, "I have . . . to admit it . . . I didn't think rap was going anywhere because the music was so bad at first. I was like, 'Get out of here, that shit's not going nowhere, it's not going to be shit.' "[12]

Irrespective of his skepticism of rap music, Marley Marl quickly adapted to the new environs of the radio studio. Much to his surprise, his console was not that of a standard DJ. Marley Marl's explanation of the excitement he felt experimenting with that station's broadcast console is worth quoting at length:

> I come from the school of "make do with what you have . . ." When it came to DJing on the radio and using the station equipment, that's all we had so I had to learn and adapt how to mix-in reel-to-reels. I had to learn to use the station turntables to scratch. There was an A/B switch on top of the fader which I used to click up and down to make transformations. They were like, "How are you doing that on the radio station stuff?" I just figured, "It's a click. It's intermitting. I can use it." Everybody's going crazy. It was great because when you put the fader all the way down, it was an automatic cue, so I didn't need headphones. There was a little speaker right there with my cue and the big speakers on top, so all I would have to do was throw it on, pull the fader down and spin it back. I can hear what I'm doing. I didn't have to switch, "Oh, let me hear the next cue, let me switch it back and forth," because automatically, once you put the fader all the way down in lock position, you hear it. I had this little speaker on the side so I learned how to do it and how to, "OK, let me spin back, throw it in, throw it in."[13]

Without lingering over the mechanical details of WBLS's studios, it is possible to see a great deal of ingenuity in Marley Marl's approach to his new environs. His experience mixing and manipulating records live, as well as his familiarity with the function and functionality of a wide range of playback technology, prepared him to adapt his live practice to a broadcast context. Yet the DJ's openness toward experimentation and inclination to improvise is only partially attributable to preparation. When Marley Marl entered WBLS's studios, the social function of DJing changed very little, as did his personal musical priorities for a mix. What did change was the technology available to realize those goals. Within the hypertechnological ecology of the commercial radio studio, Marley Marl imagined and realized new combinations of recorded sound. Referring to the DJ's technical virtuosity as well as to his taste in records, Magic noted that "Marlon's strength was that he mixed disco and rap DJ styles: he could scratch, blend, edit, splice, anything!"[14]

By the close of 1983, the format of *Rap Attack* was set. Magic would address his super listeners in the style of commercial DJs, and Marley Marl would mix the show live from WBLS's state-of-the-art studios.

The Sound of Early Hip-Hop, 1982–1984

The first broadcasts of *Rap Attack* were an exploration of the new possibilities rap records brought to the "megamix" format. To unpack how Marley Marl and Magic adapted rap to the radio, it helps to dive into the tapes. When we listen closely to a December 1983 broadcast, we can hear that the way Marley Marl and Magic mixed the music was as important to the overall experience of a transmission as were the individual tracks.[15] We can gain purchase on a distinctly radiophonic style of mix. The tracks Marley Marl sutured together on this 1983 tape are synthesizer driven, electro-adjacent. In their soldering of highly technologized dance music to rapped vocals, these tracks are as indebted to the circuits-and-switches craft of Kraftwerk, Giorgio Moroder, and Yellow Magic Orchestra as they are to the minimalistic, austere production aesthetic of Def Jam's early catalog.

For Magic and Marley Marl, a successful mix communicated the energy and individuality of each record. It also structured a musical experience over time not reducible to the appeals of any constituent track. DJs achieved this long-form musical experience through a number of techniques, worked out in clubs and radio studios over the last decade. Marley Marl's most common mixing technique was a smooth blend, in which the DJ matched the tempo and pitch between two adjacent records in order to fade-out the first while leveling-in the second. When well executed, this technique smudged the boundaries between each record, binding listeners to a new track before they realized the previous had ended.

The transition between the Russell Brothers' "Party Scene" and Whodini's "Rap Machine" is perhaps the best example of this style of mixing in this set. In the final minute of "Party Scene," the track's synth ostinato fades from the mix. Only a drum machine beat remains. Over this beat, Marley Marl layers the introductory synth melody from "Rap Machine." At this moment, what the listener hears belongs equally to each track. The drum beat from "Party Scene" and the melody from "Rap Machine" meld into a new whole existing only in the space between the two. While Marley Marl completes this transition, Magic plays a *Rap Attack* logo, sounding "This is a Mr. Magic (Magic) Super (Super) Blast (Blast)" in the fore of the transmission. Facilitated by the simultaneous broadcast of two tracks and a prerecorded feature, this transition shepherds the listener's attention from one track to the next.

Other transitions are stark. For example, between the Art of Noise's "Beat Box" and Shotz's "Fresh," occurring roughly thirty minutes into the mix, there is no blending. Instead, Marley Marl cues "Fresh" into the mix at the end of an iteration of the outro beat of "Beat Box," effecting a sudden, but not jarring, transition. One track simply replaces the other. A similar, though perhaps more sophisticated, technique is used to mix "Fresh" into Run-DMC's "Hard Times." During the track's outro, hand claps and sixteenth-note synth toms pan from left to right, ear to ear, and back again. Marley Marl takes this four-measure idea and loops it. With each new repetition, Marley Marl decreases the tempo of the beat. The effect of such repetitions is subtle: if you're not purposefully attending to the slowing tempo, you'll probably miss it. After four successive decelerations, Marley Marl abruptly cuts "Fresh" from the mix and releases "Hard Times," allowing the record to enter the broadcast with one of the single's iconic synthesizer hits. It becomes clear, in retrospect, that the changes in tempo were the DJ's way of creating a clean transition between the adjacent tracks—a classic tactic of aligning beats per minute (BPM). There is no simultaneity, no point when both "Fresh" and "Hard Times" sound in concert. Instead, the DJ effects a juxtaposition that keeps the listener's attention on the music, uninterrupted.

While most of the transitions on these tapes fall into these two camps—those with or without two records sounding simultaneously as the DJ mixes from one to the next—there are glimmers of more daring techniques strewn throughout. For example, Marley Marl takes a capacious view of both simultaneity and adjacency as he mixes from Run-DMC's "Hard Times" to "It's Like That." The two tracks are strikingly similar in tempo and beat, both featuring hard, reverb-washed snare punches on two and four, and thick, lingering synth chords every downbeat. Rather than mix one into the next, Marley allows both records to spin in sync with the other on opposite turntables. With only one record sounding, he switches between the two channels rapidly, oscillating between the two records. The effect is such that the listener hears "It's Like That" and "Hard Times" on alternating beats—a trick that emphasizes the sonic consanguinity of the records. One can't help but smile at the virtuosity it takes to hear the cut, align the records, and toggle between decks with such speed and precision.

A more ambitious mix occurs after Keith LeBlanc's "No Sellout." About halfway through "No Sellout," something curious happens: the unmistakable voice of Martin Luther King Jr., proclaiming his people "free at last," enters the mix. The studio recording of "No Sellout," however, contains only vocal extracts of Malcolm X. At no point in the single is King's voice featured. At this juncture, Marley Marl has interpolated one orator beside the other, allowing them to exchange exhortations and aphorisms over LeBlanc's driving beat. The two civil rights icons are joined in a posthumous dialog. In between their locutions, Marley eases in the synthesizer melodies from the impending record, TC and the Dangerous Three's "You Can Do It." The juxtaposition of Leblanc, X, King, and TC and the Dangerous Three is an ingenious one. The Dangerous Three's verses all narrate structural inequality and daily hardship from a perspective of optimism and community. Together, all sound as a single ensemble espousing solidarity, if from the divergent languages of militant nationalism, nonviolent liberation, and individual affirmation. This mix evinces a technical and thematic daring uncharacteristic of the period, and one ideally suited to the radio mix. From the comfort of their homes and cars, listeners were free to attend to the finer nuances of layering, mixing, and thematic continuity characteristic of broadcasts of *Rap Attack*.

These techniques—smooth mixing, abrupt cuts, and longer, more involved stretches of mix—were the foundation of Magic and Marley Marl's megamixes. As the duo refined and stretched their sensibilities in the years that followed, these moments of simultaneity and uncertainty would be the places where the duo imagined new possibilities for recorded sound and influenced the aesthetic trajectory of the genre. But, in 1983, the place of rap on commercial radio, and of the genre as a whole, was far from assured. In the following years, Magic and Marley Marl continued *Rap Attack* without the comforts and capabilities of WBLS's studios.

Canceled: *Rap Attack* Returns to WHBI

If the 1980s had begun auspiciously for UC stations, by 1983 the outlook had darkened. By the first month of 1983, Arbitron calculated the total market share between WBLS, WKTU, and WRKS to be 14.3, down 2 percent from the previous summer and 4 percent from the same period in 1982. Some commentators explained the dip as an artifact of a recent change in Arbitron methodology. It wasn't really a decrease in share, they argued, so much as a recalibration. Still, the stakes were too high for program directors to accept that reasoning without also adjusting strategy. Lower ratings, even if temporary, meant fewer advertising dollars. WRKS programming director Mayo spoke with palpable exasperation when asked what caused the shift. "None of us really has a clue," he told *Billboard*, "but there are millions of dollars and jobs riding on all of this. No matter what Frankie [Crocker] or Carlos [DeJesus] and I do, all we really can do is guess and hope."[16]

For the remainder of 1983, WBLS's ratings languished below their competitors'.[17] Reeling from their first significant decrease in ratings since the mid-1970s, tensions mounted in the station as management debated how to reverse their course. The matter was made worse by internal turmoil at the station. Crocker faced renewed scrutiny as independent labels accused him of giving preference to "white records" and taking payola. Management fought to dispel allegations of employee abuse and unfair labor practices.[18] The situation grew dire when, in May 1984, WBLS's ratings dipped to 3.3, nearly half of those earned by WRKS and 6 points lower than their 1979 apex.[19] Percy Sutton, reflecting on WBLS's declining fortunes, defended the station's ratings by arguing that promotional costs incurred sustaining the number-one position quickly hit a point of diminishing returns; with carefully controlled programming and promotion, he argued, you can make more money from the number two or number three spot than the top.[20] But in 1984, as WBLS's ratings plummeted toward their nadir, the station's dilemma appeared less a product of careful design and more a reflection of a media market evolving beyond their control.[21]

Thus, while it came as a shock to Mr. Magic and Marley Marl when WBLS's management canceled *Rap Attack*, the cut makes sense as a rash decision by a station in crisis. Magic recalled the events that precipitated his departure from WBLS, beginning, "In 1984, our show . . . had the highest numbers ever in New York City so we wanted to renegotiate our contract."[22] He continued, "Charles Warfield, who was the station's general manager, hated hip-hop. We had a meeting and he said, 'The major labels are giving me a lot of hassles. They don't have any rap artists. They aren't making any money on rap. Magic, all the kids are listening to you. We got a new format we call Quiet Storm, and we want you to do that.'"[23] It's hard to tell whether or not Warfield was forthright with Magic, and just as hard to tell whether or not Magic exaggerated his show's ratings. Faced with a decision to switch formats or leave, Magic and Marley Marl left WBLS to return to WHBI.

Commercial Sound on Noncommercial Radio

The return to WHBI meant a return to more meager production resources. Still, the duo carried their signature commercial broadcast sound with them to time-brokered radio. An extant recording of *Rap Attack* helps us hear how.[24] The tape begins with "Roxanne's Revenge"—likely the first-ever broadcast of the track—played in its entirety. Where the studio record ends, the radio mix continues, with the beat supporting Shanté's takedown of rap group UTFO abiding in the background. As the track comes to a close, *Rap Attack* "world premiere" logo—the prerecorded bit used by Magic to signal the broadcast of new music—sounds repeatedly over the beat. Magic's voice, echoing so that each word sounds simultaneously, speaks, "A world premiere . . . A world premiere!" After this brief intervention, Magic addresses the audience, beginning, "And you know it like a poet, it's Magic 106-FM WHBI. It's called 'Roxanne Speaks Out.' I hope you got it on tape because you might never hear it again. Coming up on ten minutes before two o'clock in the AM." Magic then delivers a list of shout-outs to listeners located throughout the tri-state area.

The sound of the show marks a significant development in the aesthetics and presentation of rap music on independent radio. Though Magic's address is looser than it was during his tenure at WBLS, his diction less precise and his vocal tone less consistent, his on-air speech is practiced—professional. His coordination of prerecorded logos with music and audience address is characteristic of the multilayered, constantly evolving sound of high-profile radio. Magic and Marley Marl's presentation is no less sophisticated for WHBI's luddite environs. Other aspects of this tape provide indications that the duo enjoyed a freedom regarding broadcast style and content not available at WBLS. When Magic did break for station identification, he referred to WHBI as "Magic 106-FM," an epithet of his own invention. Where WBLS strictly enforced a "decency standard" for the language in a given broadcast, Magic allows "Roxanne Speaks Out" to play without censoring language unsuitable for commercial radio. Still, their broadcast is, in a word, surprisingly commercial for noncommercial radio, betraying his experience at WBLS and a broadcast style informed by attempts to adapt rap music to mass market radio.

Another tape of *Rap Attack* demonstrates this continuity in the sound and character of Marley Marl's mixes between the two stations.[25] Labeled "WHBI Mr. Magic & Marley Marl (1985)," the tape begins with a kaleidoscopic progression of Grandmaster Melle Mel and the Furious Five cuts, mixed deftly together with skillfully placed scratches, stereo pans, and seamless transitions between fragments disunited in tempo, harmony, and instrumentation. After a progression of records sequencing "The Message," "New York, New York," and "World War III," Marley Marl mixes the final Grandmaster Melle Mel track, "It's Nasty (Genius of Love)" into a long-standing *Rap Attack* logo (e.g., "This is Mr. Magic Super Blast"). He then proceeds directly into a prerecorded station identification, a freestyle rap performed by MC Spyder-D. Spyder-D's freestyle concludes with the MC rapping, "So Marley Marl, if you're in the place / Just put that drum beat in their face." Here, Marley mechanically stutters a recorded voice imploring listeners to "turn their radio up" on one turntable, while gradually mixing in the next track, Grandmaster Flash and the Furious Five's "The Truth," to the fore on the other. In total, this sequence unfolds over eight minutes of the broadcast. Though brief, it gives a sense of the kinds of mixing, layering, and production qualities that defined *Rap Attack*, irrespective of its specific broadcast context. Even from WHBI, Marley Marl and Magic cloaked *Rap Attack* in an aura of technological plenitude, technical virtuosity, and the situational awareness characteristic of the most compelling live DJs.

It is unclear from this broadcast whether or not Magic and Marley Marl performed their mixes live in WHBI's studio. Yet it was important to the hosts and DJs of *Rap Attack* that listeners perceived the show as live. From their earliest broadcasts together, Magic often asked listeners,

"Is it live, or is it Marley Marl?" Moments such as the DJ's response to Spyder-D's line "Marley Marl, if you're in the place," were among many when the hosts attempted to demonstrate the real-time performance of the musical mix. When Magic reminded listeners to stay tuned after *Rap Attack* for *The Awesome 2 Show*, for example, he made sure to inform listeners that "DJ Teddy Tedd will be live in the studio." The best indication of the stakes and function of liveness comes near the end of the broadcast, "ten minutes before three in the AM." Magic comes over the air to announce, "Check this out: Mr. Magic maxin' and relaxin', Marley Marl doing the waxin' . . . this is Marley Marl's beat of the week. And I know right about now you're wondering whether or not it's live. Hold it up, Marley." As if on command, the persistent scratching embellishing the beat from Kurtis Blow's "AJ Scratch" ceases. Magic reenters, asking Marley, "Can I get a 'Yo, yo?'" In conversation with Magic, the turntable echoes a clear and intelligible "Yo, yo." The game continues, "Say, 'Yo yo yo.'" The turntables return a "yo yo yo." On the third time, the duo fall out of alignment. Magic asks Marley, "One more time: 'Yo,'" and the turntable speaks "YOwiYOwiYOwi." To this, the DJ retorts, "Man, you talk faster than me, I can't keep up." Whether or not this was a coordinated skit, with Magic performing liveness against a prerecorded mix, or a spontaneous moment of interaction, the effect on the listener would likely have been the same. Indicators of liveness were a powerful means of communicating the simultaneity of experience that enables an audience to feel as though they are listening as a collective.

It was this sense of collective that Magic attempted to confirm during his brief return to WHBI. No matter the venue, Magic addressed his audience in the same trained patter. His sign-off from the "WHBI Mr. Magic & Marley Marl (1985)" tape begins,

> Super listeners, we are not leaving you. If we wanted to leave you we would have gone soft and walked. We would never have abandoned our friends and family here in Money Making Manhattan, or, for that matter, all of Metro New York. So we will be back on Tuesday night, starting at one o'clock in the AM. Anyone driving in the car please proceed with a little extra safety and care. Super listeners, whenever you do your homework, always do it to the best of your ability. And also remember that persistence always overcomes resistance. Any fool can learn from his own mistakes, but it takes a wise guy like Fly Ty, Will, or a wise guy like *you* to learn from the mistakes made by others. Quick reminder: be yourself or you might find yourself by yourself. And that's

definitely no fun, ask CW down the dial. For the entire Juice Crew, I am of course Mr. Magic, reminding you, once again, in 1985, to go for yours. *Awesome 2* is next. The station of the new generation is of course Magic 106- FM. And a special last minute shout to Renee.

1985–1986: Protosampling, The Limin, and the Aesthetics of (Re)Combination

In the spring of 1985, *Rap Attack* returned to WBLS. Magic, vindicated, was blunt in his assessment of the factors that led WBLS to reverse their decision, stating, "'BLS brought us back cuz Red Alert was killing them in the ratings."[26] From their national platform, Magic and Marley Marl shaped the cultural and sonic contours of rap music at a critical moment.

Throughout the entire broadcast run of *Rap Attack*, Magic dabbled in controversy. By 1983 he had designated Red Alert "Red Dirt," among other weekly disses.[27] His propensity to stoke controversy was no less apparent in 1984, seen in his readiness to air and promote "Roxanne's Revenge." But upon his return to WBLS, his stunts grew in scope. The DJ used *Rap Attack* to intensify a beef that has since become known as the "Bridge Wars." Beginning with an alleged slight in the Marley Marl–produced MC Shan track "The Bridge," DJs from the Bronx and Queensbridge volleyed rebuttal tracks across the East River. For his part, Magic jabbed at Bronx duo Boogie Down Productions on the air and, for a time, refused to play their records. Even after his return to WBLS, Magic's on-air feud with Red Alert continued unabated. Magic had a sense for radio spectacle; he also had a sense of humor. This was particularly evident in the harsh way he broke an early Public Enemy record. After premiering the group's single "Miuzi Weighs a Ton," Magic declared the track "garbage" to his listeners before taking a pen to its surface. He cut the record across the grooves beneath the studio microphone, broadcasting the physical and metaphorical destruction of Public Enemy's music. Magic was savvy, however, about the disputes he picked and slights he issued. Controversy, when performed correctly, sold records. Yet Magic's propensity to instigate and prod had implications beyond sales. In passing harsh musical judgments, in imagining disputes and asking listeners to take sides, Magic offered hip-hop as a citywide culture with a shared set of references, allegiances, and home places.

If Magic's persona endured the change in stations, rap music itself was changing. Magic remained in lockstep with the evolution of the genre. While much of the country nursed a vogue for the hard-edged, stripped-down aesthetic of Run-DMC, LL Cool J, the Beastie Boys, EPMD, and the Fat Boys, Magic and Marley varied their selections. In 1986, listeners could hear selections from Funkmaster Wizard Wiz, MC Shan, Doug E. Fresh, Steady B, B Fats, the Main Attraction, Lil' Jazzy Jay and Cool Supreme, Fresh 3 MCs, the Boogie Boys, and the Classical Two, among many, many others. Magic and Marley Marl incorporated early singles by up-and-coming notables Audio Two, Big Daddy Kane, Kool G Rap, Public Enemy, and Erik B. and Rakim into heavy rotation. But *Rap Attack*'s most significant aesthetic contribution wasn't its playlist; rather, it was in the way those tracks were mixed. In the space of uncertainty arising before one track ended and the next began, Magic and Marley Marl helped listeners conceive of new ways recorded sounds might intermingle and layer.

More than just mixing one selection into the next, Marley Marl staged long stretches of encounter between two adjacent selections. To illustrate this, let's go back to the tapes. One 1986 recording, labeled "Mr. Magic's Rap Attack (1986) Pt. 1," opens with the DJ Davy DMX showcase "Have You Seen Davy," in which the turntablist virtuosically cuts and stutters the horn hits from funk outfit Uncle Louie's "I Like Funky Music."[28] The studio recording of "Have You Seen Davy" features the era's paradigmatic spare production—a minimalist drum machine loop with an occasional chorus of female voices. The radio broadcast of the track, in contrast, layers additional sounds from the moment Marley Marl mixes in the track. For the first minute of the broadcast of "Have You Seen Davy," Marley Marl adds vocals to the mix, a first repeating the words "wanna go," and a second sounding "rap attack" between scratched sputters and stops. "Have You Seen Davy" in this instance is a palimpsest, bearing the writing of the original musicians' work as well as Magic and Marley Marl's annotations.

For the next three minutes of the broadcast, "Have You Seen Davy" continues, with Marley Marl varying the vocal embellishments. The commercial release of "Have You Seen Davy" runs for about three and a half minutes. Marley Marl's mix, in contrast, shows no sign of ceasing after five. Instead, Marley Marl gradually levels-in the hard-rock beat and distorted guitars of Chubb Rock's "Rock 'n Roll Dude" until the new track abruptly overtakes the previous. It is a subtle shift: the tempos match, the formal boundaries of each track align so that the end of one coincides with the start of the other, and there is no audible seam between the cuts. In many mixes, this progression would serve as the transition from one track to the next. In Marley Marl's hands, however, this shift initiates a long transitional space.

In this space between tracks, neither fully "Have You Seen Davy" nor "Rock 'n Roll Dude," Marley Marl places elements of each track in combination and conversation. Once the beat from "Rock 'n Roll Dude" has overtaken the foreground of the mix, Marley Marl reintroduces the female chorus from "Have You Seen Davy," first pitched down into an ambiguously gendered chant and then at the original pitch, each with a generous application of echo. The effect is such that vocals from the first track, now altered and stripped of their original context, assimilate to a new beat. In a subsequent section of transition, Marley Marl brings the vocals from both records into dialogue. The DJ extracts the pornographic moans of "oh, baby" from the bridge of "Rock 'n Roll Dude" and splices them within and among the female chorus's persistent inquiries as to whether or not the listener has seen Davy. This conversation between the two tracks' vocals continues for nearly a minute, until all material from "Have You Seen Davy" is absent from the mix. Marley Marl repeats the bridge from "Rock 'n Roll Dude" multiple times, dropping voices and layers in and out of the mix and repeating measures without repeating the form. After a sufficient period of play, he introduces Chubb Rock's vocals to the mix. The track then plays without alteration.

In this example, we see two approaches to the combination of prerecorded sound evident in Marley Marl's mixing. The first is characteristic of his interpolation of prerecorded vocals on top of a single record. In this approach, the DJ allows one record to play while manipulating another layer of sound on top of it, in this case the words "wanna go," "rap attack," and "rock it." This technique was, by 1985, common across hip-hop. We might call this approach "protosampling," or the extraction of small units of music or sound from one record to be interpolated over another without the aid of digital sampling technology. But something different is happening in the transition from "Have You Seen Davy" to "Rock 'n Roll Dude." In this uncertain space, both records are subject to constant manipulation. Both records are altered in timing, leveling, and cut such that they create something new between them.

Outside of music, such intermediary, transitional periods have been productively theorized as *liminal spaces*, or spaces of ritual transformation through which an object or person passes from one fixed and stable state into another. Liminal states are, in a sense, places of margins and boundaries, of formlessness and unpredictability, with no guarantee of successful transformation. Anthropologist Victor Turner defines a "limin," or the period of transition itself, as "a threshold, but . . . a very long threshold, a corridor almost, or a tunnel which may become a pilgrim's road, or, passing from dynamics to statics, *may cease to be a mere transition and become a set way of life, a state*."[29] We might productively view the transitional spaces between two tracks in Marley Marl's mixes as limins, the process of mixing one of creating liminal spaces. In these moments, the heightened intensity and instability of music-in-transition can be heard not just as the threshold between two adjacent records, but as musical states, ways of life, of being in and of themselves. The period during which "Have You Seen Davy" and "Rock 'n Roll Dude" mix does not register as categorically different from those characterized by the dominance of either record. Rather, their intermixture naturally extends the same procedures and techniques already audible on each record to create something new as—quite literally—one becomes the other. The importance of these liminal periods is evident in the length of time over which they unfold. While both tracks play without interruption from the other for about four minutes, the period during which one has begun but the other has not yet ceased lasts for over three. These periods of transition on *Rap Attack* often last as long, or longer, than the tracks that they putatively separate.

These liminal moments in *Rap Attack* were important devices in the development of hip-hop's aesthetics of extraction and recombination. They required DJs to hear the similarities and differences between tracks in terms that explicitly appraised their ability to mesh or conflict. Like a game, it forced DJs to make decisions about how to mix music within the constraints set by the records in their crate and the sound system at their fingertips. In the era before the widespread availability of digital samplers, DJs were already altering, blending, layering, splicing, and manipulating sounds into new composites in nuanced and sophisticated ways. The "horizontal" mixing techniques deployed to great effect in "The Adventures of Grandmaster Flash on the Wheels of Steel," in which the cuts and breaks between adjacent records were the stuff of play, gave way to "vertical" mixes characterized by layering, stacking, and simultaneity. These extended liminal areas of mixes could only be composed to full effect in the context of a radio mix. The musical devices DJs explored in radio assumed a stationary listener. They trafficked in subtleties and minutiae that would easily be lost in the pounding volume and throb of bodies at a club or park jam. And they unfolded over periods of time not amenable to the three-to-five minutes allotted a commercial record release. They relied on two commodities only available at the moment of broadcast: time and attention. This style of mixing, in short, only made sense within the expanded temporal frame and intensified listening context of mix-show radio.

In this way, the radio studio acted as a musical laboratory just as primed for experimentation as the recording studio. Given the kind of sonic and tactile work radio DJs performed weekly, it's not hard to hear the advances ascribed to the golden era telegraphed in the broadcasts on the mid-1980s. Indeed, Marley Marl was responsible for remixing and arranging many of the tracks on *Paid in Full*, and Hank Shocklee of Public Enemy's production duo the Bomb Squad has credited the pause tapes and sampled mixes he produced for broadcast WBAU as occasions through which he developed his approach to beat production. The sonic revolution audible in Eric B. and Rakim's *Paid In Full*, Public Enemy's *It Takes a Nation of Millions to Hold Us Back*, and De La Soul's *Three Feet High and Rising* were less breaks from the past than the continuation of a tradition painstakingly worked out over the air. What I mean to suggest here is that the unique context of radio—long-form mixes; an audience more likely to be engaged in stationary, contemplative listening rather than in social dancing; and a production context of technological sophistication and possibility—encouraged DJs to mix recorded sound in ways that preceded, presaged, and inflected the ways in which producers assembled beats in the late 1980s.

Golden Era? Rap Radio and Racial Politics

At the end of 1988, Magic retired from *Rap Attack*, leaving New York to decompress in Baltimore. Magic left at what should have been an auspicious moment for the music. Labels' profit statements were strong, consumer sampling technology democratized beat production, and markets for the music were popping up all over the globe. Just as the music was poised to break the outer atmosphere, however, a slate of incendiary media coverage brought it crashing into the uniquely American substrate of music, race, and violence. A new wave of debates figured rap as something of a Rorschach test. That listeners consistently heard rap music as either an expression of Black creativity or threat reveals as much about American racial attitudes in the Reagan era as it does about the music.[30] These debates, as well as UC radio's inability to steer national discourse, changed the terms by which media outlets marketed and broadcast rap as a popular music.[31]

A series of heavily covered incidents of violence at rap concerts in the mid-1980s set the tone for the national conversation surrounding rap in the years that followed. In December 1985, Def Jam's "Krush Groove" Christmas party, a sold-out Madison Square Garden event featuring rap acts Run-DMC, Doug E. Fresh, Kurtis Blow, Dr. Jeckyl and Mr. Hyde, and the Master Rappers, drew national attention for a slate of alleged gang stabbings and shootings that occurred within and around the arena. Though many firsthand accounts disputed police narratives of the concert, the event sparked a wave of negative coverage incommensurate with the scale and severity of the assaults. In the wake of the Krush Groove incident, venues charged exorbitant security fees and increased the insurance costs for rap shows. When rap shows were allowed, they were often patrolled by large and eager police forces.[32]

In the following years, two further cases of violence at rap concerts in the greater New York metro area solidified rap's reputation, for the mass media, as violent music. These incidents are notable not just for the coverage they received, but for the burgeoning associations that journalists argued connected rap music and gang activity. In November 1987, disputes at a New Haven, Connecticut, concert headlined by MC Dana Dane resulted in stabbings and tramplings, leaving one attendee dead. Speculation immediately turned to the involvement of "Jamaican gangs . . . from Bridgeport and Hartford."[33] A 1988 stabbing death at a Long Island concert featuring Erik B. and Rakim and Doug E. Fresh ran on the front page of the *New York Times*. Coverage of the September Nassau Coliseum concert focused on the appearance of the suspects and their apparent organized nature. "It looked like these men had a discipline, a leader, and a plan," the Nassau County detective investigating the murder noted, "and they carried it out with some precision."[34] The *New York Daily News* reported the same incident as a "Rap Rampage," equating the music and fans with "black gangs" maneuvering like "sharks at feeding frenzy."[35] By the close of 1988, New York and national media regularly reported on violence at rap concerts. Despite the infrequent nature of these incidents, commentators appeared primed to associate rap music with violence, pathology, and criminality. That there may have been gangs present at concerts was tantamount to rap music's tacit approval of violence. With the euphemism seemingly ready to hand, national media outlets coined a phrase for these incidents: "Rap Attacks."[36]

The increase in local and national coverage of violence at rap concerts was met by a decrease in the broadcast of rap music from UC radio outlets.[37] Stations around the country, both gradually and abruptly, lessened or eliminated rap from their broadcasts, save for crossover hits such as LL Cool J's down-tempo R&B single "I Need Love."[38] Breaking from its competitors, WBLS gradually integrated rap into its daytime playlists. One program director justified this shift in direction by noting that, "during the day, our emphasis is on [the] 18–49 [demographic]. . . . Rap is 12 or 13 years old in this market, so the kid who was 12 when it started is now 25, and they can easily tolerate it if it comes down to a toleration level."[39] WBLS's decision to increase the number of rap singles in its playlists was not roundly applauded, nor was it emulated at other stations in the city. New York radio personality and Black radio advocate Bob Law, for example, did little to hide his distaste for rap music or WBLS when he penned a letter to the editor of radio periodical *Cash Box*:

> Black Radio, the primary information source in the Black community boasts of "Rap Attacks" and "Hippity Hop." When you consider the diminishing audience the ratings reflect, it may be a signal that Black Radio has misunderstood. Perhaps the needs of your community have changed far beyond a rap attack. Perhaps the pursuit of news and relevant information has your audiences searching elsewhere. Perhaps the Black community has grown up leaving Black Radio with the challenge to catch up![40]

Despite continued reticence from the radio and record industries, it soon became clear that rap was on a course to become one of the most salable popular musics of the 1990s. Commentators in radio and music industry periodicals considered what impact the presumptively violent predilections of rap artists and fans might have on the social and commercial prospects of the music. Nelson George, who often played the role of cultural broker for hip-hop artists, wrote a series of articles, admonishing in tone, disentangling rap music from its reputation as a generator and expression of "black-on-black violence." In his first article, George developed his argument carefully, delineating rap's merits and purpose to a general readership. "Like no other current cultural expression," George began, "rap music speaks to and, at its best, for the underclass of black and brown teen who is locked out of the economy by awful schools, reactionary social policies, and a job market that forces too many to choose between messenger work and crack dealing."[41] He explained to readers that, though rap might sound "hostile and foreboding," it does not mean that "[it] or its audience is inherently dangerous," and the violence at these shows is not new or categorically different from the violence endemic in the places where many rap artists grew up. In short, rap was neither a cause nor justification for violence. In his later columns, he attempted to redeem rap's reputation, focusing on the close association between hip-hop artists and the Stop the Violence movement, the charitable efforts of rap artists and promoters, and nascent attempts to use rap as a tool to promote literacy among young people.[42]

The question of what role Black and UC format radio might play in the development of rap music continued to generate commentary. For those who believed Black radio had a responsibility to steward rap music, the history of "race records" loomed large. Public Enemy manager and vice president of Def Jam Records Bill Stephney rendered the stakes of the debate in clear terms when he warned that Black stations content to ignore "the music of [their people]" will eventually find themselves "providing janitorial services for a white pop station."[43] For some involved in the day-to-day decisions of programming a UC station, such notions of solidarity were naïve and idealistic against the realities of operating a business. "An audience . . . is not a musical form's cultural roots," retorted WRKS program director Tony Gray. "For us to remain a successful station, we have to service the core of our listening audience."[44] Further, the content of rap records remained a barrier to broad radio. "Only the most accessible, least offensive rap records on the market" found themselves integrated into drive-time playlists, according to one *Billboard* reporter, and those that did find radio play were most often by artists that had "crossed pop," espoused a "literate rap style," or composed songs with a "mellow mood."[45] The most damning criticisms centered on the issues of race and class. "Black Radio is run by 'buppies' [Black Urban Professionals]," a representative of Rush Productions contended. "They made a commitment to a lifestyle that has nothing to do with the street. . . . They may have started on the streets . . . [but] they know nothing about the streets of today, and they don't want to know."[46] And while some radio industry personnel were sensitive to the fact that rappers claim "they're just attacking societal problems in their own language," they struggled to shake its associations with "obscenity," "violence," and "gang warfare" in their minds or those of their listeners.[47] It seems fitting, then, that the most prescient commentary was aimed at the media itself, with one writer arguing that "lopsided coverage is the foundation on which stereotyping thrives."[48]

These arguments unfolded with no small measure of animosity on both sides and, as UC stations delayed taking decisive action with regard to rap music, pop stations did not. Perhaps the most enduring consequence of rap's protracted trial period on Black radio can be seen in the vacuum it left for larger, well-financed stations to position themselves as leaders in the broadcast of rap music in the early 1990s. The internecine ratings wars and the debates over the ethics and economics of rap music of the 1980s gave way to intensified format fragmentation—the division of a format that appeals to a large cross-section of listeners into multiple subformats targeted at hyperspecific demographics (e.g., urban country, rhythmic contemporary, modern jazz)—and corporate consolidation, eroding the terrain that UC had once held so firmly. In 1989, with RKO General's acquisition of a second license in the New York market, WRKS split into two stations, with 98.7 targeting older demographics with a "Black gold" format and the new Hot 97-FM featuring rap and youth-oriented R&B. Though WBLS continued with its UC format, it never successfully reconciled its station image and sound with rap music. For a brief period in 1993, on the heels of a community violence crisis brought to a boil by the insurgence of "gangsta rap" into American popular culture, WBLS publicly denounced ties to the music and eliminated all rap from its playlists.

And yet rap music thrived in the 1990s. If Mr. Magic and Marley Marl had help set the creative, cultural, and commercial stage for rap's emergence as a commercial music, carefully shepherding it into the forefront of popular culture, they left radio at a time when outside forces threatened to wrest control of the music and its meanings from those who made it. While Hot 97 and underground DJs like the Awesome 2 and Stretch and Bobbito continued to broadcast rap music to growing and enthusiastic audiences throughout the 1990s, UC outlets on commercial radio, with their greater capacity to inform and direct national issues, abdicated an opportunity to disseminate hip-hop from a sensitive, informed perspective. After contributing to the acceptance of rap, Magic ceded his platform to broadcast and comment on it.

"I Miss Mr. Magic": Legacy

Though Magic had retired from radio, he was not quite ready to leave rap. Magic remained active as an advocate for artists and the genre until his death in 2009. For his part, Marley Marl leveraged his successes as a DJ and record producer into a long and storied career.

After *Rap Attack*, Magic tried to keep its brand relevant, releasing a four-volume collection of rap tracks featured prominently on his radio show. Sales, however, were lukewarm. Part of the release's poor success can be attributed the fact that many of the tracks on these releases were already widely available. But a more significant factor was a competing offering by WRKS competitor Red Alert. "[DJ Red Alert's] Next Plateau record . . . gets the edge over Magic's package because it contains original Red Alert Mixes and maintains the feel of his popular rap program," *Billboard*'s record review noted, lending credence to the idea that radio offered an experience not reducible to the music programmed on a given show.[49]

If Magic's business ventures stagnated after radio, his image did not. Beginning in the 1990s, New York based MCs began to incorporate mentions of Mr. Magic and *Rap Attack* into their verses, strategically deployed as a way of playing their newfound success off their humble upbringings. "I rap in front of more niggas than in the slave ships," Queens-based rapper Nas begins in the present tense on his 1992 track "Halftime": "I used to watch *CHiPs*, now I load Glock clips / I got to have it, I miss Mr. Magic."[50] Notorious B.I.G. adopts a similarly nostalgic mode in his 1994 single "Juicy." On this track, Biggie places Mr. Magic within a sequence of references to the 1980s in his rags-to-riches anthem, rhyming, "It was all a dream, I used to read *Word Up! Magazine* / Salt-N-Pepa and Heavy D up in the limousine / Hangin' pictures on my wall / Every Saturday *Rap Attack*, Mr. Magic, Marley Marl."[51] As late as the mid-2000s, artists continued to drop Magic's name as a quick signifier of hip-hop in the 1980s. Producer-rapper Quasimoto—one of the aliases of the producer also known as Madlib—differed from his predecessors in the 1990s when he, over a skillfully anachronistic, boom-bap-with-a-wrench-in-it beat, rapped, "I remember Ultramagnetic and Stetsasonic / Afrika Bambaataa and Soul Sonic / MC Shy D, Public Enemy/ Boogie Down, MC Shan, MC Ren, the Disco Three / Mr. Magic with the *Rap Attack*."[52] For those who came of age in the 1980s and 1990s, hip-hop in New York was inseparable from *Rap Attack*. Simply speaking, Magic's name was enough to conjure a time and a place.

But, more than looming large in historical memory, Magic and Marley Marl helped define the sound of rap music during a critical period in the music's development. Their efforts selecting, mixing, and presenting rap music helped a generation of listeners hear new possibilities for recorded sound. The skill and care they took in adapting this new, at times raucous music to the "professional" broadcast standards of commercial radio extended the boundaries of listeners and labels alike. In helping the music reach new heights of complexity and acceptability, they conferred to it more legitimacy. Though this legitimacy would, in the years that followed Magic's departure from radio, be transformed into an affirmation of corporate hegemony and a tool for policing Black voices, Magic and Marley Marl helped pry open a door for political and cultural expression that may otherwise have remained locked.

FOUR

Programming the Street at WRKS

From its 1981 inception to its change in format in the late 1980s, New York's WRKS-FM 98.7 remained remarkably consistent in its branding. KISS-FM sold itself as the sound of the streets, *the* sound of New York City. Full-page ads printed in broadcast trades touted the station's presence on streets across New York, from "Broadway . . . to Second Avenue . . . to the Bowery . . . throughout the Five Boroughs."[1] In interviews across the decade, KISS's programming staff attributed the station's success to their sensitivity to street-level musical developments. Buses with KISS's signature "big, fat, juicy, red lips" painted large on their side—"subliminal seduction," as one KISS manager described the campaign—coursed the streets of New York.[2] The message, to anyone looking or listening, was clear: KISS is the sound of your city, now.

At first blush, KISS's branding is consonant with the messaging adopted by its competitor urban contemporary stations. If you keep the pressure on, however, this rhetoric seems surprising coming from WRKS-FM. A subsidiary of broadcasting behemoth RKO General, itself a subsidiary of transnational corporate conglomerate General Tire and Rubber, at an institutional level KISS couldn't boast of the same organic connections to the streets as did its competitors. WBLS was owned and operated, after all, by a cadre of African American professionals with deep roots in many of New York's Black communities, even if their class and generation at times insulated them from the young people making and living "street music." The DJs at WHBI, too, could claim an immediate connection to the streets. Their self-produced programs were quintessential community affairs, a megaphone amplifying the sounds of New York's African American and Latin youth cultures. KISS's ability to cement a connection to the streets into a ratings-topping market position appears to have been pure, if brilliant, marketing.

Yet to dismiss KISS's claim to the streets as nothing more than marketing would be to miss the unexpected truth behind the statement. While some of KISS's representatives may have exaggerated their connection to the streets, the station's programming staff and weekend hip-hop DJs each, in their own way, cultivated and maintained an intimate, on-the-ground connection to New York's musical cultures. From program directors who frequented the city's underground dance clubs and one-stops, to the increasingly sophisticated listener and market profiles developed by the station's research department to the musical and social networks that fed new singles into the playlists of DJs Red Alert and Chuck Chillout, at all levels KISS was concerned with knowing and representing New York from the asphalt up.

What, then, does it mean to represent New York in music? What are the sounds of the street? At KISS, the folks involved with programming came to know and define "street music" in their own ways and, in turn, converted that knowledge into a station identity. Consider, for example, the different perspectives registered in the following statements. "We deal with that part of New York that is New York."[3] This is how KISS-FM program director Sonny Taylor described the station's decision to foreground "street records." For Taylor, the fledgling, highly local musics that KISS broadcast captured something unspeakable yet essential about New York, and his equation of these records with the city's identity echoed throughout the trades. In another *Billboard* piece covering WRKS's programming, Nelson George ventriloquized the impressions of many listeners and industry insiders when he wrote, "WRKS is openly acknowledged to be New York's most street-oriented urban radio station."[4] This rhetoric was not limited to the historical period under consideration, nor was it limited to those with close connections to station strategy. When, in 2014, I asked Chuck Chillout to describe the programming philosophy behind his weekly WRKS mix show, his answer resonated with those of others at KISS in the 1980s: "You kept it to-the-street."[5]

Program director, journalist, hip-hop DJ. Three different individuals, three different ways of being and knowing the streets of New York. A genre of music, a marketing category, and a set of social relations. Three different ways of invoking "the streets" to grant meaning to musical sound.[6] Programming decisions speak to the musical, political, and industry trends affecting stations and communities across the country and provide a means of orienting a history more ambitious in scope around the sound of a single station.

From WXLO to WRKS

In many ways, the 1981 founding of WRKS-FM 98.7, better known as KISS-FM, is a case study in how closely radio tracked the latest advances in consumer marketing. Gone were the days of "unformatted innocence" on the FM band.[7] Program directors and sales managers evinced a new vigilance in their attention to listener behavior. Demographics, market research, and experimentation informed every facet of their stations' sounds. In this, they modeled management strategies of America's consumer goods titans, who designed products and services around nuanced, meticulously researched consumer profiles. In a short window, radio programmers and researchers conceded that listeners evince subjectivities more complex than those rooted in the traditional categories of age, gender, race, and income. Product differentiation, they reasoned, would stem naturally from an accurate understanding of their station's listeners and their market's desires. In order to understand how KISS-FM built its format around claims to an unparalleled knowledge of New York's musical alleyways and undergrounds, we need to begin with the corporate strategy that informed its sound.

Before it became KISS-FM, 98.7 New York went by the call letters WXLO. Featuring an album-oriented rock format that leaned Top 40, WXLO was best known for its broadcasts of deep cuts and full sides from an expansive catalog of rock and roll. WXLO's audience affectionately referred to the station as "99X," and it enjoyed both impressive ratings and a high degree of listener loyalty into the mid-1970s.

But come 1978, the station's ratings began to falter as a greater number of listeners migrated toward WBLS and WKTU. America's disco fever was spiking, and stations ignored the symptoms at their own peril. For WXLO, the choice to ignore disco hurt. The station's mild ratings decline of 1978 multiplied into an asymptotic nosedive by the summer of 1979. WXLO's owners took the station's new low as an opportunity to clear house, firing the managers and programming staff who had not already left.[8] As 1980 loomed, the new management agreed that a change was in order, though exactly what form that change would take remained uncertain. The leading speculation in the trades hinted that the station might revert to its old call letters, WOR-FM, in an effort to rebrand the station while maintaining its AOR format.

WXLO's new management opted to do the opposite, keeping its call letters and tweaking the format. Whereas previous wisdom counseled programmers to work from a format toward a target demographic, WXLO bucked the trend in broadcast marketing and reversed the priorities. The management first elected to "deemphasize teens" in order to pursue the twenty-five-to-thirty-four demographic, citing advertisers' complaints about weak returns on campaigns directed at teenage listeners. Then, rather than double down on their rock and roll roots, they determined their new programming based on research that indicated there was room for another adult contemporary (AC) station in the New York market.[9]

The results were disastrous. The station's ratings continued to decline, and advertisers continued to spend their money elsewhere. The decision to institute an AC format was rooted in the premise that WXLO had lost its identity as a rock station. The switch to AC only hastened this identity crisis. What was once an instantly recognizable AOR powerhouse commentators now referred to as "insipid," "milquetoast," "innocuous," and "less ambitious in its programming since it adopted the rock format in the late 1960s."[10] What's more, the vaunted twenty-five-to-thirty-four demographic turned out to be a more fragmented category than programmers had anticipated, and WXLO's lack of a differentiated appeal did little to win their sympathies. When the station's ratings showed no sign of improvement by August 1980, WXLO's management hired Ken Burkhart, a seasoned broadcast consultant whose claim to fame was his purported invention of the disco format, to help revamp the station's programming and image. The station's contract with Burkhart raised new speculation that WXLO would coast along with the cultural currents and adopt a disco format. While WXLO program director Don Kelly remained adamant that the station would not pursue the disco format of WKTU, he hinted at the set of changes that would eventually birth KISS-FM. "We will be urbanizing the format," he told *Billboard*, "for both black and white listeners."[11]

The stakes of WXLO's 1980 reinvention were high, for reasons unrelated to programming or market segmentation. In January 1980, the FCC announced that it had revoked three of RKO General's broadcast licenses and initiated the process of suspending thirteen more. This action was a response to what one judge referred to as a "staggering variety of corporate misconduct" on the part of RKO parent company General Tire and Rubber (GTR).[12] The Securities and Exchange Commission, among other federal entities, had found GTR guilty of "misconduct over a twenty year period" that included "illegal domestic political contributions, systematic overfilling and denial of rebates to partly owned foreign affiliates, bribing foreign officials to gain business advantages, and financing illegal activities through secret accounts and then covering up those activities through falsification of records."[13] While most of the charges against GTR did not concern activity regarding or within their broadcast holdings, the FCC intervened when it was discovered that RKO itself had "knowingly engaged in an improper reciprocal trade program that was uncompetitive . . . knowingly falsified financial statements . . . and was not entirely honest and forthcoming with the [Federal Communications] commission."[14] Broadcast industry analysts estimated the total price of RKO's threatened licenses at over $400 million.[15] WXLO stood among the RKO stations jeopardized by the ruling.

Response to the FCC ruling was heated, and most broadcasters counted themselves supporters of RKO. Though he spoke strictly on behalf of his company, one GTR executive voiced the opinion of many in radio when he inveighed that the FCC decision was "the most unfair and discriminatory ever handed down by a government agency . . . the largest 'fine' ever levied against a company in the history of American Enterprise [*sic*]."[16] A dissenting commissioner agreed with the consensus in industry, defending the minority opinion by jibing that the FCC had appointed itself "national nanny." To others, the punishment fit the crime. These observers and policymakers rejected the argument that the FCC was "punishing the child for the sins of the parent." One commissioner described the reasoning behind the FCC's admittedly drastic action, retorting, "If there is any truth to the concept of a trustee, these people just went too far. . . . [We are] nowhere near the position that the 'sins of the parent' company are visited upon the child. If the 'child' is a puppet, that's different."[17] Irrespective of whether or not RKO or WXLO were innocent, guilty, or unknowing pawns, RKO's license for 98.7-FM rested on the chopping block. The corporate-level turmoil had the effect of clarifying station-level strategy for RKO's threatened broadcast properties: whatever direction RKO determined for WXLO, they would need to do so against a smog of gross corporate malfeasance, be scrupulous and transparent in every detail, and proceed without the guarantee that, after the verdict, there would even be a station to program.

Thus, WXLO's transition into an urban contemporary (UC) format occurred parallel to RKO's reimaging as a responsible, avuncular media company. In the interim, RKO took several measures to win the favor of the FCC, including transferring a portion of their holdings into a new holding company, propitiously named NewCo.[18] WXLO, for its part, did more than attempt to dissociate from its parent company. They took the occasion to change management and initiate measures to build trust with the broadcasting community. In February 1980, RKO appointed Lee Simonson, a career RKO employee, to head WXLO.[19] The station purchased full-page ads in *Broadcasting* magazine to introduce Simonson to others in the industry. Here was Simonson, husband, father, foster parent, and baseball fan, ready with the clarity "necessary to manage in the polyglot environment [of New York]."[20] The ads put forth an image of level-headed leadership that begged listeners and the FCC to identify with the Rockwellian line-drawings of the new manager. Simonson's track record of successful management and RKO's all-American portrayal of the new manager stood at a far remove from the accusations of corruption looming over the station: they were a signal of virtue from a station mired in vice.

On the programming side, WXLO began the arduous work of unrolling its new format. In addition to Burkhart, they poached top WKTU jock Paul Zarcone to host the morning drive-time slot, as well as Wanda Ramos of WBLS. Gradually, the new programming team updated the station's playlist, and the on-air talent sounded a personality for the new format, making good on the "urbanization" they had prefaced in previous months. In the fall of 1980, the station officially announced its change in format from AC to UC, on the air and in the trades. For listeners, the change in format would have been clear in the station's new sound, especially audible in the quantity of R&B, soul, disco, and electro now populating its playlists. It would also have been evident in the station's tight, energetic production quality. It would have been easy to miss in the trades, however, tucked as it was toward the bottom of a page insert in the back matter of *Broadcasting*'s radio section. "RKO Radio's WXLO (FM) has changed its format from adult to urban contemporary," the announcement opened, continuing in the style of a telegraph: "According to Program Director Don Kelly, change is attempt to gain more listeners in city's five boroughs where 60–70% of records sales are of black crossover product. Station also helps to gain a ratings boost from Arbitron's telephone retrieval of diaries completed by minorities. . . . With new one, it goes up against market leader WBLS (FM) and WKTU (FM)."[21] Though short, this description is telling. Not only does it reveal the outsized market share enjoyed by Black artists in the early 1980s, but it also points to an important industry consideration: to the greater ratings impact of minority listeners in the early 1980s as ratings systems tweaked their methodologies to account for previously ignored populations. Their decision to target minority listeners was now a viable tactic for luring in advertisers. With its new format, WXLO appeared to steady itself from the missteps of its previous format change. Moreover, the new format architects decided on a target listener more specific in her preferences and lifestyle than the nebulous twenty-five-to-thirty-four group. With the UC format touted by the trades as a "growth format for the eighties," and in naming WBLS and WKTU as competitors, WXLO advanced a clear vision as to where their supporters would be gained.[22]

Following the formal format change, WXLO's transitional activities accelerated. In June 1981, the station officially announced a change in call letters to WRKS, breaking with the tainted sign WXLO and aligning the station with the national KISS brand of radio stations.[23] Throughout 1981, WRKS worked with several research firms to develop their format, nuance their understanding of their listener, and tighten their sound. During this period, WRKS also unfurled their campaign to identify the station with New York itself. There was little original in the tag lines the station chose, or the idea that their broadcasts were unique reflections of their environs. As early as 1978, spokespeople across town at WBLS leaned on the phrase "We believe we are New York" when describing their racially and ethnically diverse audience and asserting their primacy of place. But KISS leveraged this stance more completely than any of its contemporaries. In November, full-page ads in *Broadcasting* laid bare this metonymic logic, loudly proclaiming that "WRKS is New York." What's more, these ads feature KISS's earliest usage of "the streets" as a metaphor. The first thing a reader scanning below the headline would see was WRKS's new mission statement, "Talk about New York and you're talking about streets." For a station brand, colonizing "the streets" as a geography and a concept was a clever sidestep from the "urban" in urban contemporary, the euphemistic nature of which fooled precisely no one. What is a city, it seemed to insinuate, if not a network of streets and the people who traverse them? It also marked a dramatic shift from previous industry definitions of "street music," which, just a year prior, signified buskers, subway musicians, and those who played outdoor festivals, musicians who, quite literally, made their living performing on the streets.[24] KISS's new iconography and slogans addressed younger listeners, for whom the streets were synonymous with racial and ethnic diversity, as well as with the energetic, iconoclastic music they preferred. Though "street" suggested youth and minority musics, KISS's slogan worked through an ongoing process of association, whereby KISS-FM played music that was already considered "street," and the music that KISS played became "street music" as it was transduced through KISS's broadcasting and marketing machinery. In 1980, KISS pushed back against those who saw "the street" as overdetermined, as reducible to race, geography, or genre. If the streets themselves were asphalt, the category "street" was plastic.

Upon the release of the summer and fall 1980 ratings books, the decision to turn to UC appeared to be working.[25] Ratings rose. Competitors WKTU and WBLS's ratings fell, and the stations began to sweat KISS's ingress into an already crowded market. KISS's outlook brightened further in May 1981, when Simonson, finding himself propelled to the vice presidency of RKO Radio, hired Barry Mayo, a young programmer and manager with a strong track record as programming director (PD) eager to prove his mettle in the country's largest radio market, to serve as assistant PD.[26] Even on the corporate side, clouds appeared to be lifting. Just as *Broadcasting*'s editor penned a screed decrying the ongoing FCC action against RKO, pointedly titled "Enough," the words seemed to reach the commission's ears: the FCC announced it would, for now, seek no further punitive actions against RKO.[27] WRKS entered 1982 a new station with new leadership and a new format. The question of programming, though, remained. How do you evolve with New York? If WRKS promised to deliver listeners the streets of New York, how would the station, to reprise Chuck Chillout's formulation, "keep it to the street"?

Ears to the Ground

WRKS's programming strategy was deeply informed by the experiences and philosophy of young programmer Barry Mayo who, less than a year after arriving at KISS-FM, was promoted to the position of program director. Before arriving at WRKS, Mayo worked his way up the programming ranks, beginning at Howard University's student-run WHBC-AM 830 and continuing with a string of early career successes in mid-sized markets. From his first engagements as a programmer, Mayo showed a savvy approach to selecting music and branding formats. When directing the programming at Little Rock's KALO in the mid-1970s, for example, Mayo maintained the station's R&B playlist while calling the station disco. At KALO, he and his staff took risks on what was referred to as "white crossover" music, records that, by genre or sound, many believed would not widely appeal to Black listeners. "'Fly Like an Eagle' on a Black station in Little Rock raised some eyebrows," he explained, "but we went from number eight to number three in one book."[28] After KALO, Mayo presided over similarly localized format conversions at WRAP in Norfolk, Virginia, and WMAK-AM in Nashville, Tennessee.

At each station, Mayo educated himself in the idiosyncrasies of his new market. While he remained sensitive to the distinct preferences of listeners around the country, he foregrounded local preferences and situated market knowledge at every turn. At no place was this education more important than at WGCI-FM, Chicago, where Mayo accepted his first PD position at a major-market station. When Mayo arrived at WGCI in the fall of 1979, the station offered Chicago a "pure disco" format. Disco, however, did not strike Mayo as sustainable in a city so strongly aligned with downtempo R&B and blues. "We were trying to do disco, and [rock format station] WDAI was getting ready to do disco, and suddenly it dawned on us that we'd be fighting for a non-existent audience. Chicago was a black town. We figured that out one day and decided to go after [W]BMX."[29] A detailed programming plan followed from this observation. By winter of 1980, ratings services placed WGCI within a point of WBMX.

Mayo maintained that intimate knowledge of a broadcast market was key to programming successfully, and many broadcasters shared this position. But Mayo seemed to go one further, outdoing his competitors by immersing himself in the community for whom he broadcast and by assessing the success of his selections with careful attention to ratings and research. "I think the key is having your finger on the pulse of the community," Mayo explained of his tailored approach to programming in Chicago. The way he finished his response is worth quoting at length.

> We get hung up so much in either calling stores over the telephone or our research. . . . Mediatrends and Arbitrons, we take the human

element out of it. I've done some things in Chicago that I would never do in other markets. I personally am not a big blues fan. But when Bobby Bland's album came out, the first thing I said to my music director is "find a cut off of it" that day and put it on, because I know that particular artist does well in this market. . . . You have to learn to separate where your head is at from the head of your market. We got into the head of our market.[30]

Mayo suppressed his own tastes in favor of those of his audience. In Chicago, he observed that programmers tended to use race as a ready-to-hand indicator of musical preference despite indications of this metric's unreliability. Black format and Top Forty programmers alike had evinced a "parochial approach to Black musical tastes," ignoring the substantial Black audiences who listened to white "crossover" records, as well as white audience who also enjoyed the music of Black artists.[31] What's more, Mayo observed that support for disco was flagging especially hard in the hometown of Steve Dahl, the radio jock who infamously detonated a crate of disco records not far from center field at Chicago's Comiskey Park. Reflecting on his tenure at WGCI, Mayo summarized, "We just did the best job reflecting what was going on in the streets."[32]

Given his success in Chicago, it was no surprise to many in radio when a New York–based RKO PD recommended Mayo for the WXLO opening.[33] For Mayo, a Harlem native, the opportunity represented both a homecoming and a chance to test his abilities in the nation's most competitive media market. He began by replicating the methods that supported his previous successes, spending at least one day a week visiting record stores and one-stops. New York differed from his previous markets in several ways. For one, Frankie Crocker's cult of personality exerted more influence in New York than had any other individual in Mayo's previous cities. Crocker was king, and his seat behind the microphone was a throne. "Frankie Crocker's musical tastes have controlled progressive music in New York for the last few years," Mayo noted. "If WBLS played it, it was a hit. If you didn't hear it, that meant it wasn't."[34] Further, New York was more diverse than most markets in the country by all relevant metrics. Though the diversity of audiences could result in an equal diversity of tastes, disco and urban radio had demonstrated dance music's broad appeal and overturned notions that mapped subjectivity onto musical taste too rigidly. "Whites, Blacks, and Latinos were grooving on the same sounds," he observed of New York. "Our ethnic mix is tremendous."[35]

While Mayo remained an outspoken advocate of qualitative methods of market research—getting out into the broadcast community and interacting with folks—quantitative and perceptual research, often conducted by specialized agencies, became central to station operations in the early 1980s. Much of Mayo's success can be attributed, at least in part, to his mastery of contemporary ratings research, demographic profiling strategies, and his stations' ongoing contracts with research firms.[36] But Mayo remained careful not to place too much stock in statistical representations of human preference. His rhetoric on the matter was charged. "You're a fool if you let any study dictate the programming of your station," he noted in response to a study that divided the UC audience into four distinct classes of listeners and offered sample programs for each. "When a man can't make a decision on a record that he throws on the turntable and immediately reacts to, he's in trouble, especially if he has competition."[37] However much Mayo and his cohort of UC programmers tried to downplay the importance of research to their operations, there was little denying the centrality of ratings and research to commercial radio in the 1980s. Though radio research was by no means new to the last quarter of the twentieth century, the 1980s saw an "explosion" of different research methods and techniques.[38] Stations allocated larger and larger portions of their programming budgets to expand their in-house audience research capacities and to contract outside research and consulting firms, who offered a veritable buffet of specializations. The trades abounded with articles and special issues introducing broadcasters to the research options available to their stations and coaching them on the merits and pitfalls of various methodologies. *Differentiation* emerged as a key term in broadcast discourse, and, in an end-of-year reflection, one *Radio and Records* columnist designated *positioning* as the single word to summarize 1981 in radio. So pervasive were these marketing concepts that Reagan-era radio formats came to evince economist Theodore Levitt's infamous 1980 dictum "There is no such thing as a commodity. All goods and services are differentiable."[39]

One result of this twin rise of market research and format differentiation was a phenomenon called "format fragmentation." On the one hand, a slate of new research techniques added nuance to broadcasters' understandings of their audience. Whereas audience research had traditionally constructed listener profiles based on demographic categories such as age, gender, race, income, or location, these new methodologies multiplied the axes along which consumer identity was represented. New consumer profiles integrated lifestyle, behavior, and hobbies as well as a host of different psychographic dimensions into their calculus—for example, a "propensity to take risks," "quick to tire with current fashion," or "likes to be the life of the party." On the other hand, radio formats grew as singular in focus as stations' target listeners did. From the tested format album-oriented rock came classic rock, adult rock, deep cuts, rhythmic rock, and psychedelic; from traditional Black formats came Black progressive, Black gold, quiet storm, current jazz, and, of course, urban contemporary. These phenomena were two sides of the same coin: new listener profiles occasioned new formats, and new formats occasioned novel listeners. They created increasingly tight relays between listeners' self-perception and a station's sound and gave researchers a new vocabulary for describing audiences. One practical effect of the hyper-specialization of target listener and formats was that stations could now "sell their audience" more effectively to advertisers. Qualitative descriptions, however speculative, about a flesh-and-blood consumer made for a convincing sales pitch when bolstered by ratings data.[40] Format fragmentation is one way of understanding how WBLS, WRKS, and WKTU could all claim a UC format yet all offer a differentiated appeal. For KISS-FM, it allowed the station to mold its sonic renderings of the street to the expectations of its audience as their tastes developed over time.

Though armed with research and ready to trust his gut, there was one rub for Mayo: he was no fan of the new youth music increasingly ubiquitous on New York's streets. In fact, Mayo hated rap music. As Dan Charnas has argued, so deep was the PD's disdain for rap that he nearly made himself the exception to his personal programming rules by banning it from KISS's playlists. Mayo may have glossed the signs of rap's popularity himself, but those around him made it impossible to ignore. When Manny Bella, a representative for Profile Records gave Mayo Run-DMC's single "It's Like That"—a cut that strained Mayo's sense of what music should sound like—it was only after listener requests inundated the station hours after the first drive-time broadcast that Mayo relented. Further, Mayo fought for months with young programming intern Tony Quartarone about the viability of hip-hop. It was only after Quartarone, Mayo's protégé at KISS, demonstrated listener demand via the massive ratings' spike WBLS had enjoyed since their addition of *Rap Attack* that Mayo thought seriously about what place rap might occupy on the station. With Mayo on board, management and programming staff at WRKS quickly arranged to program a hip-hop mix show, a measure to siphon some of WBLS's listeners to KISS and to maintain their reputation as the single home of street music.

Mayo charged himself with the task of securing DJs. To do so, he did what he had done in the past: went to where the music was.

"Yo! It's real! It's real!"

In 1982, the year that Mayo began scouting for a hip-hop DJ, one home of hip-hop in New York was downtown club the Roxy. With its mix of uptown and downtown, hip-hop and punk, Black and white, old guard and new wave, the Roxy epitomized Mayo's understanding of the streets of New York: musically, stylistically, ethnically, and racially diverse, but united in dance and sound. Presiding over hip-hop events at the Roxy was Zulu Nation founder and DJ Afrika Bambaataa. As the leader of the Zulu Nation, Bambaataa acted as a gatekeeper to hip-hop culture. In securing a DJ for KISS, Mayo first consulted Bambaataa.

Bambaataa, busy preparing an overseas Zulu Nation tour, first recommended his "son," DJ Afrika Islam, to Mayo. At the time, Islam enjoyed some renown in New York's dance music circles as the headliner of the weekly "Wheels of Steel" parties at the Roxy. Further, he had experience producing a hip-hop radio show for WHBI-FM, which he based on his Roxy parties. He was a natural fit to compete with Magic and Marley Marl. But Islam proved unwilling to adapt to the strictures of corporate radio. DJ Red Alert, Islam's friend and studio assistant on the *Zulu Beat*, recalled, "They asked for Islam to come down [to the KISS offices] several times. Islam would miss the appointments. So they asked who was the next person Bam had?"[41]

The next person Bam had was star Zulu DJ Jazzy Jay, and Mayo wasted no time in inviting him to audition for a spot in KISS's line-up. The pitch, as Jazzy Jay remembers it, was simple. "Listen," Mayo instructed. "We want to program KISS's music behind what you guys are doing over at the Roxy." If the pitch was simple, it was also enticing. "At the time we didn't know how to break into radio," Jazzy Jay recalls of the early 1980s. Prior to Mayo's offer, Jazzy Jay's attempts to enter the radio industry were discouraging. They included encounters with well-appointed program directors who, in no uncertain terms, expressed their belief that hip-hop's moment had come and gone. Radio seemed out of reach. So he quickly took up Mayo's offer to broadcast a weekly hip-hop mix show, airing from 9 PM to midnight on Saturday—not coincidentally the same slot occupied by Magic and Marley Marl. While Magic and Marley Marl spun live in WBLS's studios, Jazzy Jay prerecorded his program, filling a homemade cassette tape with a full set of hip-hop tracks and club singles. Still, Jazzy Jay believed his sets no worse for wear: "As far as what we programmed and what we played for our people, at the parties, at the clubs and jams or whatever the deal is, it was something totally different [from contemporary DJs]. We were the personality, the programmer and the technician." The arrangement seemed to be a felicitous one. Mayo had secured one of the leading figures in street music, and Jazzy Jay gained an outlet for broadcasting his art to audiences around New York.⁴²

But the arrangement quickly imploded, and Jazzy Jay left KISS only a few months after his first broadcast. What appeared, on the surface, to be a mutually beneficial arrangement proved lumpy at best, exploitative at worst. While there's disagreement about whether or not KISS promised to pay Jazzy Jay, what is clear is that no money—or, in any case, not enough—exchanged hands. When Mayo and Tony Quartarone, who had since been promoted to assistant PD, insisted that the DJ was gaining exposure, their argument fell flat. After weeks of arguing with the station, Jazzy Jay decided that his efforts were better placed performing live shows, producing records, and touring with the Zulu Nation. For Jazzy Jay, this departure marked a turning point in his long and accomplished career as a DJ. For Mayo, it marked a return to the drawing board.

As Jazzy Jay severed his ties with the station, he recommended his cousin up-and-coming Zulu Nation turntablist Kool DJ Red Alert to fill his slot. In order to fill the Friday night vacancy, Mayo approached DJ Chuck Chillout, a northeast Bronx DJ with a reputation in the downtown scene. These DJs, in their own way, had come to embody "the streets" in New York's club scene. Given the duration and impact of their tenure at WRKS, it's worth introducing them in some detail.

Chuck Chillout, born and raised in the northeast Bronx, began DJing in the mid-1970s. As early as middle school, he began saving his lunch money to buy records, with his first purchase being a 45 rpm of the Ohio Players' "Skin Tight." In high school, he saved the money he earned as a camp counselor to buy a boom box and batteries.⁴³ It wasn't long before he saved enough to purchase his own turntables and speakers for his growing record collection. As a teenager, he expressed interest in learning to DJ, though he had little patience for the disco records currently filling the crates of most DJs in his area. He found a musical education close to home. "My uncle, Richard Fernandez, [taught me]," he said. "He was always playing, like, the disco shit. I didn't want to hear that, you know?

But if it wasn't for him teaching me how [to DJ] I wouldn't know how. So I'm teaching him the rap stuff and the break beats." Though Chuck was drawn, first and foremost, to the music, he's clear about the role DJing played in his life's trajectory: "It kept me off the corner."[44]

Between 1977 and 1979, Chuck Chillout integrated into the northeast Bronx hip-hop scene. At that time, according to Chuck, hip-hop was still a community affair, featured at block parties in public spaces during hot New York summers, and school gyms and community centers when the weather turned cold. To hear him list the places where he attended shows is to encounter a personal geography of hip-hop's early years: Evander and DeWitt Clinton High Schools, Olinville's Public School 21, Valley Park. Further, two of the clubs to first feature hip-hop were both located in the northeast of rap's home borough, the T-Connection and the Stardust Ballroom. Chuck recalls that hip-hop was segregated by neighborhood when he was coming up. One could attend parties throughout the borough, but DJs were careful not to overstep their territories. "If you didn't know any of them people [Flash in Harlem, Bambaataa in the South Bronx, Herc in the West Bronx], you couldn't play in certain areas. They'd take your shit and beat you up." For Chuck, a crucial connection came through DJ Breakout, a local northeast Bronx DJ who played the role of gatekeeper through the region, and who helped Chuck discover breakbeats and hone his craft. Through Breakout, Chuck Chillout met Grandmaster Flash, DJ Doc La Rock, Pete "DJ" Jones, and Afrika Bambaataa, who in turn connected him to shows and artists across the city. Before the turn of the 1980s, Chuck headlined his first gig at Twin Parks on 180th Street in the Bronx. By mid-decade, he was spinning at clubs throughout the city, from gymnasiums in the Bronx to infamous Chelsea club the Tunnel.

The son of West Indian parents, as a child Red Alert lived in Harlem and went to school in the Bronx, where he earned his nickname for the danger he posed on the basketball court. Red Alert was an early and fervent listener to New York radio. Rolling the dial between WWRL and WBLS, Red considered himself and early student of jocks Hank Span, Eddie O'Jay, Jerry Bledsoe, Ken "Spider" Webb, and Frank Crocker, who the DJ recalls "dominated" New York in the 1970s. As a teenager, he was equally inclined to travel to midtown dancehall club Nell Gwynn to hear its mix of "disco and radio records" as he was to cross the Harlem River. Like Chuck Chillout, he was an early and insatiable record collector. "After every payday I wasn't thinking about getting dressed," Red Alert remembered. "I was going around the corner to two stores, Rock and Soul and Discomat. They were right there on 35th street and I was picking up the latest twelve inches of disco and R&B and funk and whatever else."[45]

When he began to DJ in the mid-1970s, he quickly became addicted to the practice. "I moved from the Colonial projects, back down to where my parents lived, which was on 113th street and 7th avenue," Red Alert recalled, aligning his foray into DJing with his family's move. "I hooked up my equipment right in my room and just stayed in there and practiced and learned the art every day and night." By 1977, he spent a majority of his time practicing and experimenting in his Harlem home, much to the chagrin of his parents.[46]

Red's propensity to travel throughout New York introduced the budding DJ to influential figures in New York's burgeoning hip-hop scene. So, too, did a key connection. Through his cousin, Jazzy Jay, Red Alert became involved in the Zulu Nation. By 1979, Red Alert was spinning at Zulu Nation parties by night and working as an assistant to a broker on Wall Street by day. On nights when he wasn't spinning, he traveled across New York, following the music, keeping up with DJs, and thinking about how he could further his own skills. But Red Alert did more than just attend shows; he developed a habit of taping them. Before long, Red had accrued a collection of hundreds of live performances, and a reputation throughout the five boroughs as the source for hot and rare tapes. So impressive was his collection that when Zulu DJ Afrika Bambaataa started his own radio show on WHBI-FM, he invited Red Alert to join him as a studio assistant. "I used to come down there and help Islam and I would bring a tape from one of the shows," Red Alert told Troy Smith. "That was another thing people knew me for. I was taping all the Zulu parties." Even before Red hosted his first show on WRKS, listeners to the *Zulu Beat* knew to expect—and to record for themselves—the weekly "Red Alert Special."[47]

And it was through Red's connection to the *Zulu Beat* that he first met Chuck Chillout. Islam and his cohort enjoyed a close relationship with several independent label scouts, who counted on time-brokered radio to circulate their product. One of those label scouts was Vincent Davis, the founder and manager of Vintertainment Records. "I met a brother at WHBI while doing Zulu Beats by the name Vincent Davis," Red narrated to Smith. "He came down with the record '2, 3, Break,' which was on Vintertainment Records. That was how I really met Chuck Chillout, because he did that cut 'Hip Hop on Wax, Volume One.' Vincent Davis came to me and asked me would I like to do the same thing like

Chuck?" The two DJs became fast friends. They bonded over their parallel careers as turntablists and recording artists, and over their obsession with DJing as the era's defining art form. What's more, they found in each other a friend willing to travel to the ends of the tri-state area, eager to close out dance clubs that didn't shut their doors until well into the work day. "We just went to hear the music," Chuck Chillout said of a typical Saturday night itinerary. "Being a DJ, you had to hear everything and everybody. We would go from the Roxy to Club Area, from Club Area to Danceteria, from Danceteria to the Paradise Garage at four in the morning and stay in that motherfucker 'til eleven o'clock."[48]

Perhaps it was their ubiquity across New York's disparate dance scenes, their ecumenical taste, and their indifference to internecine battles over genre, style, and fashion, that made them appealing flag-bearers for "the street" to Mayo. Perhaps it was the strength of their own live performances, or the depth of their crates. Either way, both DJs' recollections of their first encounters with Mayo evince how appeals to "the street" were a fundamental component of Mayo's approach to the DJs, and suggest that each understood the proposed hip-hop mix shows as representations of New York's street culture. They return, in surprising ways, back to the Roxy.

Both Chuck Chillout and Red Alert remember the evening they met Barry Mayo. "So, one night I happened to be in Roxy's and a cat named Barry Mayo was in there," Chuck Chillout recalled. "Me and Red was standing there, [listening to] what's going on with the music. So he hands me his card. [Says] he wants to put this shit on the radio." Red Alert's telling also begins in situ at the Roxy. "The whole Zulu Nation was down at the Roxy roller rink. We were being successful, we had just launched some records out," he described. "The program manager [of WRKS] would come down. They wanted to add what they called quote-unquote the 'street element' to what they had."[49] Chuck Chillout was incredulous. "Yeah, whatever! We didn't believe him, I didn't believe him." But Red Alert was less so and pursued Mayo's offer. The programming team at KISS requested a demo tape, and he wasted no time in supplying one. No sooner had he submitted a mix to KISS than he received an offer to produce a monthly program, airing Saturdays during Magic's slot.

Red Alert called Chuck Chillout moments after the DJ signed his contract at KISS: "Yo! It's real! It's real!" Eager for the same opportunity, Chillout recorded a demo tape and took it to WRKS's midtown studios. To his appraisal of the situation, Mayo was less than forthright:

I got down there one time, two times, three times. [Mayo] still left me with the receptionist. "I don't know where blah is or where blah was." He was playing games with me in the beginning. So she went to the bathroom, and I got up and walked down the hallway. I didn't know where I was going. So I walk back there, and he's sitting back there! He says to me, "I was wondering when you were going to walk back here." So now he takes me to a guy named Tony Quartarone, who was the program director. So he goes, "Yo, I wanna put this hip-hop on the radio." But Tony was my age, he was young, you know, white kid from Allentown. So he goes, "Yo, I'mma take your tape, I want that real hip-hop street shit." I give him the tape. You know, I'm thinking, "What's gonna happen?" I was hoping he was going to listen. Usually they take your tape but don't listen. But he listened. Before I got home—I came home on the 2 train—my mother goes, "Some Tony Q guy called." I said, "What!?" I called him back, he goes, "Yo, I wanna put you on, once a month."[50]

Through 1983 and into the beginning of 1984, the two DJs did just that: they recorded tapes for broadcast on WRKS. If Jazzy Jay quit KISS due to his dissatisfaction with "exposure" as a form of compensation, Red Alert adopted a realist perspective on the matter. "Put it this way," he continued in his interview with Smith. "The name of the game is you have to pay your dues! It was all good for me because I was gaining exposure, I started getting gigs."[51] For Chuck Chillout, too, the name recognition and label attention the DJ garnered through radio show translated into studio production opportunities and high-profile live performances around the country. "Roll tape for a minute," Chuck Chillout said of the moment. "Now it's blazin' hot, people are listening." Their programs on KISS-FM propelled Red Alert and Chuck Chillout to the center of the music industry, positioned at the precise point where label, artist, and audience interests intersected. It was from that place of convergence that the DJs selected music for broadcast.

Prerecording for Live Radio

The time Red Alert and Chuck Chillout spent listening to other DJs was not idle entertainment. Rather, it was an education in the potential moods, feelings, and sound worlds one might coax out of records in sequence. To Red Alert, all DJs, not just radio mixers, offered clues to the successful execution of a mix, and he took a practical approach to his listening. "What I was doing was paying attention to what other people were doing in their mixes. Not only what Jazzy had done or what Marly did, but what other guys did in the past, namely the Disco DJs."[52] There were few places other than New York in the 1980s where such ready exposure to high-level DJs would have been possible. Since the early 1970s, New York–based DJs had taken the mix to new heights, and spinners like David Mancuso, Nicky Siano, Frankie Knuckles, and Larry Levan found new and innovative ways to create community experiences through sound.[53] By the Reagan era, there was a wide field of artists opening doors to new heights of expression with two records and a mixer. "So I always used to listen to people like Larry Patterson, Ted Currier, and Sergio Munzibai," remembers Red Alert. "I mean the list is long. These were mostly live broadcasts from a club or just straight up mixes. . . . I had learned . . . all the different types of music [Zulu DJs] played in the Roxy. I would play R&B, Disco, Dance music, quote unquote hip hop sounds, and some rap records all mixed together."[54]

In his early sets on KISS-FM, Red Alert's programming drew from this combination of genres and styles. Some sets were top-to-bottom explorations of the era's rap tracks, like a 1984 set that mixed Grandmaster Flash and the Furious Five's "Step Off" into the Fat Boys' "Place to Be" into "AJ Scratch" by Kurtis Blow.[55] Another rap-centric Red Alert set extended the Cold Crush's "Fresh, Wild, Fly, and Bold" into T La Rock and Jazzy Jay's "It's Yours," milking the two tracks' breakbeats for all they had to offer. Other sets moved from rap into distant domains, creating different sonic and emotional terrains for listeners to traverse. One exemplary 1984 set opened with rap tracks by Divine Sounds, the Fearless Four, Doug E. Fresh, and the Ultimate Three MCs and then continued into a half-hour of synth-heavy R&B jams. Listeners ascended from rap valleys all the way up R&B mountains like Ashford and Simpson's "Solid as a Rock," Charme's "Georgy Porgy," "Feels so Real (Won't Let Go)" by Patrice Rushen, and the Force MDs' "Forgive Me Girl," an apology anthem more likely to move the body than the heart of its addressee.[56] Though it was a title devised by KISS's marketing department, Red Alert's sets lived up to their title of "Mastermix Dance Party."

Chuck Chillout, too, mixed rap with other genres for his KISS broadcasts. For Chuck, this openness toward genre was a matter of aligning his show with his club practice. "I was playing break beats and rap songs and couple of R&B joints that were happening like Joyce Sims, Keith Sweat, Guy," he noted. "You mix it up with the rap, 'cause basically what you was playing on the radio was playing in the clubs. So you wanted to keep your show, you know, aggressive, and to the point where people are listening." Club play proved an extremely important reference for both DJs, and with good reason. Watching DJs mix and integrate records in the club gave Chuck and Red an opportunity to see how audiences might react to a track on the radio. Hearing a track played on budget-crushing sound systems such as those at the Roxy, Funhouse, or Danceteria allowed them to hear a different set of nuances than you'd hear on a domestic system. There was unexpected power in volume. "You, basically . . . you played what was in the clubs on the radio and you kept it to the street. That's why people turned to it. You was a part of it," Chuck argued. For Chuck, his connection to the clubs represented the difference between ears-to-the-ground DJs like he and Red, on the one hand, and DJs who played on rotation, on the other. "Basically, my whole show—the difference between me and these cornball DJs now—I was always looking for the hottest and newest shit that was coming. A lot of these guys now have to play a playlist. That's not what a DJ's supposed to do. You're supposed to play what's happening in the street. That's the only way you can be competitive and be on the cutting edge of what's going on with the music."[57]

But not all club records would play well on the radio. For Chuck Chillout and Red Alert, there were strict criteria about what kinds of records would make good radio records. To describe these records, Chuck invoked a language that lost its technical specificity to something ineffable in the sound. "Shit's gotta be aggressive," he told me, clapping his hands insistently. "It ain't have that, then what's it for? Gotta be boom bangin', you know what I mean? See, I sit there and the way it sounds in the club doesn't sound the same way to me in the studio. So it has to be sounding right. Because you gotta feel it." I pressed Chuck to describe what he meant, and he elaborated in the form of an example, "George Benson . . . I can remember that album, *Give Me the Night*. That was the best fucking album ever. The mix on it was incredible. There's so much shit going on that album, if you actually listen to it loud you can hear all these things moving." For these DJs, an album's visceral impact, postproduction sophistication, and club audience response all contributed to whether or not it made it from the dance floor to the radio. In the end, their methods weren't so different than that of Mayo or KISS's other programming managers. Selections had to land with KISS's constituents. One had to research and test records. And those records had to sound right.

Chuck and Red's early 1980s programs on WRKS differed from their live practice in a significant way—their radio sets weren't broadcast live. This point requires some clarification. To say that these DJs' sets weren't "live" also seems to suggest that they weren't performed live. This is not the case. Rather, the DJs recorded a performance of their sets at home and brought the tapes to KISS's studios to be adapted for broadcast. The paths their tapes took to air reveal an unlikely chain of media linking performance to broadcast. "When I recorded my show for radio," Chuck began, "I would take my two turntables, record my show onto cassette, and I would give it to the [studio tech], because they wasn't playing our cassettes over the radio. It was reel-to-reel and carts [8-tracks]. So they would take me and Red's show, tape it to a reel-to-reel and then play it across the radio." Air personalities Jerry Young and Yvonne Mobley greeted listeners from KISS's studio during the 9 PM–12 AM broadcast slot, giving a voice to the two DJs' work. During broadcasts, Red and Chuck were likely to be in a club somewhere, continuing their own education while they schooled listeners.

Prerecording did not give the duo license to stretch the truth, however. Anything they broadcast on the radio, they were accountable to in the club. Red Alert explained, "[Program director Fred] Buggs and Mayo were really listening, because they asked us questions like 'how come y'all don't do the same type of style like [dance DJs and remixers] the Latin Rascals?' See the Latin Rascals were known for doing the editing with the special effects and other stuff. So we explained to Mayo and Buggs that the reason why we don't do it like that is because the same way how they hear us on the radio, they expect to hear us like that in the club. If they see that it's not the same like on radio then they feel you are a fake."[58] Audiences expected radio DJs to live up to their broadcasts. While the creativity and technology may have been in place for DJs to research new styles of sonic collage in their studio-laboratories, the culture of reception was not. So these DJs staked a middle ground between verisimilitude and imagination. They created long-form musical journeys that, like Orpheus, took listeners deep into New York's underworld with a song.

Going Live

For Red Alert and Chuck Chillout, radio opened doors to new performance opportunities. As a fringe benefit, it brought them closer to the decision-makers at record labels. By the mid-1980s Red had toured with new wave and alternative acts such as Devo, Talking Heads, Bow Wow Wow, and Nina Hagen. Moreover, many labels began to recognize that play on one of the major mix shows determined whether a particular piece of vinyl would become trash or treasure. In a reversal of the 1970s orthodoxy, which privileged club over radio play, labels and individuals began to send KISS's hip-hop DJs new product in force. "Everybody was bringing us records," Chuck remembered. "They was bringing us vinyl. I was getting mountains of records every week. I had to play through them, hear the whack, hear the bullshit. . . . It was coming like that in the mail. There'd be stacks of them!" Other artists approached the radio DJs about producing records for them. Eager to put their own work on vinyl, Red and Chuck cut their own records for Vintertainment's "Hip-Hop on Wax" series, with Chuck's contributions released under the prankish alter ego DJ Born Supreme Allah. These performances and recording activities began to seep into their radio shows in unexpected ways. For example, in 1985, Red signed on to be the DJ for Brooklyn-based MC Sparky D. In 1985, the two recorded the single "He's My DJ," in which Sparky D, in her aggressively melodic style, builds up Red Alert's skills in verse while he demonstrates those same abilities through a fast-paced, quick-cut tour of classic breakbeats. Soon after its release, Red Alert incorporated the record into his radio broadcasts. What better display of achievement for Red Alert than a "showcase" record on which a top MC lauds his skills, broadcast during his own radio program on the nation's highest-rated station?

109

Other opportunities came as competition heated up between New York's rap radio DJs. One event in particular looms large in popular memory of rap radio in New York: the highly audible beef between Magic and Red Alert. When Red Alert went on the air during Magic's broadcasts, Magic took it as an opportunity to taunt his competition. The insults weren't particularly sophisticated ("Red Dirt," "Red Duck"), and only in some cases were they personal ("Woody Woodpecker," an allusion to the DJ's red hair), but they succeeded in getting under Red Alert's skin. When Red Alert complained to Mayo that his competition was disrespecting him on-air, the manager helped Red Alert view the altercation from a new perspective. Red Alert recalled of the discussion,

> As I am telling Mayo all frustrated, he is standing there laughing as I am talking. As he is laughing I am getting madder and madder, because I am thinking he is laughing at me. So I ask him why are you laughing at me. He closes his office door and says "sit down." He says I respect that

you are mad, the reason why I am laughing is you have to learn some-thing, while that man is spending time dissing you, he is advertising you. Think about it, instead of spending time talking about his show, he is spending time talking about you. What he is doing is his own listeners are going to start leaving his show just to hear who you are. So take it in hand that he maybe dissing you, but he is advertising you.[59]

If Red and Chuck shied away from overselling their talents in their early broadcasts, this was only to remain a concern for a short period. In 1986, management arranged for the DJs to broadcast their sets live from KISS's studios. In part, this was a response to evolving station strategy. It was also part of a broader push to keep up with the competition. In 1985, RKO shook up their personnel. They promoted Mayo to the position of general manager of KISS, and Tony Quartarone and Fred Buggs stepped in to lead KISS's programming department. When Tony Quartarone left KISS midway through 1985 to tend to his health, Mayo poached Tony Gray from Philadelphia's UC WUSL. To Mayo, Gray fit the KISS mold to a T: "He's a person who is heavily research-oriented *and* has ears to the street. That's a rare breed of programmer, and that's what Kiss is all about." By mid-decade, KISS's brand was synonymous with "street music," so much so that Russell Simmons could laud Mayo's work in *Billboard* with "Every time a young program director comes and starts playing street music—the people's music—the station does well." Still, competition cut into their ratings, and going live was a way to bring in key listeners. To Chuck, the transition to live broadcasts was an obvious one. "We went live to go up against Magic and Marley because Magic and Marley were live, you know, so we had to compete."[60]

Though it would be accurate to say that Red and Chuck's sets con-sisted of "playing records," that phrase does little to capture the virtu-osity and imagination with which they mixed their selections. By 1986, the KISS hip-hop DJs composed mixes that chopped and repeated verses, layered new rhymes over old beats, delivered sly commentary on New York's rap scene and social issues, and proceeded rapidly through clas-sic, rare, and fresh-off-the-press breakbeats. They added sound effects in obvious and surprising places, let spoken-word records dialogue with sung and rapped melodies, and elevated sonic juxtaposition to an art reminiscent of the finest visual collagists. Chuck, in particular, reveled in the repetition of particularly strong rap verses, repeating them with successively involved scratching, thus trapping listeners in uncanny periods of progress-by-stasis. He mixed the chorus of Tears for Fears'

"Shout" over a Quiet Storm track oozing sensuality at 96 BPM, a combination of strife and sex as ear-perking as it is discomfiting. And he toyed with his listeners, repeating Dynasty and Mimi's "*Dynasty* Rap," a rhymed summary of the serpentine plot of the ABC soap opera, about as many times as it would take for a listener to catch up on missed episodes. That Arista signed and produced the record is more surprising than Chuck's relish in it.[61] Red Alert, for his part, often mixed long stretches examining the sonorous depth of a single sample, turning it over and examining it from many angles as one might a precious stone in light. In these DJs' hands, "the mix" had come a long way from hip-hop DJs' early 1980s experiments in adjacency and simultaneity. They had forged a style of composition that pressed at the harmonic, rhythmic, and emotional boundaries of common musical practice.

Broadcasting live came with its own perils. For one, programming staff could object to the DJs' selections as they sounded over the airwaves. "[Mayo] thought I was crazy when I played Public Enemy," Chuck remembered. Public Enemy was not the only group to raise Mayo's suspicions, and so invested was Mayo in the kinds of tracks being broadcast from his stations that he was prone to rejoin a DJ in the studio, mid-broadcast. "Man, I remember one night I played [the Beastie Boys'] 'Fight for your Right to Party,'" Chuck began. "'Who are these white guys? Who is this? What's going on?'" Chuck continued with an impersonation. Though they briefly debated the merits of the track and the skin color of its performers, Mayo had little reason to doubt Chillout's judgment. "By that point my boss was like, 'Yo, do what you want. He's got a track record. He's making a point.'"

In Chuck's telling, the critical turning point in his relationship with Mayo, the moment when the manager learned to trust his DJ's selections, came at the end of 1986. Chuck narrated:

> I remember when I first got [Joeski Love's] "Pee-Wee's Dance." I had that shit on a reel-to-reel. And I played it, and my boss came in the room and was like, "What is that playing on the radio, and why is it not a record?" And I said, "Yo, this is the biggest shit right now.' You know I always kept my head to the street. I say, "Yo, this is the dance everybody's doing." "I don't care . . . da dada da da. What's going on? Why is it not a record?' So I said, "Yo, listen to this. It's big." He thought I was crazy. So I played the reel-to-reel Friday night. Phone was going crazy Saturday, 'cause I was the only one that had it, 'cause my man Vincent Davis at Vintertainment Records down in Bronxwood, we grew

up together. So my phone rings at 10 AM in the morning, "Yo, what in the hell did you play on this radio station, that these kids are calling up?" "Yo, that's the thing I was telling you about!" "Yo, I will never ever bother you again about a record, because they're calling crazy."[62]

As Chuck's story about broadcasting an unsanctioned reel-to-reel of an unreleased single demonstrates, Mayo learned to trust his DJs because they did precisely what he had hired them do to: they represented the latest hip-hop had to offer, on a timetable faster than record labels could market and distribute. In this way, the DJs' personal relationships with artists around the city proved vital sources of new music for their programs. Indeed, it was Chuck Chillout's longtime friendship with Vincent Davis that enabled the DJ to acquire an advance cut of "Pee-Wee's Dance." In some cases, artists would approach Chuck out of the blue to deliver a tape. "I would walk down the block and I would see Slick Rick," Chuck said of one such occasion. "He gave me a record, *The Ruler's Back*. He had that on cassette. I met him in a fucking supermarket, around the corner from my girl's house. He had that album a good three years before it came out. Before he got signed to Def Jam. He gave me *Ruler's Back*. I think that helped him get his record deal because I was playing the fuck out of that song."

Chuck had a similar relationship with Chuck D of Public Enemy. The two had met each other and become friends through their involvement in hip-hop. Chuck D, the promoter and budding MC with the group Spectrum City, recently rebranded as Public Enemy, found himself at many of the same parties as Chuck Chillout. When Public Enemy cut records, Chuck D delivered them to the radio DJ, who was eager to help his friend out. "So he brings me 'Public Enemy Number One,'" Chuck recalled of the exchange. "You know it had James Brown in it, 'Blow Your Horn' in it. That was a typical breakbeat. Not too many people knew about it. You had to be old school to know it. I played it. It wasn't a real big response. But I played it because I had a relation with him."

By 1987, Public Enemy had recorded the first tracks for their second album and were looking to test-play some tracks to gauge the response. Chuck would remember that a few months after he aired "Public Enemy Number One," he received a call from Chuck D notifying him that he was delivering a record to KISS's studios. "So he brings me the acetate of 'Rebel without a Pause,'" Chuck said, singing the iconic whistling-radiator saxophone sample from the track through his teeth. "Listen, before he got downstairs I threw that shit on [the air]. . . . Then I played it again. So the next day everybody was *blasting* that shit." In Chuck Chillout's telling, Chuck D could hardly believe it when he heard the song coming through his car's radio on the curbside of KISS's studios. "Oh, my god, I didn't expect you to do it!"

What does a golden era sound like? Here's one answer: a disembodied squeal copped from a James Brown record supporting Chuck D's defiant bass, emanating from every home, car, and boom box, for blocks.

The story of Chuck Chillout broadcasting an acetate of "Rebel without a Pause" captures a paradox at the heart of the golden era: radio was both a boogeyman and booster for the genre's success. More than perhaps any other record, "Rebel without a Pause" represents the borderline between hip-hop's putatively inchoate transitional period and the dawning of the first rays of light of the golden era. The iconic sax sample, Chuck D's overtly political rhymes, avowedly uninterested in an R&B-adjacent or drive-time complacent aesthetic of smoothness, and the track's crowded, noise-driven production style—all have been cited as heralds of hip-hop creativity to come. More than just these musical features, a single lyric from Public Enemy's single has come to act as a summary of rap music in the 1980s. "Radio," Chuck D raps at the beginning of the second verse, "suckers never play me." In the dominant historical narrative, this line encapsulates rap's struggle for legitimacy. It poses the history of early commercial hip-hop as one between "suckers," here represented by drive-time DJs, programming managers, and the major label execs who passed on Public Enemy and their sibling acts, and those in the know, the artists, independent labels, and underground jocks who believed in the music and worked toward its success. This is a heroic history, and one in which the two Chucks' circumvention of traditional industry gatekeepers stands as a triumphal moment. But how might we reinterpret this story, and the place of "Rebel without a Pause" in hip-hop history, to provide a more nuanced account?

For one, we can reconsider the tension at the center of this oppositional account. To be sure, salaried broadcasters were hesitant at best, hostile at worst, when forced to decide whether or not to incorporate rap into daytime rotation; to be sure, there was racism, classism, and other assorted chauvinisms inflecting their decisions just as much as there were disinterested financial calculations. And it stands to note that the impression of opposition between listeners and artists, on the one hand, and gatekeepers, on the other, would galvanize hip-hop in the year to come as it became an essential component of a burgeoning countercultural identity. Nevertheless, measuring rap music's success in terms of rotation saturation might miss the point. DJs like Red Alert and Chuck Chillout on WRKS were able to accurately represent street music on one of the highest-rated stations in the United States for over half a decade. If rap music failed to saturate daytime play, it was utterly ubiquitous on Friday and Saturday nights, and in the following days on cassette. It didn't matter if suckers didn't play Public Enemy. They didn't have to. With Chuck, Red, and Marley on commercial radio, and the Awesome 2, Hank Love and DNA, P-Fine, and others on time-brokered and college radio, those who wanted to hear rap could and did.

Further, placing "Rebel without a Pause" in the context of adventurous radio mixes, rather than as a sonic outlier on a chart of contemporary record production, forces us to hear the single as part of a creative continuum rather than as a radical break with music practice. This is not to detract in any sense from the wildly inventive production of Public Enemy's Bomb Squad. It is a call, however, to listen in context. In the years leading up to Public Enemy's *It Takes a Nation of Millions to Hold Us Back*, rap music grew steadily in sophistication. Following the electro-rap one-offs and rock-and-roll minimalism of the first years of the 1980s, groups like the Stetsasonic MCs, Ultramagnetic MCs, and Erik B. and Rakim grew more sophisticated and daring in their beat production. A parallel development occurred every week on the radio. Chuck Chill, Red Alert, and Marley all offered their listeners highly technical and no less imaginative mixes, upping the ante across the decade. Between incremental development of beats and radio mixes, "Rebel without a Pause" is better heard as a significant increase in firepower in an ongoing musical arms race than an unanticipated detonation at popular music's foundation. Its techniques, subjectivities, and sounds all emerged from an ongoing process of experimentation and evolution. And that process was performed on Friday and Saturday nights with the broadcast and mixing of rap records.

Heard within the context of KISS-FM's branding, "the streets" emerged as a tool for organizing rap's new oppositional politics and the raucous sounds that reflected them. As, over the course of the 1980s, rap became synonymous with "street," the broadcast of Chuck D's intensified vocalization of discontent can be heard as another way in which radio helped amplify the concerns of young people, as another way in which Chuck Chillout fulfilled his self-assigned mandate to "keep it to the street." Though Mayo surely could not have foreseen that his efforts to keep KISS-FM relevant to its listeners would result in the broadcast of a record that openly insulted him and his milieu, the space he begrudg-ingly created for rap music, and the framework for reception he helped to institute, gave coherence and force to the genre as it developed year to year. These are the real paths that "the streets" carved in 1980s New York: lines of connection and exchange between institutions and indi-viduals with a mutual investment in the broadcast of rap.

FIVE

Broadcasting the Zulu Nation

If you spend any time searching online, it's not difficult to locate MP3s of the *Zulu Beat*, a hip-hop radio show airing between 1983 and 1985 on WHBI-FM 105.9, Newark. Finding digitized cassette recordings of hip-hop from the 1970s and early 1980s usually requires one to wade through dead links and inactive message boards. Sketchy metadata, often as evocative as it is inaccurate, complicates the search. There is a deep cache stranded in the derelict spaces of the web, a modern form of dusty crates of vinyl languishing in the attic.

In the case of the *Zulu Beat*, however, recordings are actively hosted and traded. Tapes of the *Zulu Beat* find ardent reception into the present, valued as musical mixes, objects of nostalgia, and documents capturing a transformative moment in hip-hop history. When the archivist behind oldschoolhiphoptapes.com, who goes by the handle "Dutch," announced that he would begin to reupload tapes after existing links went dark, requests for broadcasts of the *Zulu Beat* were among the first that fans and collectors submitted.[1] Strewn across web-streaming sites YouTube, Mixcloud, and Sound-Cloud, as well as a dizzying array of niche forums and blogs, collectors have made a substantial portion of *Zulu Beat* broadcasts available to contemporary listeners. Spend enough time clicking and it's easy to accrue a wide sampling of the show's broadcast history, an introduction to host DJ Afrika Islam's experiments transposing hip-hop into broadcast sound.

Download and play any tape of the *Zulu Beat*. Whether a fragment or a full broadcast, the contents tend to follow a similar trajectory. It won't take long before Islam lowers the volume to address his listeners. Perhaps it's just to interject, to deliver a shout-out, or to remind listeners that dedications are coming up after the mix of the week. They should have their cassettes cued up and ready. Perhaps it's to announce an upcoming Zulu Nation party or to inform aspiring DJs and MCs how to mail a demo tape to WHBI's 80 Riverside Drive studio. "If it's fresh," Islam often says, "you can get it on the air." Fragments spun from newly pressed acetate tantalize with the knowledge that a world premiere awaits just after the next station identification. Banter with studio assistants Donald D and Kool DJ Red Alert invites listeners to join their late-night camaraderie, and selections dedicated to "all the newborns in New Jersey," "to all you homeboys in Manhattan, the Island of Satin," draw the audience within the affective bounds of WHBI's broadcast territory. Afrika Islam's address demonstrates how hip-hop radio animated social life within New York just as radio scattered hip-hop beyond the five boroughs.

A world emerges in the transduction of sound and sociality on the *Zulu Beat*. For Islam, the *Zulu Beat* provided an opportunity to reflect hip-hop in New York. "There wasn't even a main thesis to the show," he recalled. "It was to get on and just present hip-hop for what it really is."[2] Radio offered Islam a distinctly new set of possibilities for sounding the outlines of hip-hop culture. And radio, in turn, gave listeners new means of communicating with one another. Audience members tuned in to deliver personal messages, to glean information about upcoming shows, and to learn more about the artists they admired. Islam encouraged listener participation, and throughout broadcasts he notified listeners when to tape, how to call the studio, and where to send their fan mail. The *Zulu Beat* became a community forum, transfiguring listeners' relationships in sound while forging new communities in radiophonic space.[3]

Recordings of the *Zulu Beat* and the communities they disclose beg a question: What can we know about the material and affective world of Black youth culture in New York from extant cassette recordings? These tapes are rich historical documents, operating as inscriptions of an event, as texts, and as objects with their own histories. Tapes tell us something about the event of a broadcast; they hint at the lived-ness and liveness implicit in any performance. As recordings, they can also serve as texts suitable for close reading, opening a window onto the culture that produced them. As much as these tapes can open up room for interpretation, it's important to remember that recordings also have lively material histories. Each circulated in a world in which they were valued, exchanged, collected, and altered. They spread rhizomatically, mailed, sold, traded, and erased along the vicissitudes excitement and gain.[4] These histories of circulation are largely unknowable. Tapes of the *Zulu Beat,* however, invite us to listen to their grooves, to the ways that community radio traced the human contours of New York with FM waves.

"Welcome to Another Beat on the *Zulu Beat*"

Airing for the first time in the spring of 1983, the *Zulu Beat* captured a moment of unprecedented social and stylistic convergences. In the year leading up to the show's initial broadcasts, the four pillars of hip-hop worked their way out of the Bronx and into music, dance, and art scenes across New York. With the help of well-connected proponents in the downtown art and dance communities—a cohort Jeff Chang encapsulates as "white baby-boomer outsiders, young white bohemian dropouts, white art rebels, [and] Black post-jazzsters"—the youth cultures of the Bronx became the focal point of crosstown collaborations.[5] Zulu DJs held court at downtown clubs the Ritz, Negril, Danceteria, and the Roxy; graffiti worked its way out of subway tunnels and into gallery spaces; dancers encircled battling breakers in downtown clubs as well as uptown community centers; and rapping captured the ears and imaginations of listeners throughout and beyond New York. In his oral history of New York dance culture in the early 1980s, Tim Lawrence describes this period as motived by a "drive for synthesis," a curiosity to see "what happened when sounds and people from different backgrounds came together."[6]

Initially funded by downtown promoter Kool Lady Blue and hosted by South Bronx sons Afrika Islam and Donald D, the *Zulu Beat* sprang directly from this drive for synthesis. Islam presented listeners with a distillation of hip-hop culture, with programming informed as much by Afrika Bambaataa's crate-digging credos as the downtown club scene's DIY avant-garde outlook. Listeners heard deep cuts from Kraftwerk, Emerald Sapphire and Gold, and Liquid Liquid spun adjacent the Jimmy Castor Group, Dyke and the Blazers, and James Brown. Announcements for outer-borough Jazzy Five MC shows flowed into plugs for downtown club dates. Islam infused his two broadcast hours with carefully selected sounds and personalities, drawing on his tenure as headline DJ at down-town roller disco and multicultural hub the Roxy, as well as his time spent repping breakdance outfit the Rock Steady Crew and boogieing at queer-of-color dance club Paradise Garage. In the months preceding the advent of the *Zulu Beat*, Islam emerged as a fixture in a scene galvanized by the potential of "creative, explosive contact" between different sub-cultures in New York City.[7]

For Islam, the success of the *Zulu Beat* lay in its connection to the music featured at New York's cutting-edge clubs. "The music that was played on the show was the music that was being played in the streets," Islam noted. "That's why everybody could identify with it."[8] Others ob-served that Islam's approach to selecting and mixing records diverged from what many listeners recognized as hip-hop. Se'Divine the Master-mind of the World's Famous Supreme Team remarked that "Islam was playing underground music. . . . In fact, the music that Islam was play-ing during that time. . . . [Some audiences] were not ready for him, at least that was the impression I got. In fact, that boy was ahead of his time. He was beyond hip-hop!"[9]

Impressions such as SeDivine's were informed by the fact that "the street," for Islam, referred to New York dance culture in a broad sense. The commonalities he observed—the musical curiosity and social inclusiveness shared by uptown hip-hop culture and the down-town scene—served as a fertile model for Islam's experiments in radio. "Friday night I was at The Roxy," Islam commented. "We were playing exactly the same thing [on the radio] we were playing in the parties."[10] Positioned between these worlds, Islam was keen to act as a representa-tive for hip-hop as he knew it.

From Zulu Nation to *Zulu Beat*

Raised in the Soundview neighborhood of the Bronx, Islam's formative years were spent in the presence of the Zulu Nation, which Bambaataa founded in 1975 in an attempt to transform his disillusionment with the violence and dead-end trajectory of gang life into a positive force.[11] The DJ envisioned the Zulus as an alternative to the social hierarchy and struc-ture that gangs provided, offering an alternative form of organization to young people fatigued by the devastation wrought on Bronx neighbor-hoods by turf wars and drug trade. The Zulu Nation combined emblems of the pan-African movement with the vocabulary of the post–civil rights moment, stitched together by a capacious interpretation of Nation of Islam theology. The organization's message of self-respect, nonviolence, and Black pride attracted a loose, fluid coalition of ex–gang members and young people. The Zulu Nation offered its members music and dance as viable alternatives to gang life, and its rapid success stemmed from the centrality of expressive culture to the organization.[12]

By 1977, membership extended far beyond the Bronx, and, by the cusp of the 1980s, the Zulu Nation boasted of chapters across the city. Estimates hold that, in 1982, the Zulu Nation included thousands. Steve Hager described the ease with which one could affiliate with the Zulus in his iconic 1982 *Village Voice* profile, writing that "becoming a Zulu wasn't difficult, all you had to do was show up at the right parties and express an interest in joining."[13] Over time, hip-hop and the Zulu Nation entwined. Each Zulu party provided evidence to support the organization's conviction that music could cross cultural barriers.[14] As hip-hop spread beyond the Bronx, the Zulu Nation spread with it. "The Zulu Nation was the heart and nucleus of uptown before coming downtown," Islam noted.[15] In 1979, MC Chubby Chub whipped a packed Audubon Ballroom into a frenzy when he rapped, "We're the mighty Zulu Nation, Bambaataa Corporation / Like rush hour at Grand Central Station." Just a few years later, the crowd at a Bronx River Houses show knew that when Busy Bee Starski called, "What's the name of this nation?" they should respond, "Zulu, Zulu!"[16]

Afrika Islam made his name in hip-hop as a breakdancer. A b-boy in the Zulu Kings, Islam learned about the sounds and styles of hip-hop as Zulu DJs spun the beats for battles against rival crews. Islam came under the tutelage of Afrika Bambaataa in the late 1970s. By the early 1980s, Islam would recall, "I got named 'The Son of Bambaataa' because I was always under him and his teachings and what was going on in the Zulu Nation at the same time in hip-hop."[17] Islam's skill as a DJ earned him his own crew of Zulu MCs, the Three the Hard Way MCs. It was with these MCs that Islam met his future cohost, Donald D.

Islam's enthusiasm for dancing quickly took him beyond the Bronx. In the early 1980s, the DJ's preferred club was the Garage, then infamous for its crisp-at-any-volume sound system and as the home of DJ Larry Levan. Islam credits his time at the Garage for opening his eyes to the potential of parties that "pulled people from all the boroughs" and for expanding his musical horizons. "At the Garage you could hear Roy Ayers, the Soul Sonic Force, and Manu Dibango," Islam remembered. "And to see such acts as the Peech Boys and Chaka Khan and Grace Jones and France Joli—all of these eclectic underground acts—it was impressionable for a kid from the South Bronx."[18]

Though younger than eminent Zulu DJ Jazzy Jay and Bambaataa, Islam's precocious turntable stylings created performance opportunities for the young DJ. When Bambaataa left his post as the headline DJ at the Roxy's weekly "Wheels of Steel" parties to tour Europe, he named Islam his replacement. "Someone told me, 'The only other person that can play like Bambaataa is his son,'" Islam said, and so Bambaataa named Islam to take over in his stead.[19] At the close of 1982, Islam presided over the Roxy's hip-hop spectacles each weekend.

At the Roxy, Islam met promoter Ruza Blue, a socialite active in the downtown dance scene and the coordinator and host of the venue's "Wheels of Steel" nights. It's not clear where the idea for a radio show originated. Some unsourced accounts suggest that Earl "Rootsman" Chin, host of a weekly reggae hour on WHBI, encouraged Islam to do the same for hip-hop. Others have insisted that Islam was a natural replacement for Mr. Magic when he left for WBLS.[20] Regardless of where the idea came from, in the first months of 1983, Ruza Blue and Islam arranged to produce a hip-hop radio show on WHBI. Blue fronted Islam the capital for the station's time-brokerage fee in exchange for promotion on-air, and DJ Red Alert recalls that journalist Steve Hager also contributed to the program. During early episodes of the *Zulu Beat,* Islam made sure to notify listeners that the *Zulu Beat* was a KLB-Fun production, a Kool Lady Blue venture.[21] In March 1983, Islam and MC Donald D produced their first show for broadcast at 1 AM on a Tuesday. Islam acknowledged the diversity of the *Zulu Beat*'s constituents when he asked an interviewee to explain breakdancing "for everybody that's in the land tonight, everybody that's on the planet, to all the Gods and all the Zulus. All the brothers on downtown, all the Ahkis . . . the Blacks and Puerto Ricans and the Trendies and Uptowners and the Punk Rockers."[22] The *Zulu Beat* staked a territory opened by synthesis. Operating at the interstices of multiple communities, the *Zulu Beat* let Islam and his listeners explore the resonances of a citywide musical culture.

Shout-Outs and the Hip-Hop Community

If the *Zulu Beat* brought new broadcast communities together in the act of listening, we'd do well to ask just how radio programs construct and attract their publics. Tapes can help us here. MP3 recordings of the *Zulu*

Beat give us a way of knowing, if only in a limited sense, just who tuned in. With tapes, we can hear how ephemeral communities formed around broadcasts of the *Zulu Beat* and locate within recordings something of those who produced and heard it, forcing us to confront a classic question in media theory: To what extent do public texts disclose their audiences? To unpack rap tapes, there's no better place to start than shout-outs.

Dedications from one listener to another were a foundational feature on the *Zulu Beat*. Within minutes of initiating his broadcasts, Islam announced to the audience that the phone lines were open, making sure to read the number for each of WHBI's two lines carefully. Calls then flooded the station. Studio assistants and cohosts Donald D and Red Alert operated the phones, fielding calls and writing lists for Afrika Islam to read over the air. Shout-outs do something important when it comes to animating broadcast publics. If all public texts perform their relationship to their audience by "elaborat[ing] . . . a particular culture, its embodied way of life, its reading practices, its ethical conventions, its geography, its class and gender dispositions, and its economic organizations," shout-outs provide direct evidence of presence.[23] They complicate radio's open structure of transmission, writing distinct communities of reception into broadcasts even as they spread along unknowable paths of reception.

For years, historians treated radio as a one-to-many medium. Thanks to a recent wave of thoughtful historical and ethnographic work, it's now commonly accepted that audiences inflect the media they consume. In making this leap, reading shout-outs against the notion of broadcast publics has been instructive.[24] While scholars have long recognized "the relationship between formal and aesthetic features of mediatized address and forms of historical consciousness and collective subject formation," as Daniel Fisher has put it, he also reminds that "to consider how forms of public culture gather audiences to themselves is also to ask how their particular forms of address may entail consequential abstractions of broader social groups, audiences, or publics."[25] When Islam spoke through WHBI's microphone, interviewed a guest, or played a prerecorded cassette mix, for example, he addressed an unknowable mass of potential listeners while revealing his and his audience's cultural commitments in the content and style of that address. Shout-outs go further, rendering this form of public-building literal. Shout-outs on the *Zulu Beat* were intensely personal, with Islam envoicing a message from one listener to another. Dedications took relationships formed and sustained in the city and staged them for everyone listening, imbuing bonds of friendship and affiliation with new public value. Though there may have been more than one "DJ Lee of 113th and 7th," however unlikely, such dedications performed the relationship between specific listeners in the transaction of the shout-out, all while absorbing others in a listening public through more imaginative, vicarious identifications.[26] Place names, nicknames, and bonds of friendship and kinship redrew the affective geographies of hip-hop in a stylized vernacular. It was this ability to interpellate listeners into a new hip-hop public, to envelop existing communities while simultaneously generating new affiliations, real and imagined, that made radio such a compelling machine for community building.

A recording of a July 7, 1983, broadcast illustrates the centrality of dedications on the *Zulu Beat*.[27] About forty-five minutes into the transmission, just a few minutes before listeners recording to TDK or Memorex 90s would scramble to flip their cassettes, DJ Afrika Islam clipped the end of a prerecorded station identification to announce that "dedications are about to be read." Islam asked Red Alert, seated next to him at the broadcast console, if he agreed that "everything is going very, very, *very* well in the studio tonight," and proceeded directly into the week's dedications. "A Red Alert Bulletin! He says peace to Shawn and Trici, to Lisa, [in a nasal growl] H-H-Hines, Greg and Stevie Steve, to DJ Lee of 131st Street and 7th Avenue." After stumbling over a sloppily written "DJ Skeezo of Brooklyn," pausing to check his pronunciation with Red Alert, Islam continued, "Tony Metcalf and Curtis of Bed-Stuy, to his main nephew EZ Money Mike of 113th Street, to his one and only son Little Red Alert . . . and to all the family in Wagner Houses. And to the Bronx River Zulu Land, also known as Home Base, also known as Home of the Gods. And to the Bodyguards of Manhattan." Finished with Red Alert's dedications, Islam read those that listeners had called in to the studio before transitioning into the anxiously awaited mix of the week. In total, it took Islam roughly three minutes to read the complete list of listeners' names and notes. During the July 7 broadcast, it took three further interludes and numerous one-off shout-outs for Islam to close the docket of listener requests.

Historians of radio have spent a considerable amount of ink detailing how radio, as a mass public medium, has impacted communities across geography and time. This emphasis on community reception goes a long way toward helping us understand shout-outs. A shout-out's value derived from the sense of publicness it carried. Through dedications, Fisher writes, "one airs a relationship, performing it in a heightened, public context, emplacing kinship in a social, institutional, and geographic landscape."[28] Broadcasting on FM radio rendered a listener's message available not just to the intended recipient, but also to anyone else who might have been tuned in to 105.9 in the early hours between Tuesday and Wednesday. It is hard to overestimate the excitement listeners felt in hearing their name or music on the radio. When I asked Teddy Tedd of the Awesome 2 about it, he told me, "Are you kidding! That was like seeing your graffiti pass by in the subway! It was huge."[29] Reminiscing about the first time he rapped live during a broadcast of the *Zulu Beat*, Donald D noted, "The first time I ever rhymed on the radio, that was an incredible moment. All my friends calling down to the station, congratulating me—whether it was Melle Mel or Rodney C or Sha-Rock—just saying they heard me on the radio."[30]

Hearing one's message or one's name spoken on the radio was significant for hip-hop audiences, predominately young people of color from New York's ghettos, precisely because it combined the publicness of transmission with the aura of technical mastery and institutional remove surrounding radio. To hear one's name in a shout-out was to be audible in a more nuanced way than ready-to-hand media languages for portraying race and poverty in America could capture. Just as graffiti was a way to make a writer seen, shout-outs were a way for a community to be heard, harnessing the electromagnetic spectrum rather than aerosol as its medium. But to focus solely on shout-outs' politics of visibility would be to miss their richness. A full list of shout-outs from a 1983 broadcast is worth presenting in order to demonstrate the range of expression hiding in dedication breaks. After segueing the Jimmy Castor Group's "It's Just Begun" into Cat Stevens's "Was Dog a Doughnut," Islam begins, "So check it out,"

Raquelle wants to hear "Rockin' It." I already played that, Raquelle, you tuned in a little too late! Pooh Bear says, "What's happening?" to the LIQ crew and Princess . . . That must be from Queens. Now Corey B from Brooklyn is rocking on! I hear you! Donald B says, "What's up?" to Donald D, and Donald D is on the phone at this time. I hope that's the same Donald D . . . And God V says peace to the Grand Force MCs, and that definitely goes out to my main man . . . Four . . . Forty Four! says peace to Afrika Islam and Bambaataa. And of course OJ along with the mysterious J5, the guy who drives you around, you know, with the sneaker prints on his neck. And of course O3, the guy with the K . . . Aries, you know? And to EZ, to Galaxy from Kool EZ. Lamonte says, "What's happening?" to Greg from St. Nick Ave. up in money-making

Manhattan. Yolanda to her cousin Lin, and Chris, they like to do the wild style . . . it's freaky stuff. And the Shine and Robski to DMC and Dandy from T-Ski, love to Rob and Norma. And of course Dee Rock of course says, "What's happening?" to Scarlet and Zalia. And Mr. Hines says [unintelligible] to . . . What's her name? Latifa? Yeah . . . I hear you, Hines . . . Scooby D says, "What's happening?" to Monty B, we all say, "Happy birthday! We wish you many more." Butchie T, Disco D, and Shaun-ski to all the New York City Rockers and Kevie Kev. And getting to the last page . . . Wisdom Allah wants to hear "Change the Beat." We already played it! DJ Tibbs and his girls listen to the *Zulu Beat*. Gordie B dedicates to Ken Duke, Calvin, and Jerry, and the game room where everybody wastes their quarters. Once again Captain Hook says peace to all because he's back out, and that definitely goes out to Mr. Hook! And Taft says, "Hello," to his sister Kim from Lynbrook Houses. "Love Rap" is dedicated to the Breakmasters from Queens, and Master K wants to hear "Sucker MCs."[31]

Dedications on the *Zulu Beat* spanned the mundane to the intimate to the humorous, with professions of love commingling with prank calls. A listener named Mina was typical in her use of dedications to "throw a big kiss to her man from Taft." Listener La Rock called in a dedication to remind "the whole of Chapter 7" to attend the following day's Zulu Nation Meeting. "You hear that?" Islam asked on his behalf, "All of Chapter 7 at the meeting tomorrow." Some listeners communicated messages that would only be meaningful to a few listeners. During a 1984 broadcast, Crazy Legs of the Rock Steady Crew left a personal message for Islam to relay, "Crazy Legs says . . . not to call out . . . or to come visit him 'cus he's got problems. Alright! So don't visit Crazy Legs!" Some listeners found a citywide audience for timeless prank calls. One dedication read, "Tim dedicates 'The Mexican' to Ben Dover." Laughing, Islam catches the prank as he reads the name aloud, continuing, "Ben Dover! That's a good one. I should have grabbed a bag for that one!"[32]

Shout-outs were also an important tool for writing community onto urban space, and as often as listeners directed their dedications to a single recipient, they dedicated their shout-outs to more general locales. Entire housing projects, streets, and neighborhoods became the object of dedications as listeners expressed their affection for their home places. Dedications such as "Mr. Freeze is in the studio, and he says peace to the Soundview," or "Papa D is the number-one listener and gives a special shout-out to the Brooklyn Crew," trafficked in a poetics of place, relying on networks established prior to their broadcast for their specificity.[33] Other listeners directed their dedications to entire boroughs, with Islam announcing, "This goes out to everyone up in the Boogie Down," or, conveying on behalf of one listener, "And this is going out, another one, to the Zulu Nation and Staten Island."[34] Shout-outs' evocations of place presage a phenomenon Murray Forman observes in rap lyrics of the late 1980s, in which the shout-out communicates "powerful ties to place that both anchor rap acts to their immediate environments and set them apart from other environments."[35] Shout-outs participated in a discourse of place-making, with rap radio providing the occasion for listeners to rework their relationship to New York City and to each other.

If you pay close attention to the list of places registered in shout-outs, you can observe the psychogeographic boundaries of New York City expanding. Listeners frequently called in shout-outs to relations in hip-hop strongholds in the Bronx, Harlem, and Queens, as well as Bed-Stuy and Brownsville, Brooklyn. Others called from the peripheries of the city. Listeners called from Westchester County, directing their shout-outs to White Plains, Mount Vernon, and Port Chester. Listeners from Long Island and northern New Jersey, at the far edges of WHBI's broadcast range, added their dedications to Islam's lists. Some dedications offered listeners an opportunity to self-identify as their referent, such as the July 17 shout-out "This is going out to everyone in the tri-state area. All Nubians, you know who you are."[36] In naming a place, and doing so in terms that highlighted its Black occupants, dedications corralled that location and its inhabitants within the imagination of the audience and inscribed those identities into their personal cartographies of the city. Other times, the ambiguity of a dedication led Islam to joke about its many possible referents. In the middle of a long chain of dedications, Islam read, "Wanda says hello to Kevin on 17th Street." Without pause, he followed with, "Now that could be anywhere in New York! All you Kevins on 17th Street, if you know Wanda, she says, 'What's up?'" In the transaction of a dedication, listeners redrew the boundaries of New York, coding their new map with the cultural affiliations of listeners.

Dedications were almost always rendered with nicknames, or stylized abbreviations such as "Butchie B, Big Al, or Little Rodney," as Islam listed during a dedication break on "Tape 8–9 DJ Grazzhoppa collection." Listeners specified their relationship to the recipient of their shout-out. They called as boyfriends, siblings, neighbors, crew members, friends, siblings, parents, as well as their own stage personae. Faye Ginsburg notes that listeners addressed by a radio broadcast may simultaneously inhabit a range of subject positions.[37] By transacting shout-outs in nick-names rather than birth names, dedications solidified the sense of community created by a broadcast. Though listeners may have occupied many different subject positions in their daily lives, shout-outs singled out the parts of their identities that intersected with hip-hop culture.

Hearing the *Zulu Beat*'s Listeners

Listening for the lived experience behind shout-outs forces us toward speculative modes of listening. As direct and as public as shout-outs are, they toggle, like so much in Black culture, between disclosure and concealment. They hide as much as they give away. To know more about the hip-hop community, we need to dwell in this obscurity. We need to mind the listeners whose voices we can't hear. Consider, for example, how we might listen for the presence of young listeners as they tuned in to the *Zulu Beat*. When researching this chapter, I spoke to numerous fans who followed the show while in elementary school. Their recollections share a common refrain: each remembers staying up late to catch as much of the show as they could before passing out from exhaustion. So we know young listeners were a core constituency of the *Zulu Beat*. What more, then, can the tapes tell us? A 1983 advertisement on the *Zulu Beat* is a useful place to begin.[38] The ad asks listeners, "Are you the next Chris Evert Lloyd? Can you fill the shoes worn by Earl the Pearl? . . . Do you possess outstanding athletic abilities?" The ad continues to instruct interested listeners to consider participating in the New York City trials for the United States Youth Games, which were open only to boys and girls aged nine to fifteen. Much like ad spots on commercial radio, this announcement reveals its target in its address.[39]

At times, Islam spoke to his young constituency directly. During a fall 1983 show, Islam sent a message to his younger brother, warning, "Don't forget, Little Islam, you better be in bed before 5." On an April 14, 1983, broadcast Islam addressed all adolescent listeners as the time approached 3 AM. "All listeners under the age of fourteen must be in bed by 3 AM," he offered in a stern tone. "If you're under fourteen, turn off your radio at 3 AM."[40] Young listeners developed intricate methods for taping late night hip-hop that allowed them to record without stirring the suspicion of parents. One fan remembers staying up late as a child in Queens, taping the *Zulu Beat* at a low volume to avoid waking his parents. "I got hip on taping the music low so my mom wouldn't hear the music upstairs," he says. "I thought you had to have the volume on high so the tape was loud, but I was wrong. . . . All you had to do was put the record level on 7 and have the volume barely on."[41] Other listeners remember setting watch alarms, splurging on ninety-minute tapes to capture forty-five minutes of broadcast before rising to flip the tape, or falling asleep with their hand placed just so on their radio. If they were lucky, the "pop" of the tape deck resetting would be enough to rouse them. They could then flip the cassette and repeat the process until the end of the broadcast.

If young listeners were relatively conspicuous on broadcasts of the *Zulu Beat*, others were less so. Early rap radio programs drew a large incarcerated audience. Indeed, if you were looking for it, you could catch glimpses of this audience in a dedication quoted earlier in this chapter: "Once again Captain Hook says peace to all because he's back out." Here, I read "back out" to mean "no longer incarcerated." Rap radio provided prisoners a means of connecting with the outside world, of feeling involved in the imagined community of hip-hop as they listened. This was true for each of the early hip-hop radio shows. Reflecting on the listeners who called and wrote to *The Awesome 2 Show*, Special K remembers, "We met a lot of cats that was on lockdown. . . . That was their thing, their ritual: 'I'm dealing with this jail time, but I know on Saturday nights I'm listening to the Awesome 2. I got a little radio.' "[42] At the opening of a 1982 broadcast, the World's Famous Supreme Team reminded their incarcerated listeners, "Not to forget that we are thinking about you," and to "remember to send some letters in to the studio." Similarly, broadcasts of the *Zulu Beat* helped ease the devastation of incarceration. Dedications such as this, delivered over a loop from Kraftwerk's "Tour de France," from a 1984 broadcast of the *Zulu Beat*, were common: "This is for all the brothers that are stuck on the rock. Anywhere, from Comstock on down the to the Rock. For working hard."[43] Here, "Comstock" refers to the Great Meadow Correctional Facility, located upstate near Fort Ann, New York, and "the Rock" to the infamous prison on Alcatraz Island, a stand-in for institutionalization more generally. For these listeners, hip-hop radio was a small reprieve. It established a vital connection to the outside, allowing listeners to participate in a culture on the outside during their sentence. By acknowledging incarcerated listeners, *Zulu Beat* created the possibility for ongoing inclusion in a community.

For many listeners, the sense that they were listening at the same time as others was essential to the experience of the *Zulu Beat*. Indeed, simultaneous listening was part of Islam's philosophy for the show. According to Donald D, "[Islam's] idea was: 'I'm going to take what I'm doing at the parties and do it on the radio. You MC on the radio, I play the breakbeats, I play the beatbox [drum synthesizer/sequencer] and we gonna just do it live on the radio so that people who can't be at the parties will be able to hear what we do all at once.' "[44] Only a few hundred people could be at a party. Anyone could tune in to a radio show. Listeners' active participation in broadcasts amplified the sensation of simultaneity. During one broadcast, Islam pressed listeners for their input on a new track. He prefaced his premiere of "Feel the Force," an electro-rap single by G-Force featuring Ronnie Gee and Captain Cee, by saying, "Something new, I'm not going to tell you the name until it's over. If you like it, give me a call. You know when, you know where."[45] As the track played—the track runs about seven and a half minutes—Islam periodically interjected to remind listeners to phone the studio with their feedback. "Now like I said," he reminded listeners, "I can't tell you the name of it, just tell me if you like it. Just give it a 'A' or a 'B.' I know what an 'A' or a 'B' or a 'C' is, just don't give it a c."[46] If this game is any indication, one way we might come to know the audience of the *Zulu Beat* is through the ways their collective preferences influenced Islam's programming over time.

From the earliest broadcasts of the *Zulu Beat*, Islam encouraged listeners to send tapes and letters to the studio, informing them how to do so. "Now check this drift," Islam told his listeners on a late March 1983 broadcast. "If you want to send your tapes in to be reviewed by yours truly, Afrika Islam, or you want to send your letters to let me know what's happening with the funkiest show on radio, the address is 'Radio Station WHBI, Afrika Islam, 80 Riverside Drive, New York, New York, 10024. . . .' That's for everyone who wants to get their tapes reviewed by me for future consideration on-air, or to let me know what's happening with their area or their crews."[47] After a few months on the air, Islam confessed to stockpiling listeners' tapes in the studio and at his home. Over the course of its two years on the air, Islam featured tapes by the Jazzy Five MCs, Afrika Bambaataa, Grand Wizard Theodore, and the DJ Whiz Kid, among many others.

Just as often, Islam played tapes from artists who didn't make it into the canonical histories of hip-hop. Islam featured one such tape on a spring 1984 broadcast. Islam introduced it: "This week a tape submitted by DJ Wanda Dee and Cisco, hot little track, something definitely new for the *Zulu Beat*. That's Wanda Dee the girl DJ—and I should have said the *lady* DJ, Elegant Lady Wanda Dee the DJ—and of course Cisco the MC from Charlie Chase." The music is buried deep beneath a low-fi wash that blends into *Zulu Beat*'s base of FM static. DJ Wanda Dee spins a mid-tempo break beneath a drum machine loop, arranging synthesizer sounds over the sequencer's analogue drum presets. Cisco alternates between rapping and a melismatic style of singing, his lyrics difficult to discern amid the noise and reverb. As the song ends, Islam pauses the tape with an audible "click," and reminds listeners to send their "freshest tapes." "If it's not fresh," he warns, "you're going to hear this."[48] On "this," Islam cues a raucous laugh track, and allows it to play without commentary for nearly twenty seconds. In this, Islam ventriloquizes his audience's standards for new music.

From the Street to the Studio

If listeners' participation in the *Zulu Beat* established the program as a community forum, a common aesthetic project spanning the physical and psychological spaces of radio, WHBI's studio itself emerged as an important social space. Donald D recalls, "Our friends [used to] come hang out at the station. Frosty Freeze from the Rock Steady Crew was a real good friend of mine. . . . He would come down to the station just to be around it and just love it."[49] Announcements like "Larry Love is in the studio at this time, stepping in right on time" populated the studio with hip-hop notables. Islam incorporated his guests into his broadcasts through announcements of their presence, studio chatter, and interviews, creating audible artifacts of WHBI's studio as a social space.

Each week, visitors descended on the 80 Riverside Drive station unannounced. During one 1984 broadcast, a wave of visitors overcrowded the studio. Islam informed listeners, "Presently right now DJ Red Alert is in the studio along with my father, of course, Afrika Bambaataa, and MC Donald D, and Frosty Freeze of the Jazzy Five MCs." Visitors trafficked in and out of the studio throughout the night, and, about a half-hour into the broadcast, Islam informed listeners that "Afrika Bambaataa has just left the studio along with the entourage from the Bronx River, better known as Reggie, Izzie, and Ahmed. . . . Red Alert and Donald D, of course, are still in the studio, I want to make that loud and clear." Islam blurred the line between metaphor and reality when, seconds later, he remarked, "This is, of course, the place to be on a Wednesday." Yet the crush of visitors tested the DJ's patience. "I don't want you to forget," Islam stated. "The studio is real crowded and a lot of people want to come down and . . . check out the *Zulu Beat* in the studio. We appreciate everybody coming down, but you know definitely next time you got to let us know you are coming. It doesn't make any sense to just come down and crowd the studio. I'm talking about everybody, of course, except my father, but that goes for everybody from my mother on down."[50]

Islam and Donald D invited friends and hip-hop community notables to the studio to be interviewed on the air. "We would have live guests come down and we would do interviews," Donald D related. "We basically had our friends come to the station and we would interview them." For Islam, conversations with his guests offered listeners the clearest glimpse of hip-hop culture at the time. "I'd been in hip-hop since day one," he explained. "So the people I had on the show were truly from hip-hop—meaning they could have been a promoter or a rapper. So when they came on the show they were talking about experiences that were going on inside the field of hip-hop—not just necessarily [promoting] a new record."[51] With deep connections in hip-hop and the downtown art and dance scenes, Islam featured interviews with breakers, graffiti writers, DJs, MCs, promoters, and visual artists. His interviews spanned the gamut of the four pillars, including the Rock Steady Crew breakers; writers Futura, DONDI, and Toxic; jacks-of-all-trades like Fab Five Freddy or MCs the 3D rappers; promoters Malcolm McLaren and Ruza Blue; and visual artist Keith Haring.

Islam adopted a conversational tone in his interviews. Many sound hardly more formal than friends hanging out in the studio. He opened an interview with his roommate, Crazy Legs of the Rock Steady Crew, with "So, Legs, just tell the people exactly what 'Crazy Legs' means." After answering that "Crazy Legs" refers to way he looks while dancing, the conversation progressed through questions inviting Crazy Legs to explain how he became president of the Rock Steady Crew, building toward a line of questions asking Legs to comment on Rock Steady Crew's recent appearance in the movie *Flash Dance*. Islam was a shrewd interviewer, aware of his interlocutors' inexperience carrying a conversation for an audience. He often feigned ignorance or omitted himself from situations he shared with Crazy Legs in order to solicit the desired response. When Islam guided the conversation toward the Rock Steady Crew's recent tour, Crazy Legs called Islam out for playing naïve. "Our third tour was in California," Legs returned to Islam, "which you was with us, too. We was *only* roommates." Islam and Crazy Legs laughed, with Islam playing innocent: "I forgot, again! I just remembered!"[52]

For a nascent culture like hip-hop, interviews were an important form of publicity. In early April 1983, Fab 5 Freddy joined Islam in the studio. A graffiti writer and promoter instrumental in uniting the uptown and downtown scenes, Freddy greeted the audience over a loop extracted from Run-DMC's "Sucka MCs." "I have a very, very, very special announcement," Freddy informed the *Zulu Beat's* audience. "Listen up: To anyone who is planning on going to the movies Friday night, there's going to be a very special film being shown. It's called *Wild Style*. The movie stars the Fantastic Freaks, DJ Theodore, Busy Bee Starski, Cold Crush Brothers, DJ Charlie Chase and Tony Tone, the Rock Steady Crew, Double Trouble featuring Little Rodney C and KK Rockwell, Grandmaster Flash, Fab Five Freddy, and a whole host of graffiti artists from New York City." Freddy goes on to describe the movie, a story about a graffiti artist "trying to get himself together in New York," attending "high-powered parties" and rap battles and tagging trains in the process. After Freddy's announcement, Islam entered the conversation, prodding Freddy for more information on the filming and the artists involved and asking Freddy to weigh in on the significance of the first hip-hop film for the *Zulu Beat*'s audience. As an added enticement, Islam spun an excerpt from the *Wild Style* soundtrack while Freddy narrated the scene for listeners. The interview ended with Islam introducing Fab Five Freddy's newest single, "Change the Beat," before exiting the conversation and allowing Freddy to rap, on air, over his own track.[53]

If Islam drew on his network of friends, acquaintances, and collaborators to secure interviews for the *Zulu Beat*, he drew on those same networks to providing musical programming. Listeners frequently heard compositions by DJ Jazzy Jay and Grand Wizard Theodore, and programmed tapes "donated" to the show, such as a summer 1983 improvisation featuring "Afrika Bambaataa on the turntables and DJ Whiz Kid on the beat box." DJ Red Alert proved an especially important supply of cassettes. "Red Alert had hundreds of tapes that he had got copies of from all the battles that he was able to be at," Islam remarked. "These were battles that we both were at, but actually having the cassette was the most important thing."[54] Tapes from Red Alert's collection featured so prominently on the *Zulu Beat* that Islam prerecorded an introductory logo intoning, "A Red Alert tape special," drenching the phrase in reverb and applying a generous amount of echo. Other times he simply announced, "Alert just walked into the studio with a boatload of tapes."[55] Listeners, in turn, recorded broadcasts of the *Zulu Beat*. They became personalized documents attesting to a moment in New York—recordings of a broadcast containing recordings of parties. It was this recording of live parties and hip-hop radio that severed hip-hop from the five boroughs. Where these tapes traveled, hip-hop set down roots.

Hip-Hop Publics Out of Time

So far I have detailed the ways in which the *Zulu Beat* functioned as a community forum during its tenure on WHBI, and I have suggested some ways in which we might learn something about the communities who participated in the show through the sound of extant tapes. But these tapes have had long lives. Tapes of the *Zulu Beat* have entailed publics in new locales as they've circulated over time. If the direct lines of circulation aren't so easy to recover, still, the fact of their historical circulation is important. Thinking through circulation allows us to understand how different communities invest and reinvest meaning in the *Zulu Beat* as it fits their circumstances.

Hip-hop proved surprisingly mobile during its early commercial phase. It took less than a decade for the genre to jump from the parks and PALs of the Bronx across the Atlantic. If early rap records brought the Sugar Hill Gang and Kurtis Blow to new audiences in 1980, emissaries of hip-hop were quick to follow. In 1981, Afrika Bambaataa led a cadre of Zulu MCs, breakers, and DJs on a tour of Europe. Bambaataa envisioned the tour as an opportunity to represent this new culture abroad and to cultivate Zulu Nation chapters around the world. He saw his Zulu envoy as ambassadors for hip-hop and hoped that exposing new populations to rapping, DJing, and breaking might encourage others to take up the practices to their own ends. In this regard, Bambaataa's tour was successful. Through this tour, DJ duo the P Brothers of Nottingham, England, acquired tapes Afrika Islam made for the breakdance demonstrations when he handed duplicates to members of the audience. They cite these cassettes as important to informing their own practice as DJs, and later for the development of a distinct hip-hop culture in the Midlands. By 1985, local but significant hip-hop scenes existed in England, the Netherlands, France, and Japan.

To illustrate how tapes birthed local hip-hop culture in the 1980s, we can return to the story of Dutch, a long-time tape collector and host of the website old-school-hiphop-tapes.blogspot.com, which, while no longer active, was the preeminent source for finding rap tapes on the internet when I researched and drafted this chapter.[56] Dutch's story dramatizes the ways tapes come to listeners in the present through routes that, although unknowable, nevertheless sediment themselves onto recordings in surprising ways. Dutch, much as his name indicates, is from the Netherlands. He grew up in the 1970s in a small town outside of Rotterdam. His first recollections of rap are of broadcasts of the Sugar Hill Gang on state radio. Shortly thereafter he remembers first hearing favorites "The Message" by Grandmaster Flash and the Furious Five and "Buffalo Gals" by Malcolm McLaren. By 1983, Dutch began to learn to breakdance. By 1985, teens in the Netherlands could go to parties like "One Night New York" in Rotterdam, which featured hip-hop films, music, and dance battles.

Dutch recalls that the best way to hear hip-hop, other than purchasing records—which might not have been distributed in the Netherlands or might have been exorbitantly priced—was to tape full broadcasts of the radio show *Soulshow*, a program featuring African American music with an occasional rap track. He taped it for nearly five years, until he could afford to buy records himself in the early 1990s. Dutch purchased rap records throughout the decade, fewer each year, but found his attention return to rap music with the advent of the internet. In the mid-2000s, he and other collectors began to upload tapes to their personal sites. Dutch notes that he very quickly developed a knack for locating hard-to-find tapes. In order to procure more, Dutch reached out to other collectors, offering to trade or share his tapes in exchange for others. What is now a banality was then revolutionary to Dutch and his fellow collectors: the internet is a remarkable tool for exchanging objects and information with folks who share your interests. Dutch's collection ballooned. By the late 2000s, it made more sense to centralize his collection on a website.

For Dutch, the most significant aspect of web-based trading, besides the pace and ease with which exchanges could be transacted, was its ability to tear down the gatekeeping and artificial scarcity he observed in cassette culture. For some collectors, tapes were often valuable precisely because they were rare. Whether original or dubs, owning the physical tape mattered to collectors, and the fewer copies that existed, the better. Tapes circulated in an economy whose currency was a collector's reputation. One gained access to newer and more valuable tapes by demonstrating their commitment to figurehead collectors, or earned access by securing new recordings of their own. In 2007, Dutch started a blog about his own cache of tapes to attract the attention of other collectors and began to upload MP3s in 2008. Shortly thereafter, other collectors supportive of his initiative began to offer their collections to Dutch in part or in full. By 2009, old-school-hip-hop-tapes.blogspot .com housed the largest collection of tapes on the internet, and between June and July of 2016, the site received over a million unique visitors.

I asked Dutch to what degree owning the physical cassette mattered in the scheme of his website and collection activities. He insisted that the digital data, the sound file extracted from a cassette, is singularly important. The cassette originals, to Dutch, remain important as historical examples and curiosities, but the real value resides in events and sounds inscribed onto magnetic tape. Not all events or sounds, however, retain the same power to elicit the flights of imagination and identification that are central to their appeal for many listeners. Radio address and other nonmusical features, in particular, are capable of invoking memories, of transporting listeners to the times and places of their youth. Like other listeners, Dutch cites the liveness of broadcasts as an essential aspect of this appeal and efficacy. "I like live performances (not battles) where there is a good interaction between the DJ and the MC," he said. "These radio tapes, including weather forecast and commercials are a time capsule from NY in the 80's."[57] The extramusical content of tapes helped listeners from around the world inhabit a New York that might exist nowhere else but their imagination. Listeners in the present, like Dutch and the thousands who continue to download and listen to recordings of the *Zulu Beat*, still find themselves interpellated by Islam's radio address though the separation of "sound from source, of voice from body."[58]

Though the precise circuits of transmission these tapes followed and publics addressed are unknowable, some anecdotes regarding circulation are suggestive. Each DJ I spoke with was eager to share stories of situations in which they encountered their tapes in unlikely locations. Chuck Chillout recalled hearing a familiar sound while traveling in the South:

> I remember one time me and Red was in Florida. We was in Jacksonville, Florida, and a kid rolls up with the car blastin' 98.7 KISS, DJ Chuck Chillout. So we stop the kid, said, "Yo, man, where'd you get that tape from?" He said, "Yo, you can't get this! It's that New York shit." So I looked at Red, and Red looked at me. . . . If he only knew. He didn't know! Them tapes went all around the world.[59]

Teddy Tedd and Special K of the Awesome 2 each shared stories of finding recordings of their broadcasts beyond the five boroughs. Teddy

Tedd remembered getting a phone call from Chuck Chillout while the DJ was on tour in Japan. Chuck Chillout was animated, rushing his speech, and hard to understand over the phone as he relayed that a small record store in Japan was selling neatly labeled tapes of New York radio programs. "Yo, they're selling your stuff in the record store," Tedd remembered the caller saying. "They got my stuff, they got Red's stuff, and they got your stuff." Special K told a similar story. One of Special K's close friends was on tour in Japan. While waiting in his dressing room, this DJ believed he heard K's voice behind him. He turned around, confused, thinking that K was in the room with him. As he continued listening, he realized that the radio in his room was playing an *Awesome 2 Show* recording.[60] What each of these stories helps to convey is the different contexts and cultures recordings of rap music have addressed over time. Though the precise nature of their appeal remains a question worth asking, we might think of tapes of the *Zulu Beat*—or any rap radio program, for that matter—sounding an extended Zulu Nation, a fictive New York realized in the publics these broadcasts continue to summon.

Sign Off: Some Notes on Hearing Radio Publics

In listening to recordings of the *Zulu Beat*, both as objects of enjoyment and historical artifacts, I found myself increasingly given to the world their sounds seem to disclose. It is hard to resist the allure of these tapes. The music is catchy, at turns driving, funky, and bizarre. The hosts are charismatic, and the direct address of radio speech transcends the historical distance between the event and its reception in the present; it's easy to feel like Islam is addressing you, some thirty-five years hence. The enthusiasm that fans brought to their encounters with the *Zulu Beat* stoked my own. Before long, I found my own sensuous enjoyment of these tapes animating my historical imagination, however problematic it is to depart into the past from one's feelings in the present.

After years of listening to and poring over these tapes, the same enthusiasm still motivates my writing, but a new sense has come to trouble it. Listening began to feel voyeuristic, like eavesdropping. Put another way, the difference between participation and surveillance seemed to shrink. It became a reminder that actions in the public sphere may be recorded to circulate without any individual's knowledge of it. The aspects of the tapes that drew me into the putative world of early hip-hop came to disquiet my understanding of the role historiography might play in recuperating it. If rap tapes comprise an archive, we would do well to heed the pessimism expressed by Kara Keeling or Saidiya Hartman and other scholars working with queer and irrecoverable histories. For Keeling, writing as an act of recuperation may do violence to those we write about, reintroducing them to a state poised to violently depose them.[61] Hartman takes a similarly pessimistic stance, noting how quickly writing about violence in the past slips beyond the aims of the author to sanction violence in the present. Even in cases where violence in the present is unlikely, what rights to privacy are those represented on these recordings entitled to? To both of these authors, historical subjects have a right to opacity, to evade disclosure in the archive even as the material traces they leave attest to the possibility of their existence.

What are our responsibilities as we listen to these tapes, to the breaks they rock and to the breaks from which their hosts and listeners appear to us? Elise Chenier has asked a similar question of oral historical collections. Chenier considers whether or not it is ethical to transfer interviews that were consented to for preinternet archives onto open-access online platforms, and what might be made of the moral gray areas researchers and archivists find themselves occupying. The distinction is not trivial. For Chenier, "telling life stories was about more than expanding the historical record to include the experiences of those who were excluded from history. By treating the experiences of everyday people as the building blocks for a new understanding of the past, oral testimony challenged traditional forms of knowledge and authority. It was a counterforce against traditional history."[62] Like Chenier, throughout this chapter I have proposed listening to these tapes as a similar counterforce against traditional kinds of sources and narratives characteristic of hip-hop history. But I might follow Chenier's lead and ask uncomfortable questions about my own sources: Is it ethical to write history from recordings that were recorded before the advent of the internet and uploaded without any party's consent? And what of the many intermediaries and brokers who transferred these recordings through time and space? On the one hand, it is easy to argue that speech in public, such as calling in to a radio show or radio address more broadly, is made with the understanding that it is delivered with an unknowable scope of reception. On the other, no one calling in a shout-out is assenting to historical scrutiny. While I have outlined the many reasons individuals interfaced with public broadcasts of hip-hop culture, it's worth asking about the responsibilities historians have to protect the privacy and rights of those who, by design or historical accident, populate these tapes. In our histories, we would do well to think with Mimi Thi Nguyen's injunction to write "against fantasies of subjective restoration and historical coherence."[63]

While thinking of early hip-hop's communities as open-ended publics allows us to see the transience and contingency of musical scenes and prevents us from reading Black communities as "closed, coherent and manageable texts," I end this chapter by reprising and amending a question I posed at its beginning: What can we know about the material world of Black youth culture in New York from cassette recordings?[64] Even if these tapes go a long way toward fleshing out this world, to what end? Perhaps it may be better to ask what we should—or what is right to—know about Black youth culture.[65] How might we construct a practice sensitive to the lines between historical listening and surveillance, if such a distinction exists?

WHBI-FM NEWARK, 105.9.
THE FOLLOWING PROGRAM
IS BROUGHT TO YOU BY ITS
HOSTS AND ADVERTISERS.

ΣΙΧ

Listening to the Labor of *The Awesome 2 Show*

In the early hours of June 15, 1983, the Awesome 2 took to the air. Following a quick spot for the Tri-Borough Youth Games and a public service announcement from the New York Coalition for Dog Control ("If you don't clean up, it adds up"), layered over the instrumental B-side of Run-DMC's "It's Like That," DJ Special K delivered an announcement, beginning, "Back at you high-poweredly and fresh, *funky fresh*. This is the Awesome 2, and we are back, surprisingly, on WHBI, Thursday mornings from three to four o'clock in the morning." Special K's cohost, Donald B, then added that WHBI "is definitely the place to be . . . most definitely . . . I'd like to say 'hello' to all the people out there, and to tell them that this show is sponsored by Specific Records. And we're going to be back to rock your mind right . . . after . . ."

As Donald B spoke the concluding "this," the Awesome 2 pushed play on a promotional cassette. From the ad, Special K's voice awash in reverb:

> Hi, I'm Special K of the Awesome 2 here to tell you about the hottest piece of wax ever to be played on your turntable this summer. It's called "It's Your Rock" by Fantasy III on Specific Records. Start your party off with this fresh new twelve-inch, available at the

nearest record shop near you. Remember, "It's Your Rock" by Fantasy III on Specific Records. Take it from the Awesome 2 . . . because it's going to be very, very hot.

Advertisements for music released on independent record labels, such as this plug for "It's Your Rock," were a staple on time-brokered rap radio.[1] These ads were equal parts entrepreneurship and radio savvy, the product of a consistent sponsorship grind and a host's ability to convert business opportunities into broadcast sound. The labors necessary to support time-brokered radio had important aesthetic consequences beyond ads, and, if we listen, we can hear the ways they inflected nearly every dimension of a show. The aesthetics of early radio programs—the sonic aggregate of hosts' negotiations of sponsorship, industry relations, audience expectations, technological limitations, and individual preferences—help us trace rap's transition from a community-based art form into a commercially viable music. They beg the question: In what ways might it be possible to listen to the labor of the Awesome 2?

Sign On: Introducing The Awesome 2

The Awesome 2 Show aired for the first time on May 18, 1982. It continued weekly on 105.9-FM until 2004. Had it stopped then, *The Awesome 2 Show*'s tenure on WHBI would have been sufficient to earn the distinction of longest-running hip-hop radio show in the history of the genre. At the time of writing, their weekly broadcasts—including satellite radio and internet streaming—put them just shy of four decades on the air. During their time on WHBI, cousins Special K and Teddy Tedd produced, financed, and broadcast their radio show on New York's home for underground hip-hop, garnering a reputation as "America's *chillest* air personalities."[2] In that time, the duo participated in nearly the entire commercial history of hip-hop as such.[3]

In 2004, when the Awesome 2 exchanged the insecurities of time-brokered radio for a contract with Sirius Satellite Radio, they found themselves thoroughly enmeshed in the music industry, occupying roles for which there were no scripts at the moment of their first broadcasts. The skills they developed during their two-decade run on independent radio allowed them to move fluidly between musical performance and promotion, from scouting for talent to managing artists' careers to broadcast consulting. Teddy Tedd described radio's centrality in the

Awesome 2's deepening relationship with the music industry succinctly when he stated, "The radio [was] the vehicle. DJing was the vehicle to radio, and radio was the vehicle to everything else. You know, automatically you're a club promoter, automatically you're a record producer. As you move into different spaces, you're allowed to be in that space based on the thing you did prior."[4]

"You had to put the cap on it," recalled Special K in one particularly apposite explanation. "You was the sales man, you was the promotion man, you was the creative guy, you know? Whatever you had to do to keep the thing moving." Funding *The Awesome 2 Show* cast the cousins in roles at all ends of the music industry, and it placed them at the center of rap's entry into musical economies within New York and beyond. When I first spoke with the Awesome 2 in January 2016, I went into the conversation hoping to learn something about radio's impact on the musical trajectory of hip-hop. I expected we'd talk about mix aesthetics, the technical limitations of WHBI's studios, and the creativity behind their longevity. As we touched on these topics, it quickly became apparent that many of the Awesome 2's most salient memories of WHBI were of the pressure to raise money to keep the show on the air. When I listened to the recording of this interview, I was struck by just how pervasive mentions of work were in Teddy Tedd and Special K's recollections of *The Awesome 2 Show*. The more I reviewed our conversation, the more it seemed that every dimension of the show was shot through with the labors that went into producing it, by the constant pressure to raise funds sufficient to purchase airtime. In a series of interviews, we spoke further about their experiences with the time-brokerage system. We talked at length about the obligations—financial, creative, and personal—idiosyncratic to funding and programming time-brokered radio. The Awesome 2's recollections reveal more than the pressures unique to a pair or a single radio station. They trace a portrait of hip-hop's economies in the early 1980s.

The Mix, Part 1: "DJing was the Vehicle to Radio"

In 1977, when Special K and his high school friends pooled their money to buy turntables, you didn't have to live in the Bronx or Harlem to hear or experience hip-hop. The Hudson River did little to stem the flow of cassettes and dancers into parks and high schools in Passaic and Hackensack, the northern New Jersey cities where Special K and Teddy Tedd grew up. "The music was everywhere," remembered Teddy Tedd.

Though the cousins began DJing separately, their forays into hip-hop followed largely parallel paths. Mutually invested in the equipment and records they acquired together, Special K and his friends formed a crew, calling themselves Ice Productions. Between 1977 and 1979, they honed their craft through group practices, taking influence from the styles they heard on cassettes. "Whoever had better skills at one thing would give lessons or help," Special K said of his time with Ice. "If someone wasn't as talented on the mic or at DJing, [we] would help one another." As its members matured, they sought audiences with whom to share their skills and music. Ice Productions booked shows at local PALs and Boys Clubs. "Wherever we could get gigs," Special K added. "And it really just started evolving . . . getting the feel [for hip-hop], figuring out if this is what I really want to do and hop[ing] people like it."

Teddy Tedd also learned to DJ with a group of middle school friends, though not until 1980. He recalled, "I actually didn't have turntables at first. I would go to friends' houses and use their turntables and DJ. We had days where five, six, eight kids would go to whoever had the turntables at their house and go spin." Like Special K, Tedd began to DJ public events as his confidence in his abilities increased. "It was really just cutting breaks," he said of his initial experiments in DJing. "Eventually I got my own turntables, started to spin, started to do local parties, started to create a local buzz, and that's how it went."

After high school, Special K attended nearby William Paterson University. Interested in a pursuing a career in radio, Special K volunteered at the campus radio station, WPSC-AM 590. Over time, Special K's desire to pursue a career in broadcasting only intensified, and he began looking for an entry point into the radio industry. Without any other leads, an inquiry to the host of his favorite radio program seemed as good a place to start as any. Late in 1981, Special K reached out to Mr. Magic, asking for advice on how to get a job in radio. Magic referred Special K to a broadcaster named Jerry Bloodrock, who also hosted a weekly show on WHBI. Special K recalled this transition:

> I was listening to Mr. Magic and trying to break into radio and so I reached out and met, through Magic, a guy named Jerry Bloodrock, who had a radio show, also on WHBI. That's how it got started for me. I met Jerry and we got cool, so I was mostly at the radio station with him, answering his phones and, maybe, the last five to ten minutes of the show he'd let me read a few names on air and I started getting a little name, a buzz from that.

Bloodrock was an active mentor to Special K. "He was genuine," Special K remembered. "He was open-minded, and he really wanted to help." Under Bloodrock's tutelage, Special K observed the defining feature of the time-brokerage format: the looming and insistent pressure to raise money to lease airtime. "The hardest thing with both [Magic and Bloodrock] I saw was getting sponsors to pay for the show in order to come on the air and be heard," Special K said of his time at WHBI with Bloodrock. "You know he had the audience. The phones rang all night, the letters come in all day. It's a matter of getting the sponsors to pay for it."

Over time, Bloodrock gave more responsibility to Special K. As Bloodrock took more work in production and management outside the radio studio, he brought Special K and cobroadcaster Donald B in as partners, allowing them to take over the program—first single episodes, then full broadcast months—as he dedicated his energies elsewhere. Early in 1982, Bloodrock took an extended absence. Knowing that he would be unable to tend to the radio show, Bloodrock met with the station manager to transfer his contract to the Awesome 2. "Jerry convinced him to cut a contract with us," said Special K of the transition, "said he'll come back in a month's time and he just kept moving."

Before Bloodrock left to pursue his other projects, he made a single request of the Awesome 2. His words would resonate with Special K throughout his tenure at WHBI: "Please don't lose the radio show."

The Mix, Part 2: Into the Industry

Bloodrock's entreaty weighed heavily on the young DJ. "[It] was a lot of pressure at the time," Special K recalled. "You know, we're young, and the fact was you had to find this money—close to two thousand dollars a month—somehow, someway, to come on the air and play these records." Teddy Tedd noted that the early days of funding and producing *The Awesome 2 Show* were an education in the intricacies of the broadcasting and music industries. "Keep in mind we're from Jersey," Teddy Tedd pointed out. "In 1982, cats is young cats. [They'd do the show], then go home. So there was no relationship with the business. At all. They bought records. We didn't know that you got free records."

Only years later did Special K realize that Bloodrock had taken efforts to prepare him to preside over the show. "The thing about Jerry I didn't realize at the time . . . he was kind of, like, grooming me to do his thing. He figured out different ways to keep money generated to keep us on." Bloodrock had a talent for identifying opportunities in the music industry. He knew that, as a host with access to broadcast time, he was in possession of a resource desirable to anyone with a record, artist, or event to promote. Bloodrock cultivated a symbiosis between time-brokered radio and local sponsors. In doing so, he juggled an array of money-making enterprises that raised money for the show and provided content for its broadcasts.

For one, Bloodrock reached a sponsorship agreements with local record labels.[5] When New York upstart Profile Records needed radio to take a chance on their product, Bloodrock quickly brought them on as a sponsor. The relationship proved fruitful for both broadcasters and label, and independent radio soon became a major advertising channel for the independent label. Bloodrock also dabbled in talent management, stewarding the careers of rap group Rock Master Scott and the Dynamic 3 and short-lived electro-rap trio Tranquilizing 3. As these groups signed record deals with Reality Records and Apexton Records, respectively, Bloodrock followed them into the studio, assuming the role of producer and arranger.[6] Such access was valuable to a radio host: it put him in a position to break records before the wax cooled. When the Awesome 2 assumed responsibility for the show, they followed Bloodrock's lead and went knocking on labels' doors themselves.

Once DJs built those relationships with labels and artists, they found other ways to monetize them. For Bloodrock, this came in the form of a record pool. The concept behind record pools is simple: they distribute new and exclusive music to their subscribers for a fee. Subscribers get early access to new tracks, and labels get distribution directly into their target markets. In the late 1970s, Bloodrock founded his own record pool and, as he receded into his own projects in the early 1980s, left the operation of the record pool to the Awesome 2. "We would be the eyes and ears of the music industry and we would get [our DJs] whatever they needed," described Special K of his record pool.

> The record companies would get their product out, would try to get their product out to different clubs, [to] DJs in clubs, [to] DJs on the streets. We would provide a service where we would actually go out and find DJs that were looking for that service and charge them a fee monthly and, you know, get them product, get them records, kind of like, really, managing their career. Trying to get them on the inside of the industry . . . They would come at us and be like, "I heard this new song . . ." That weekend they got it. So that kept them sharp.

Just as Bloodrock took care to steward the Awesome 2 through the early stages of their career, the Awesome 2 readily mentored the DJs in their record pool. "We would bring them to parties," Special K said. "We were grooming them as Jerry was grooming me."

Special K's first independent sponsorship arrangement after Bloodrock's departure was, after his mentor, rooted in close personal relationships. While living in Passaic, Special K frequented the Record City Record Shop, a local store specializing in disco, R&B, and soul records. Over time, he became close with the owner, Joseph Hunter. Hunter and Special K struck a sponsorship agreement between Record City and *The Awesome 2 Show*, bartering WHBI's rate-advertising fee or records in exchange for sponsorship on-air. Of the early years of *The Awesome 2 Show*, Special K remarked that

> I got all of my records from a local guy in town, in Passaic, Record City Record Shop. [The owner] knew that I played hip-hop on the radio, and that was my in. I was buying records at the time, but gradually he would say, "Take this new record." So it helped us establish a store, so we shout a store out, they sponsor us for a little while with commercials, and that kind of made the store blow up along with we blew up getting the music to the people.

Record City Record Shop became an early and enduring sponsor of *The Awesome 2 Show*, one that Special K considered reliable during periods when the support of record labels was wavering.

Through the ways in which DJs financed their radio show, a picture of early hip-hop's musical economies comes into focus. Built on overlapping commercial incentives and networks of mentoring, aid, and friendship, it defies models of the industry that cede too much agency to large record companies. Understanding the commercialization of rap thus forces attention to the small enterprises and the quotidian labors that funding a weekly radio show entailed. These daily hustles bring us closer to hearing each of the strands—commercial, technological, personal—of early rap radio.

The Mix, Part 3: The Hybrid Economies of Early Rap

In the months following Bloodrock's departure, the Awesome 2 adjusted to running the show on their own. Airing at 4 on Tuesday mornings, *The Awesome 2 Show* drew large audiences despite its inconvenient hour.

"People stayed up," Teddy Tedd recalled. "That's the strength of the music. People had to have it." Special K, fighting his nerves, became more comfortable speaking to the invisible audience. He developed a rapport with listeners, fielding phone calls, taking shout-outs, and fulfilling requests. With the record pool operational, and with minimal competition from other radio programs for record labels' support, funding for the show proved relatively consistent. The Awesome 2 filled their hour playing new rap tracks alongside steadfast favorites. Each week listeners could expect to hear music by Cold Crush Brothers, Jimmy Spicer, Grandmaster Flash and the Furious Five, Whodini, Crash Crew, Fantasy III, CD III, Jazzy 5 MCs. They mixed in cassette recordings of live events alongside classic breakbeats and R&B for good measure. During the same period, the Awesome 2's entrepreneurial activities in the radio studio tracked the expansion of rap's economies.

While the economic impact of rap is usually measured by deals signed and records sold, it helps to look at the peripheries of the industry. The concept of the informal economy, defined by sociologists Manuel Castells and Alejandro Portes as "all income earning activities that are not regulated by the state in social environments where similar activities are regulated," provides a useful tool for understanding how rap fostered a range of enterprises in the 1970s and early 1980s.[7] During rap's first decade, motivated promoters turned a profit from an event's cover charge and alcohol sales at their community center parties and park jams. Artists and enterprising fans spawned a cottage industry out of their tapes by dubbing and selling recordings. Other DJs developed a thriving trade in spare electronics and speaker parts, creating commerce out of salvage. While each of these ventures could be lucrative, they were hardly part of the mainstream musical economy. Put differently: no one paid taxes on the tapes they sold at shows.

Slowly but surely, rap's informal economies intersected the aboveground music industry. The two spheres of commerce came to complement each other.[8] Anthropologist Anna Tsing has usefully called these overlapping worlds "pericapitalist" economies, which she defines as the "lives and products [that] move back and forth between non-capitalist and capitalist forms [in ways that] shape each other and interpenetrate."[9] This notion is helpful for thinking through the ways radio connected informal, street-level activity to the commercial recording and broadcasting industries. For example, the Awesome 2 often broadcast cassette recordings of artist demos, live events, or prerelease singles, putting them into wide informal circulation when listeners recorded and distributed the broadcast. As independent label personnel learned that new artists could be heard on time-brokered radio before making their live or commercial radio debut, A&R representatives turned to programs like *The Awesome 2 Show* to scout talent. When the Awesome 2 played a commercial record, they anticipated listeners would record it, thus creating both illicit trade in a label's product and encouraging a kind of grassroots advertising. Ultimately, radio DJs set a foundation for labels, influencing who they signed, where and how they marketed their rap acts, and how they distributed product.

As they came of age, the Awesome 2 found themselves caught between the street-level grind and the rarified air of FM radio. Nearing the completion of his studies at William Paterson, in 1983 Special K began an internship at WBLS, working under star DJ and program director Frankie Crocker. He recalls most of his responsibilities being grunt work for Crocker, retrieving records from the library, purchasing new records at Crocker's request, and assisting WBLS staff around the studios. Yet, at WBLS, Special K saw how a large and successful station operated. He met and observed disco and house DJs Sergio Munzibai and Timmy Regisford. From these observations, he developed a sense of what worked on-air, devised strategies for mixing and interacting with the audience, and saw firsthand the less glamorous points of a DJ's working life. More important, he credits his time at WBLS with introducing him to a number of representatives from record companies. Taking these connections back with him to WHBI—something he notes had the potential to get him fired from WBLS—Special K found himself more extensively involved in the music industry, more aware of its inner mechanics.

Street-level salesmanship also turned up new sources of sponsorship for *The Awesome 2 Show*. The roller rink United Skates of America in Queens advertised with the Awesome 2 weekly for a period. When beepers became a cultural-technological phenomenon in the mid-1980s, the Awesome 2 tried to get numbers on the hips of their listeners. By the mid-1980s, the cousins had an overflowing portfolio of sponsors for *The Awesome 2 Show*. Before long, the Awesome 2 found themselves coordinating a complex matrix of interests, each concerned with turning rap music into profit. The Awesome 2 brokered between record labels looking for outlets for their product, audiences seeking to hear new developments in music shunned by daytime radio, advertisers targeting precisely that audience, and new artists breaking into the music industry. At the heart of their salesmanship, however, was an undeniable sound.

The Mix, Part 4: Broadcast Aesthetics

The Awesome 2 shaped the sound of their radio shows to differ from their live hip-hop events. Live crowds had different expectations from radio listeners. Playing selector in a club entailed an entirely different set of conventions from mixing on the radio. That meant a DJ needed to draw on different techniques and pursue different goals. "I think it was different. . . . Radio is always different than the club," Teddy Tedd summarized of the two contexts. "You can play anything over the radio. Not anything . . . but you have more flexibility because you're not trying to drive the dance floor. Driving the dance floor is a different thing. . . . Because when people listen to the radio they're in the car, they're at home, they're not on the dance floor so you have that attention. . . . There were a lot of records we play on the radio that we wouldn't necessarily play live because they weren't dance-floor-driven." In practice, radio allowed the Awesome 2 to experiment with a much broader range of sounds and programming than was feasible live, bringing homemade and prerecorded mixes as well as vinyl records into the fray. The duo also incorporated interviews with notable hip-hop artists, event announcements, and advertisements all while communicating with the audience through a mode of address equally indebted to broadcast formalisms and hip-hop vernacular.

It's one thing to have a clear sonic vision for a radio show; it's another thing to bring it to life in the cramped quarters of the radio studio. For the Awesome 2, cultivating a contemporary hip-hop radio aesthetic on outdated equipment was an enduring challenge. Indeed, the Awesome 2 consistently returned to the limitations of WHBI's studios when discussing how they programmed their shows. Teddy Tedd's first impression of the single-room, basement studio was that it felt "foreign." The radio studio confronted a DJ with a new level of technical complexity, and navigating it felt like "going from a car to a plane." In addition to operating the usual mixing board and turntables, the radio studio presented young broadcasters with multiple microphones, a cassette deck, telephones, and a broadcast mixing console with more channels than a DJ might traditionally use. The studio's turntables were models Teddy Tedd estimates dated to the 1950s. These were workhorse decks great for playing records, but not, however, for the sophisticated scratching techniques Teddy Tedd had worked so hard to master.

Even something as straightforward as addressing the audience was fraught from WHBI's basement studios. That imagination-laden space, stripped as it was of conversational feedback, was a consistent source of anxiety. "It was kind of nerve wracking," Special K said of his mic breaks, "because just . . . right before you got on the air you're trying to figure out what you're going to say, how you're going to say it. You know, hopefully you're going to say it right. You know what I mean? It was a lot of getting my nerves together, to [snaps repeatedly], to say what I'm going to say." After the first few months of weekly broadcasts, he felt able to speak with a conviction that belied his timidity. He refined his timing, finding the right moment and tone with which to enter on the microphone as a track or mix concluded. Teddy Tedd echoed Special K's anxieties about the uncertainty of reception. "We're on the air, we're in this little room," Teddy Tedd recalled of the experience of isolation in the studio. "You don't really know what's going on in the streets. You're not in everybody's house."

Teddy Tedd took charge of assembling the musical mixes each week, but the process involved collaboration. First, the duo conferred. Together, they decided which tracks would go into the mix and then arranged places for Special K to come in on the microphone. During these mic breaks, looped grooves or instrumentals might replace rap tracks in order to create enough sonic space for the voice to cut through the mix. The DJs debated how to keep the mix moving forward and how best to carry each groove through their announcements while building anticipation for the next feature. After they agreed on an outline for the broadcast, Teddy Tedd assembled the mixes at home on his bedroom setup. When they described the goal for their radio mixes, Special K and Teddy Tedd consistently returned to the word *flow*, or a sense of continuity where each track and unfolds in one unbroken current. Flow, to the cousins, was the mark of a mature, well-produced radio program. Flow separated the DJs from the dilettantes.[10]

While the Awesome 2 invoked flow as an aesthetic distinct to radio, their sense of what worked over the radio was never fully divorced from the knowledge acquired spinning in clubs, gyms, or parks. As much as they argued that the club and the radio studio were different spaces, they were just as clear that what they learned at the club made its way into the studio. Teddy Tedd drew on his knowledge of live dancers' reactions and of the radio audiences' preferences, combining sounds he believed would excite both without the direct response of dancing bodies or the radio studio phone. Mixing business and pleasure, personal preference with sponsorship obligations, Teddy Tedd allowed kinesthetic and aesthetic judgments sedimented in intuition to guide hands. In this mobilization of intuition in performance—kinesthetic, aesthetic, and business—lay the foundation of the Awesome 2's radio aesthetics.[11]

....

Despite the ardent support of listeners, there were many periods when funding for the Awesome 2 Show was inconsistent or insufficient. "A lot of times there were no labels," Teddy Tedd said. "A lot of times we funded it out of our own pockets." The Awesome 2 were candid about their periods of difficulty. In our first interview, Teddy Tedd suggested that there were periods when the cousins fell behind on their payments by thousands of dollars. When I broached the topic in a later interview, the cousins slipped into a characteristic exchange, Teddy Tedd beginning with a slight, uneasy laugh, "We were never current."

"Never."

"Never current."

"Actually, when we left we weren't current," Special K added.

"We were always a thousand or more behind."

This admission is a significant departure from the rags-to-riches rhetoric and narratives often used to historicize the careers of hip-hop entrepreneurs.[12] Their difficulty meeting funding deadlines also raises questions about the motivations and expectations of WHBI's managers. Why, if the Awesome 2 were never current, did WHBI allow them to air week after week?

Part of the answer is that a slightly delinquent known is a safer bet than the unknown. Turnover at WHBI was high. For a variety of reasons—notably the difficulty of acquiring and sustaining sponsorship and the gap between the perceived ease of producing a radio show and the difficult reality of broadcasting—most broadcasters at WHBI tended against longevity. Many DJs, hip-hop and otherwise, broadcast just a few shows before going off the air. When hosts terminated their shows, the onus fell on management to replace the vacancy left in their station schedule. Empathizing with the management's perspective, Teddy Tedd recalled that

> it's not just us. I think it was so damn hard, you know? It was tough . . .
> the eighties was tough economically. For someone to come on the radio
> for an hour, to play music, they [management] don't how financially
> serving that would be to someone. It just so happens that we were on
> the cusp of this new thing. But who knew? But I guess they said, "Well,

these guys have been playing something, and they obviously are consistent so let's not lose them, because that slot will be empty."

The Awesome 2's financial difficulties directly bore on the practical decisions they made regarding when and for how long their show aired. For many years, *The Awesome 2 Show* aired for just one hour—between 4 and 5 AM on Tuesdays in the early years, and later between 12 and 1 AM on Saturdays, an arrangement they preferred because it placed their show in direct succession with sister rap-radio programs by DJ Red Alert on WRKS and the Mr. Magic and Marley Marl on WBLS. There were times when exceptional label and business support allowed the Awesome 2 to purchase more airtime and more desirable broadcast hours. During these times, WHBI's management perceived a sense of financial security not shared by the Awesome 2. "It changed through the years. We'd get more time, we'd get less time . . ." Special K continued the thought:

> Because it really was a matter of us trying to afford it. We didn't want to overextend ourselves. [Management] would always come to us: "Do you want more time?" Because they knew we had a big audience. And a lot of the regular guys that were on there had a lot of time because they had a lot of sponsorship. But we didn't, so we did what we could do and kind of just made our mix from there.

Although the prospect of adding more airtime to match their audience size and loyalty was appealing, they took a conservative approach to purchasing it. "They worked with us," Special K remembered of their relationship with WHBI's management. "I mean, the money would come. From somewhere. Every week we would be like, we would wonder, 'I wonder where it's coming from this week!?' And it would come and we would be like, 'Wow! I wasn't expecting that!'"

The way the Awesome 2 describe the unstable, irregular funding of their show draws our attention to the precarity of much work in the music industry. The Awesome 2's career and success beg a host of questions about how we tell the history of hip-hop. How would our narratives of work, entrepreneurship, and success in hip-hop change if they were told from a perspective that foregrounded uncertainty? What might change if the self-sufficient telos of rap-video wealth weren't the driver of hip-hop history and hagiography? What might it mean to tell the story of rap's commercialization from the perspective of these prior and necessary small projects, of mutual aid and collective action?[13]

The Mix, Part 5: Programming the Unexpected

At the close of 1985, the Global Broadcasting Group (GBG), having recently purchased WHBI-FM from the Cosmopolitan Broadcasting Corporation, leased new studios for the station. Trading 80 Riverside Drive's underground studios for more spacious facilities in Midtown Manhattan, the move transferred WBHI to the DuMont Building, situated on the corner of Madison Avenue and East 53rd Street. The DuMont Building projected opulence through its sand-colored marble walls and intricate art-deco ceiling recessions. The new facilities were well positioned for hip-hop DJs looking to break into Manhattan's club scene—the new studios were just a short walk from many venues in the heart of midtown.

With new studios came new call letters. The initial phase of GBG's rebrand of WHBI included implementing the call sign WNWK, a reference to Newark, New Jersey, the city in which 105.9-FM was licensed. The new facilities boasted of two broadcast studios and an engineering booth. The playback equipment, however, was still outdated, still unable to accommodate Teddy Tedd's increasingly virtuosic turntablism. The Awesome 2 continued to prerecord their mixes, bringing cassettes into the studio along with whichever records they agreed to spin that week.

Prerecording, however, was no guarantee that the show would run smoothly. The Awesome 2, after years of producing the show, adopted an open attitude toward the unexpected. Each week, the Awesome 2 explained to me, they could count on something unpredictable happening while they were on the air. Yet the unpredictable, they hinted, might offer future business opportunities or invite sonic experimentation. The Awesome 2 stressed that, if encountered with flexibility and generosity, chance events could be incorporated into *The Awesome 2 Show* or their business ventures to great effect.

For one, they never knew who'd be waiting for them at the studios when they arrived. "It wasn't like today where . . . in these studios today there are so many things happening you can't even go to the studio without having a week's notice and credentials and all that," Teddy Tedd said. "When we was on people would just show up! You'd get to the studio and people would be downstairs." Special K picked up the thread: "A bunch, a bunch of people. In the hallway waiting on us, you know? 'Here's my new stuff, man, check it out.' 'Here's my new mix.' And we're going to check it out and, sometimes, they'll wreck it." Teddy Tedd developed a clear, if subjective, framework for deciding which tapes to air: "[If] it's dope, it's on." More often than broadcasting a tape, the duo would seek a live outlet for the artist, matching his or her abilities with the occasion. This arrangement benefited everyone involved. The Awesome 2 filled a bill. An artist got a break. And they both developed a relationship that could pay off down the line. This was a lesson learned the hard way, they noted, after watching many artists pass through their show only to sign to a competitor's production.

Years at WHBI made the Awesome 2 flexible operators in the studio. "We were able to do anything," Teddy Tedd recalled. "Let's say someone came into the studio who we wasn't expecting. We would take a record, blend it with what was playing on the premix, and take the time to interview them, and bring that into the mix. So obviously it's not as easy as doing it right there on the fly, because it's a premix, but we were still able to do stuff like that." For the Awesome 2, the deciding factor in whether or not a visitor could be put on the air was whether or not the audience would be interested. "I don't know if we ever just took somebody and just put them on the air," Teddy Tedd said. "'Cause at the time we'd be rushing and there'd be no time to really hear their stuff. Unless it was, like, a Chuck D or a . . . [something] that the audience would want to hear." Teddy Tedd continued on their openness toward the unanticipated: "We kind of prepared just in case things would happen. We would always come to the station with records and other things just in case something presented itself." I asked if, over time, they learned how to improvise and maneuver on the fly. The answer they gave was a motto I had come to expect: "You had no choice."

One of the most difficult aspects of incorporating chance events in real time, the cousins repeated, was framing them in the most appropriate manner. When MC KRS-One and DJ Scott La Rock called the studio during a 1986 broadcast, for example, there was no question that the Awesome 2 would put them on the air. The dilemma was how to incorporate their call within a prerecorded mix. The artists behind Boogie Down Productions had recently released two singles, "The Bridge Is Over" and the title track from their first album, *Criminal Minded*. Special K took the call and, coordinating with Tedd, brought a track from their recent release to the fore while he prepared an interview. With KRS's and La Rock's music in playing in the background, the Awesome 2 proceeded to connect their call into the mix, allowing them to annotate their music and then weigh in on the "bridge wars" controversy to the sounds of their own beats.

Over time, these chance phone calls and drop-ins could be harnessed to great effect. When Chuck D of Public Enemy used moments in his interview to express his adoration of the Awesome 2 in 1988, he was one of many artists to do so. Such performances of gratitude at once affirmed that the speaker had made it, so to speak, and cemented the Awesome 2's status as tastemakers and genuine people. In our interviews, the Awesome 2 reflected on that shared gratitude as one of the most rewarding aspects of their show. Teddy Tedd discussed these relationships in superlative terms: "Probably the greatest thing, or one of the greatest things, was the relationships, you know? Meeting people early in their careers." An unexpected 1987 call from the Stetsasonic MCs to *The Awesome 2 Show* shows how the duo presented performances of gratitude in ways that were both authentic and strategic. Special K initiated the exchange. He began, "Hello, you're live on *The Awesome 2*."

"Yo, this is Daddy-O from the Stet, yo, we got the whole Stet posse in the place."

With that introduction, a chorus of voices comes in over the line as each member of the crew yells, "Yoooooo," and "Whaaat's up?" into the receiver.

Daddy-O reenters: "We're out here listening to the Awesome 2."

"Out there and in effect, huh?"

"Yea. Chillin'."

Teddy Tedd joins the conversation, attempting to steer the interview toward the topic of an upcoming tour. "What's happening fellas? Big things is happening with y'all?"

"Yo, man, we getting ready to go on tour with LL, Whodini, Public Enemy, Erik B., Doug Fresh, the whole posse, man, we goin' Rambo, man! Taking the Brooklyn show on the road."

"Now, didn't we say things was going to be kicking live?" adds Special K.

"Yeah, most definitely," Daddy-O responds. "We know y'all was always in our corner. That's why we in y'all's."

"Believe that," concludes Special K, offering Daddy-O the opportunity to issue a round of shout-outs before leveling-in the next record.

In this short, unanticipated exchange, the Awesome 2 and the Stetsasonic MCs helped establish one another as important pillars of the hip-hop community. In doing so, they demonstrate how artists worked with one another, helping each other climb one rung after another.

The Mix, Part 6: Live from the Latin Quarter

With artists visiting the studios each week, the Awesome 2 accumulated more promising tapes than they could play, even with an hour or more of airtime each week. To accommodate the overflow, they looked to their other ventures. By the mid-1980s, the Awesome 2 established themselves as club DJs and promoters and, eager to expand the business, were always looking to book artists for their events. If they were lucky, an A&R scout might catch one of their artist's sets. Soon, live shows were a new source of revenue and opportunity. As *The Awesome 2 Show* gained momentum from its new Midtown studios, the duo went lobbying around the neighborhood.

The Latin Quarter, located at the corner of 48th Street and Broadway, stood just a few blocks southwest of WNWK's studios. The way the Awesome 2 tell it, the impetus for canvassing clubs came as much from an entrepreneurial spirit as it did from boredom. "So not only was the show on at four so we'd have to come into the city early—'cause we live in Jersey and the bus service is whack," Teddy Tedd began. "Then we'd have to wait for the next bus to leave at six in the morning . . ."

"[Or] seven in the morning," Special K went on. "We'd finish the show around five . . ."

"Then you got nothing to do but walk around or sleep or whatever."

"It was a good thing too," Teddy Tedd continued. "By having that extra time in the city we was able to go to the Latin Quarter and start hip-hop at the Latin Quarter. . . . We went there, it was a regular club and they weren't playing hip-hop and we said, 'Give us your whackest night, let us do something.' Which was a Tuesday. And we turned it into something."

The Latin Quarter was a small club that loomed large in the city's imagination. During its mid-century heyday, the club took an ecumenical approach to genre and billed a who's who of the top acts of the postwar period. When not performing themselves, the Rat Pack could often be found at the Latin Quarter. After a few changes in identity and ownership, the 1980s saw another musical renaissance take place within the walls of the Latin Quarter. You'd hardly know, however, from the press coverage of the club. In the mid-1980s the *New York Times* reported on a string of robberies and shootings outside the club that attracted, in a neighboring business owner's words, "the worst elements of society" to prey on unaware clubgoers. The Latin Quarter's fire code capacity capped its attendance at five hundred, though by some accounts many more would pack in on a busy night. Like much club coverage of the time, reports of violence did little to capture the venue's musical ferment.[14]

Celebrity Tuesday at the Latin Quarter functioned as a conduit for the demo tapes the Awesome 2 received and for the artists they met through the radio show. Special K said of the coupling between the radio studio and the Latin Quarter, "What happened was we had so many demos from people that wanted to establish themselves, wanted to rhyme . . . they could do this, they could do that. And eventually some of them were handpicked from some of the ones we thought were the better ones, and they would come perform." Celebrity Tuesdays caught on quickly. The open-door policy they fostered for their radio show carried over to the Latin Quarter. Artists came to shows, unannounced, and asked if there was a slot available to spin or rhyme on stage. Special K continued, "That was kind of the idea we had, you know, some of the new acts come there and eventually what happened was when the artists that come there that didn't send us no demos we ended up meeting the Heavy Ds of the world, the Super Love Cs of the world . . . And they got signed from rocking with us on Celebrity Tuesday night." For years, the Awesome 2 had been pounding the pavement—hanging at the Funhouse, the Roxy, Disco Fever, the Rink. For years they parlayed their connections on the air and in the clubs into opportunities in both domains, a feedback loop made possible by being present, being genuine, and bringing their skills when it counted. At the Latin Quarter, they brought that hard work to bear.

As savvy as the Awesome 2 had become regarding the workings of the music industry, they reflected on this period as one where their enthusiasm, and perhaps naïveté, obscured the business potential of Celebrity Tuesdays. In retrospect, they note it as a period during which they made the acquaintance of many artists on the verge of promising recording careers. Special K reflected,

> That was a whole 'nother side of the business we didn't look at, we didn't look at, you know? "We got to sign these guys before they sign with someone else because they come to our production first!" We was just like, "Yeah, want to come up and get down, you know, get up there and go." It then occurred to us that there were other incentives. There's nothing wrong with that, but it was a business move. We had to learn as time went on, like, "Wow, we really had that guy first and we really had this guy first and that guy."

Even as they took stock of their missed business opportunities, they found that their openness and affability paid future dividends. Reflecting on the maturation of the genre in the mid-1980s, Special K noted that the Awesome 2 "kind of started [artists'] careers" by playing them on the radio, or by inviting them to perform live. He pointed out that, for a period in 1984 and 1985, before his break, Big Daddy Kane answered phones for the Awesome 2 in the studio and continued, "Then, gradually, the Big Daddy Kanes, the KRSs were ready to blow up. We were such outgoing guys, we would meet people, say, 'Hey, you're cool, come to the station with us,' and we started a relationship like that, a bond." Later in 1987, Big Daddy Kane recorded a promo track for the Awesome 2, a track they used to open their broadcasts. "And you go around town and you hear people playing it, like, whoa, you know we have good tapes," Special K noted. "And you know what else? People start requesting it like it's a song."

The Mix, Part 7: Freedom and Competition

By the mid-1980s, New York's commercial radio powerhouses moved into territory the Awesome 2 and other independent broadcasters had so painstakingly staked out. "So, I mean, you got to figure we're in this little station, and in the [early] eighties, that was cool. Because there was no other station," Teddy Tedd reflected. "But as time progressed you got KISS-FM, you got Red and Chuck Chillout, and you got BLS. And they've got a better signal and bigger audience." With a crowding landscape of rap-radio programs, the Awesome 2 set to work differentiating themselves. In doing so, they created a distinct sonic identity for their show, drawing on their labors in and around the music industry to keep their show on the cutting edge.

One way to ensure their show was not cutting edge was to play the same music as their competitors. This proved difficult in practice. Because the Awesome 2 prerecorded their mixes the day of the show, at times days before, they had little opportunity to make changes if a competitor programmed the same tracks. "I know at times we would do our mix in the daytime before [the rap shows on WBLS and WRKS] would come on the air," Special K remembered. "Two days before they even whatever, we were already set." In order to avoid the embarrassment of broadcasting a full program of repeat tracks, the Awesome 2 tried to predict what their competitors would play. Over time, they learned to hear whether or not a new track would fit their competitors' styles. The pressure to stand out, to cultivate a sense for the underground, the ear catching out-of-the-ordinary that Teddy Tedd calls their show's "essence."

For Teddy Tedd, anticipating what a competitor might play was just a first step in differentiating their show. "In the beginning we just wanted to play hip-hop," he said. "But as competition came around we knew we had to be better. We had to be edgier." Teddy Tedd frequently invoked the descriptor *edgier*, or *cutting-edge*, as a guiding principle for the show. For Teddy Tedd and Special K, to program a cutting-edge show was to turn to B-sides while other DJs spun the popular cut. It was excavating a little-known breakbeat and looping it beneath a spoken-word record. It included raiding hip-hop's unwieldy and expanding cassette archive of live shows and battles, or inserting a demo track from an artist on the cusp of a record deal. "Dope and creative," Teddy Tedd summarized. "And if that meant playing an a cappella over a hip-hop beat, or playing a live battle, or a live show, then that's what it was." Special K continued,

> And we had that freedom, we had the freedom to do that. To look for stuff like that. We'd be playing EPMD's "You're a Customer." After we played that, [we'd play] "It's My Thing," because that's one we [coproduced]. We'd start playing the accompaniment, the b-side, and it was like, "What's that?" We kinda, when you think of the competitiveness of it radio-wise, it felt like we would kind put them on alert. Like, "Oh, shit, what's that, what's that?!" Or we might hear them play something and it kind of went hand in hand, and it kind of established us together as time went on. You know we got a friendly competition, but we both have respect. We both broke records and did our thing.

This freedom came directly from WHBI's time-brokerage business model. Teddy Tedd picked up the thread of their freedom, and its limits, at WHBI, saying, "We didn't have, you know, no pressure with regards to what to play. We could go on there and play anything, but we wanted to still be cutting-edge and we still had to deal with our competition." As much as possible, the Awesome 2 tried to program exclusive material, including from the events they hosted. Teddy Tedd reflected, "So we get tapes at [our] events, we might get tapes from events that we don't have anything to do with. But if it's dope . . ." "The Cold Crush battle," Teddy Tedd continued with an example. "Something different. Something people know but that they can't hear on the radio."

Celebrity Tuesdays at the Latin Quarter became a particularly fertile ground for the radio show. "A lot of stuff we would take from Latin Quarter shows," Teddy Tedd recalled of their events. "We started recording some of them—what we were playing at some of the shows—and those shows would come out, someone would take what we did and put them on a record." This last point—putting the broadcast on a record—requires some unpacking, but it shows the unexpected connections between the club scene, radio, and the record industry. Here, Special K was referring to the path one particular performance took from party to platter. The night in question began with the 1987 birthday party for Kool Moe Dee at the Latin Quarter. During his set, Teddy Tedd spun an instrumental B-side of Erik B. and Rakim's "My Melody." He invited Kool Moe Dee to the stage to freestyle. Teddy Tedd taped the honored guest's performance and broadcast that tape as an Awesome 2 exclusive hours later. Within weeks, that performance was available as a single in record shops across the tri-state area.

When exclusive material proved thin, the Awesome 2 would look for lesser-played tracks by major artists. "I'm thinking Run-DMC," Special K started. "I remember [commercial DJs] was playing 'Walk This Way' during the daytime, at the same time a lot of cats were playing 'My Adidas,' [and we], like, play[ed] other cuts off the album, to be a little different, a little cutting-edge, to get people saying, 'I didn't know that was them!' And that kind of made our show." The Awesome 2 also leaned heavily on the groups they managed in programming their show in the mid-1980s. In 1987, after a string of strong singles, MC duo and Awesome 2 protégés Audio 2 were poised to land a major recording contract and touring deal. Teddy Tedd remembers the Audio 2 single "I Like Cherries" rising to popularity. Capitalizing on the strength of that single, the Awesome 2 flipped the record over, breaking the B-side "Top Billin'." To their estimation, many listeners liked the B-side better.[15]

Later in the decade, when the group began to produce, coproduce, and remix singles for rap groups EPMD and Ed OG and Da Bulldogs, they brought the first pressings with them into the radio studio. By the close of the 1980s, the Awesome 2 worked closely with several record labels. They introduced artists to these labels, helping artists secure recording contracts, and securing production or management work for themselves. Of their work with Ed OG, Teddy Tedd noted that "Ed OG is our own family. So obviously if we're working with them we're getting that music first, so we're breaking all those records. 'Not Going to be Able to Do It' [he says, singing the hook], we're breaking, 'Knock 'Em Out Sugar

Ray,' we're breaking, 'I Got to Have It.' Because we're working with all these guys." Special K encapsulated this utilization of their business enterprises in multiple, mutually edifying ways and is worth quoting at length:

> That was our thing. Our thing was to dig deep and get that new stuff that they probably wouldn't go get or that they couldn't get. Like I said, at that time it helped establish our roots. Audio 2 was our group, and they started to blow. Ed OG, later on down the road, they was our group and they started to blow. EPMD, we produced their record and they starting to blow. So we tried to capitalize on that by playing them more, getting them out there more, and getting an awareness factor with people saying, "We did that," and then get more production and get more work.

By digging deep, as Special K put it, by spinning their work with artists into exclusive records, live shows, and production opportunities, the Awesome 2 helped steward hip-hop to maturity as they built their own careers.

Sign Off: On Listening to Labor

By the mid-1990s, the Awesome 2 had built a career on top of the lessons Bloodrock imparted over a decade before. Through years of working in and around the radio studio, they'd turned two hours of airtime into an international presence. In following their career, we see seemingly minor activities performed over a long period time that give shape to a genre. We see how musical economies are born.

For one, we see that the Awesome 2 didn't do it alone. Economies are fundamentally systems of exchange, and as much as the Awesome 2 were broadcasters and entrepreneurs, they were also facilitators. Out of love for the music and necessity, they constantly sought out collaborators, leveraging the mutual incentive structures inherent to the music industry. They had a gift for identifying the potential of activities and individuals and built their career in part by providing opportunities to others. It's important here to look at these activities in the aggregate. The Awesome 2 were never done working. Rather, day in and day out, they worked their radio show along with any other activities they needed to make a living while living hip-hop. Cuing into these labors lets us see that hip-hop emerged as a commercial force not just because of its intrinsic appeals or because audiences had to have it. Rap became a commercial force because artists like the Awesome 2 stoked desire for the music and relentlessly linked supply and demand. Yet their success was less a product of heroic individual effort, as we so often read in rags-to-riches stories—though, if I'm honest, the work they put into hip-hop comes pretty close to clearing that bar—as it was the product of individuals who understood the power of mutual aid, goodwill, and business savvy.

The closer we follow their career, harder it is to ignore radio. When the Awesome 2 describe the trajectory of their work, they describe picking up work in the clubs, in the studio, on tours, as managers—a host of opportunities not limited to the studio. And yet all roads lead back to radio. Without the ability to speak to audiences collectively each week, without the ability to make taste and break artists to an amassed listening body, each of their endeavors would have been less effective. There would have been—very likely—less demand for the music, or at least demand would have accrued more gradually over time. Further, there would have been fewer endeavors in the first place. Ultimately, radio organized all of the various economic activity around rap in a way that was nothing short of generative. It allows us to see the connective tissue, as it were, that gave birth to a functioning system of valuation, marketing, and exchange.

Finally, broadcasts of *The Awesome 2 Show* allow us to hear rap's burgeoning economy—the purest mark of its commercialization—over time. In their broadcasts, we hear the Awesome 2's relationships with artists and labels. We hear the audience as they express their preference for the music and convert their fandom into consumption. We hear how artists relied on radio for exposure just as the Awesome 2 relied on artists for raw content. We hear how two individuals who worked to buy weekly airtime to play records can pull the recording studio, the club, the park jam, and every other context into the broadcast studio with them. Ultimately, in tuning in to the Awesome 2, we hear how labor makes music.

Epilogue

In the spring of 1993, Reverend Calvin O. Butts, pastor of Harlem's Abyssinian Baptist Church (ABC), redoubled his organizing efforts in the face of a worsening "urban crisis." A lifetime advocate for New York's Black communities, the reverend led a generation of congregants from Sunday pews into the streets, as willing to agitate the political establishment as he was to cooperate. While Butts aspired toward a community of action national in scope, much of his organizing took place close to home. In the 1970s, he expanded the ABC's youth ministry. Throughout the 1980s, Butts led campaigns against offensive billboards for liquor and cigarettes in Harlem and fought for civilian oversight of law enforcement. Over time his influence grew, and by the early 1990s he presided over a task force convened to address the catastrophic spread of AIDS, as well as persistent levels of homelessness and joblessness in New York.[1]

From his earliest crusades against stereotypes in advertising, Butts proclaimed the power of images to sway the perceptions of viewers. In this, he found himself allied with Percy Sutton—perhaps unwittingly so, given that Butts was one of Sutton's loudest critics—whose waxing media empire had already done much to re-sound and re-present African Americans in the popular imagination. Butts rarely declined a media appearance, and the *New*

York Times described the pastor's indefatigable engagement with news, radio, and television as a "one man media-blitz."[2] It was with this belief in the power of media to effect change that Butts championed a boycott of gangsta rap.

On Mother's Day 1993, Butts decried gangsta rap to his parishioners. According to the *New York Times*'s coverage, Butts argued there was a "direct relationship" between depictions of women and sex in gangsta rap lyrics and a "9-year-old girl bumping and grinding on the street after school . . . becoming the next casualty, if you will, of an early and untimely pregnancy." He condemned the young men he saw on the streets, now common throughout the city, whose postures, vocabularies, and dispositions mirrored those of gangsta rap personas. Butts concluded his sermon with a call to action: all those similarly concerned should bring him records, tapes, and CDs of harmful rap music, to be squashed beneath the drum of a steamroller. "It will be a symbolic crushing out of these negative words and images that are eroding the moral fabric of our community and society at large. We just can't deal with it anymore."[3]

Butts's call to arms polarized New York's Black communities. The reverend claimed that he received over two hundred letters and calls expressing support of his initiative within days of the sermon. In an interview on WLIB, Mayor David Dinkins offered his approval, stating, "I think Reverend Butts is right and courageous to take this stand." Radio host and community leader Bob Law agreed with the aims of the protest, if not the fervor with which Butts pursued it. "Butts has tried to raise some difficult questions," Law told the *Times*, "whereas some leaders have raised the obvious questions." Opposition to Butts was fractious. Fans rushed to the defense of artists. Ambivalent sympathizers tried to cultivate a middle ground, insisting that Butts was not attacking rap writ large, just "vile rap," though to many observers it was all the same. Label executives defended their interests by contending that many rap artists had experienced violence and held regressive attitudes toward women, and therefore it was natural that they rhymed about it.[4] Gangsta rap had become a musical shibboleth.

When the morning came, Butts's protest did not go according to plan. On June 1, as Butts and his supporters gathered at the intersection of 137 Street and Adam Clayton Powell Boulevard for the demonstration, a chanting group of counterprotesters joined the scene. Just as the steamroller was set to render symbolic destruction upon Ice-T, NWA, 2 Live Crew, Tupac, and Scarface, among others, the counterprotesters blocked its path, the most vehement among them pressing past the police barricade toward the vehicle. Amid the unraveling protest, Butts addressed the crowd with his practiced oratory, but it did little to deter his opponents. As the morning gave way to afternoon, the anticipated destruction dissipated into a strategic dump. If Butts couldn't flatten the offending records in public view, he would do the next best thing: deposit them in a sloughing pile in front of the corporate offices of Sony's music division.[5]

Confusion ruled the day. According to the *New York Times* coverage of the event, many present weren't sure whom, or what, exactly, they were protesting. The *Times*' reporter had a finely tuned ear for sound bites issuing from the din. One Butts supporter argued that the reverend "was not attacking rap or rappers. He was attacking negative rap!" A counterprotester insisted that Butts's efforts would be better spent "attacking the white power structure, who own the record companies, who own the cable stations." Another attendee suggested that the protest alienated those with a personal connection to hip-hop. In steamrolling rap, he argued, "You're steamrolling our dreams, you're steamrolling our aspirations, you're steamrolling who we are. . . . Music is not the killer, it's not the ill. The ill is the streets."[6] In the end, Butts conceded to the protesters, but not without first issuing a rejoinder: "If the rappers think they can raise the standards of their music and unite our community for our redemption, then we are willing to hear and willing to work."[7] Whether or not one felt Butts's protest was a success or a failure probably had more to do with one's relationship to hip-hop than the merits of the reverend's arguments. But levying a judgment of success or failure isn't a good reason to dwell on this event. It's better to ask: Why now? Why, in May 1993, did Butts decide that enough was enough?

Butts's comments leading up to the protest suggest that it had something to do with mass media. Butts disclosed to the *New York Times* the discomfiture he felt seeing the portrayal of women in music videos and admitted that the prevalence of these videos on cable compelled him to act. The reverend's actions following the protest, however, suggest that it had something to do specifically with radio. Radio, in what Theodore Adorno called its ubiquity—the de facto standardization that results from the simultaneous, dispersed repetition of music through broadcast receivers—could have distorted Butts's sense of proportion. If enough radio stations played the same offending tracks, it could have lent a minor cultural movement massive cultural cachet. If every time he turned on his radio he was greeted by music that chafed his sensibilities, radio could have inflated a minor threat into a major crisis. On the radio, gangsta rap could have seemed to be everywhere, at once.

Irrespective of radio's role in instigating the protests, the Harlem demonstration grew into a national movement, as advocacy groups nationwide adopted Butts's cause as their own.[8] In the following weeks, activists turned their attention toward broadcast media, intensifying their pressure on radio stations to ban the gangsta subgenre and to remove what audiences perceived as the most offensive words from all broadcasts.[9] Protests continued, and advertisers did their part by threatening to pull sponsorship. In an exercise of their leverage over stations, some even threatened to join the boycotters.

Whether the pressure came from concern for their constituents or their bottom line, large radio stations acted decisively. The only move, they felt, was to sever ties with "vile rap." From a PR perspective, it was easier to censor the genre than confront its ugly truths. It was even harder—perhaps impossible—for radio stations to face their own complicity in this bubbling crisis. After all, they had control over which singles were broadcast. Their programming managers and DJs had say over the commentary and language that introduced and contextualized music. By December 1993, several of the nation's most-listened-to stations withdrew gangsta rap from their playlists. Others found it expedient to cut ties with rap all together. WBLS counted itself a leader among stations now opposed to violent and misogynist lyrics. Though they averred that they would continue to play most rap music, the station agreed with the logic supporting Butts's campaign, and they had high hopes for the ameliorating effects of the ban. Said general manager David Lampell of the decision, "The impact is going to be obvious."[10]

Sign-Off

There are no good places to end a book like this. The window of 1979–87 represents less of a real historical boundary and more of a historiographical tool that allowed me to tell the story of a time and place in a manageable way. In another draft, I might have concluded with a reading of an important broadcast from 1988 or 1989, chosen for its ability to demonstrate how thoroughly DJs and MCs had internalized the previous years' experimentation, carefully marking musical differences and tracing continuities from the early decade into the golden era. Perhaps I could have stretched the artificial timeline till it snapped and ended with the first broadcasts of *The Stretch Armstrong and Bobbito Show*, New York's quintessential golden-era rap radio program. In yet another I might have ended with the passage of the 1996 Telecommunications Act, which extended Reagan-era regulatory reform to its logical conclusion (surpassed only in 2014, with the FCC's first public auction of an FM frequency), enabling the formation of broadcast monopolies on an unprecedented scale and effectively precluding independent stations from operating on FM frequencies.

But this 1993 anecdote, replete with protests and counterprotests, spread-eagle rhetoric, and heavy machinery loosed down a major artery in Harlem, encapsulates the decade that preceded it. It's all there, embodied in a ferocious generational conflict centered around the recording, distribution, and broadcast of a Black, masculine youth music. And what more fraught way to frame this conflict than as one of "redemption"? (Who is redeemed? From what? By whom?) This story provides something of an unhappy apotheosis, with all roads leading back uptown, where the status of rap music in American life might be settled once and for all. The main reason, however, that this anecdote is worth ending with pertains to how Butts and others shifted the terms detractors used to oppose rap music: no longer was rap's suitability for radio debated in musical terms (musical terms are never just musical, but the linguistic shift is significant). It was now a moral issue.

It's easy to be unkind to Butts. His reactionary response to gangsta rap is easy to write off as just that, and critics have repeatedly pointed out the shortsighted, divisive effects of his calls for censorship.[11] But it's worth asking why Butts was drawn to this music, delivered through this medium, at this moment. Given the failure of many key civil rights reforms in the 1980s, the carnage of the AIDS epidemic, the twin blades of the crack crisis and mandatory minimum sentencing laws, the fact that Butts and others likely felt their lives' work embattled by new and old problems, did gangsta rap sound like society in regression? If so, what about gangsta rap, when broadcast, *sounded* like a crisis?

This is not a question I can answer here, though it deserves detailed historical treatment. It's a question still worth asking, though, because it reveals something in the negative, namely: Why didn't rap sound like something else? Given the diversity and creativity of rap radio in the previous decade, why were audiences and activists so ready to hear gangsta rap through the lens of pathology? (Heard through the intractable racial logic of American popular culture, though, it seems like a foregone conclusion that they would.) When I suggest that the movements of the early 1990s sounded a crisis and thus rendered a flourishing, varied music in black and white and red, it is against other possible historical outcomes, a history of rap music and Black radio otherwise. It is with this "could have been," this history-in-the-conditional, that I want to end this book.

Dan Charnas, writing of the 2012 merger of WRKS and WBLS, has argued that the stations' failure to accept rap, above all of their combined achievements, is their lasting legacy—more so than the beauty of the early "Crocker" format; more so than the mission of minority media ownership; more so than the birth of the urban contemporary format and the decades-long shadow it cast over popular music, crystallized in the Grammy category of the same name. He's worth quoting at length:

> The fact is that the demise of 98.7 KISS-FM did not have to happen at all. Both Kiss and the station that swallowed it, WBLS, were sabotaged from within. Their swift rise and slow decline is the 30-year story of one of the greatest cultural and management failings of our time: How stations that purported to serve broad audiences with the power of Black culture ended up forgetting those audiences and ignoring that culture. . . . The history shows that both stations, year after year, made decisions that killed their stations' future by fighting a cultural war against Black youth and by refusing to understand the broad appeal of the music they did program.[12]

Charnas goes on to track the unhappy denouement of these stations over three decades, but he lingers on the end of the 1980s. To him, this was when WBLS and WRKS "missed their chance." I share his sense that these years were something of a critical window, one that closed permanently early in the 1990s. The question, then, is: What would an alternative outcome have looked like? What are the outlines of a world in which WBLS and WRKS took rap and its adherents seriously?

For one, it's possible that broad-based, cross-generational, and institutionally sanctioned support of rap could have provided a bulwark against the protests of the 1990s and opened a door toward genuine debate. There may have been no need for protests if rap were viewed as an expression of ingenuity rather than the embodiment of racial menace. Indeed, given that one of the dominant features of Black politics in the post–civil rights era has been the absence of a unifying voice who could speak to and create common ground among African Americans across class, generation, and geography, it's tempting to imagine a world in which rap was that unifying voice, an expressive rallying point for a new solidarity. It's important to note, however, that the concerns that gave rise to the protests were real and deeply felt. As Tricia Rose has argued so well, there were real conversations to have about the treatment and representation of women in rap.[13] There were real conversations to have about enduring structural poverty and violence. And there were real conversations to have about white corporate ownership of Black cultural production and the channels through which it reached listeners. Calls for censorship paved over this complexity.

In strictly economic terms, these radio stations missed an opportunity to stake a claim to ownership of rap by ghettoizing it. In the early and middle years of the 1980s, there were significant opportunities to feature the product of Black-owned and independent labels on daytime rotation. These stations' equivocation created a vacuum quickly filled by majors with no investment in the communities that produced rap, labels that would go on to use their resources to consolidate their control over the genre as it erupted in the 1990s. Further, it's possible that an American populace familiar with rap from its presence on daytime rotation would be less susceptible to the myth that rappers are violent thugs spreading the wreckage of America's inner cities. Rap wouldn't sound as dangerous. More than anything, these stations missed an opportunity to introduce daytime listeners to the depth and breadth of creativity in rap in the 1980s.

If there's a sense of wistfulness in this epilogue, it stems from the sense that much of rap's social, political, and ameliorative potential went unrealized. At the time of writing, rap requires no defense. It's not an overstatement to say it's been the most influential popular music of the last half century, and historians have helped us see the capital "D" Diversity represented in and by the music. Still, rap remains a sonic marker of difference in a present when Black bodies are still vulnerable, and Black lives still matter less. In some ways, rap was damned from birth, its mass appeal portended no sooner than the popularization of minstrel plantation melodies in the antebellum North. Critic Greg Tate has best summarized the ambivalence that edges in when celebrating a cultural form as thorny as rap music. Writing in 2004, ostensibly in celebration of the thirtieth anniversary of hip-hop, Tate steps back to ask what, exactly, was the cause for celebration. His answer: "Nothing less, my man, than the marriage of heaven and hell, of New World African ingenuity and that trick of the devil known as hypercapitalism. Hooray."[14]

This book has been an attempt to showcase how that ingenuity collided with American hypercapitalism by focusing on a space shot through with both: the radio studio. Hip-hop was never one thing. But rap radio in the 1980s reveals many of the things rap was and could have been, at least in its most public form. Under the pretense of the megamix, rap was beats, cut-and-pasted samples, and records played without interruption or commentary. Selecting and mixing records was a display of taste, savvy, and skill. In the hands of Chuck, Red, Marley, Islam, the Awesome 2, and many others, rap could tell stories beyond those in MCs' lyrics. Layering, adjacency, timing, selection, protosampling, signifyin'—through the mix, these DJs spoke with a rich and varied musical vocabulary and helped audiences all over the world hear music in a new way. To the MCs of the 1980s, as those after, rapping was a mode of expression capacious enough for every perspective and every experience. Radio introduced listeners to those experiences. Lost in the gangsta rap fray were the Afrofuturist science fictions of "Planet Rock," the twists and turns of Slick Rick's rapped narratives, the confidence and occasion rapping gave young men and women to express themselves, rhymes as a vehicle for Black Muslim theology, and the surrealist poetry of MCs like Kool Keith. It was these broadcasts that stretched the boundaries of hip-hop and intensified the creative expansion of the music. By the time Magic went off the air, there were so many rap singles of such impressive variety that they couldn't possibly be contained coherently in a three-hour showcase.

As the broadcasts from WHBI demonstrate, radio was also a vital part of community making. To those who stayed up to tune in, it meant something to be listening to that particular music at the same time as your city. Listeners—particularly minority listeners—felt a sense of cultural ownership over this music, and broadcasts of rap validated its worth. Radio gives us a way of thinking about historical communities not limited to neighborhood or borough. As Charnas has winningly pointed out, the megamix was more than a genre of broadcast: it was a metaphor for rap radio's audiences.[15]

For listeners, broadcasts were events. They were a reason to call into the Riverside Drive station. They were a forum for delivering shout-outs and performing affiliation. It was a way to get your track heard or your name on tape. Broadcasts from WHBI formed their own public sphere. From here, we can ask a set of questions to move hip-hop historiography into new terrain: What do event-based communities look like? Is it going too far to think of communities of reception as cities within a city? Are groups of affiliation coalesced by radio any less real than those born of race, class, geography, gender, or any other intersectional subjectivity? The communities of the air that formed around rap radio may have dispersed long ago, but the tapes give us a glimpse of just how vital they were.

And because of these broadcasts and these tapes, rap radio in New York was everywhere. Gangsta rap's ubiquity may have been one of the reasons that community leaders mobilized against rap writ large in the 1990s, but, during the 1980s, rap in New York was ubiquitous in a different way. Any Friday or Saturday between 9 and 12 PM you could walk for blocks and never be out of earshot of WRKS or WBLS. As one tape collector I spoke with remembers, you could hop from pool hall to bar to street and never lose track of a Friday night broadcast. Listeners were fickle, though, and if you lost a broadcast in the din of the city, you might find yourself listening to Red instead of Magic by the next block. The next day, the spread of tapes was metastatic. Chuck Chillout's recollections are worth reprising here: according to the DJ, you could hear "Pee-Wee's Dance" all over the Northeast Bronx the morning after he broke the single, and "Rebel without a Pause" through the five boroughs and then some. The reach of these radio stations was best summed up by a lifelong Brooklynite who listened to WBLS throughout the late 1970s and 1980s, who spoke to me about his experiences with the station as a teenager. After listing off his favorite artists from the era (more an R&B and quiet storm fan, he liked Smokey Robinson and Lionel Richie best), he asked me, "John, can you imagine? Saturday night, cruising King's Highway. All you'd hear for miles was WBLS."

Perhaps the most significant legacy of rap radio in New York is the fact that it was never really limited to New York. As Dutch has so convincingly shown, rap radio in New York is one of the main reasons why the hip-hop scene emerged in continental Europe and in the United Kingdom. In doing the final leg of research for this book, I came across yet another YouTube confessional attesting to the lasting import of rap tapes from New York, this one more direct than others. Written in the "description" field beneath a stream of a 1985 Red Alert set, the poster wrote,

> The reason im posting this tape is because this has a great historic significance to the hip hop scene in my city of Halifax, NS. (Canada) This is the very first NYC radio tape that was widely distributed in Halifax and a huge reason why not only we have a scene in Halifax to this day, but this tape also is the reason I became a DJ myself in 1985. Thanks to E__ M__ who taped DJ Red Alert Live on 98.7 KISS-FM & brought this

BASF cassette tape from NYC back to Halifax, circulated it, let all his friends tape a copy of it. and their friends let their friends tape it . . . and so on . . . and changed many lives.[16]

Put another way: Rap radio in New York was a global phenomenon.

For many of the individuals featured in this book, rap was something best left in the 1980s. Sutton went on to fund philanthropic efforts, many of which were innovative beyond their time. In the early 1990s, he had the foresight to organize a program to teach minority children computer literacy and basic programming skills, which still lack a place in curricula nationwide, even though knowledge of computer science is a prerequisite for many jobs. His son went on to turn Inner City Broadcasting into a successful media conglomerate. Mayo, for his part, had an accomplished career in media consulting, broadcast property ownership, and philanthropy. Dorothy Brunson moved on to a storied career in media ownership, and Wanda Ramos stayed in radio for many years after she left WRKS.

As for the DJs chronicled throughout, they're still hustling. Chuck Chillout hosts a radio show once a week on WBLS, and his signature mix of new rap, classic beats, and R&B too slick to age makes it worth seeking out. The Awesome 2 are still spinning and doing radio, with weekly shows streaming online. Marley Marl and Red still perform regularly in clubs across New York. Teddy Tedd is working on his own history of hip-hop DJs, one that only a DJ with his immersion in the history can tell. Few of them came into the wealth that some hip-hop moguls generated over the years, and that we believe will come to those who get in on the ground floor and build the company, as it were. They share a sense that, when hip-hop history was written (and it was written not just in print but also film and legend and discography), it wasn't written all the way. So as much as I've tried to avoid hagiography and have, in my own way, written many people out of this book, what I hope is that their stories will spark a revision of which histories count as hip-hop history. There are still many stories—of women, of queer hip-hop, of regional scenes, of transmission, of the families and caretakers of artists who nurtured the music just as much as those behind the turntables—that remain to be written.[17] The work is just beginning.

If there's any single takeaway from this book, I hope it's this: we need to pay attention to minor media and personal stories to understand hip-hop history. This book would not have been possible without the tapes and the unwieldy archive that brings them together and that they constitute. Simply put: tapes sound the history in new ways. They move us beyond discography, beyond biography, and into murky territory where a music was made, collectively, by a host of named and unnamed listeners. They move us away from histories where success is measured in records sold and toward one in which serial play and community status, however fleeting, are the goals. And they give us unparalleled—if never fully transparent—accounts of a music in motion, en route to where later studio records have led us to believe it arrived.

When I write of the early 1990s and its foment as a period of missed opportunity, it is fundamentally a missed opportunity for hip-hop to have been celebrated in all of its myriad forms and perspectives. It is a period when the many narratives extant in a genre reaching its height, too full of creativity to contain, were flattened by one of the oldest stories in American history. To the extent that I can fully describe this moment of missed opportunity, fittingly, I can do so only with recourse to the tapes.

On Thursday, June 10, 1993, Stretch and Bobbito took to the airwaves of Columbia University's WKCR for the weekly broadcast of their eponymous mix show. The duo greeted their listeners with an apology for their absence from last week's broadcast—Sun Ra had died days before the previous week's program, and they forfeited their slot to celebrations of the musical-spiritual polymath's memory. If Butts's protest had rankled the hip-hop community in New York, there was little indication of it on the June 10 broadcast. During the course of Stretch and Bobbito's two hours, not a single time is Butts, a steamroller, gangsta rap, or a boycott mentioned. Stretch spins a set of New York singles, many street-edged and no less mob-centric than Los Angeles or Miami's inflections of the subgenre, and there are frequent breaks to converse with studio guests Black Moon and Smif-N-Wessun. When they do spin West Coast rap, it's back-to-back tracks from the Pharcyde's *Bizarre Ride II*. Listening to these shows, I always get the sense that Stretch and Bobbito were starstruck by the artists who would come through the studio, no matter how many famous and up-and-coming rappers they worked with. The artists were just as psyched to be played on the radio. The hosts' joyful, ball-busting rapport is infectious.

To my hearing, an important moment in the tape occurs around forty minutes into the broadcast. Availing himself of the critical mass of MCs in the studio, Stretch cues DJ Evil Dee's instrumental to Black Moon's "Black Smif-N-Wessun," a track featuring Black Moon MC Buckshot and underground duo Smif-N-Wessun, to support an in-studio cipher. The

MCs take turns spitting their verses to the single and then exchange free-style verses. The lyrics are violent. They're about what you'd expect from a New York gangsta rap single. Body shots to dissing MCs, reports of quotidian ghetto violence, the ebbs and flows of the drug trade, misogynistic asides—these are some of the defining tropes of gangsta rap, and they're all here. When I listen to this tape, I think of how someone like Butts would have heard the lyrics "Check the drums of death as I break what's left of your face / Cuz you're selling out the rap race / Your family cried as your body lies in the casket / I keep a black Smith and Wesson in my Polo Jacket / Sixteen shots for all you hardrocks / And if your bitch is a dime she can get the cock."[18]

But the graphic nature of this passage isn't what stands out to me when I hear Black Moon deliver it on *The Stretch Armstrong and Bobbito Show*. Rather, what strikes me in these raps, and in the following freestyles, is how violent themes provide the stock for verbal fireworks. They're the raw material for an intensely social, competitive, and fun exchange between the MCs present. All of the MCs and DJs present play hype man to one another, joining each rapper on accented syllables, interjecting to add encouragement, whistling and shouting and howling as MCs bring particularly virtuosic freestyles to unexpected conclusions. There's so much more going on here than hood-hardened reportage.

The violence isn't trivial. If your ears aren't tuned to this genre's conventions, it can be unnerving. But I suspect that guns, sex, and drugs are where Butts and his milieu stopped listening. For these listeners, the rappers' craft, to say nothing of the DJs', was lost behind what sounded like exhortations to commit acts of heinous violence, or at least admissions of past acts. Their virtuosity, creativity, and sheer relish in performance get swept to the side. The thrill of hearing these rappers bring this art form to life on the radio was lost in the disappointment they felt at Black youths' perceived inability to rise to the political moment. I wonder what they would have thought about the music and the young people who made it if they heard what I and countless others heard in the show. I wonder what they would have heard if they listened, knowing that a city full of other folks like them were tuned in at the same time, just as excited by what was coming through the stereo. I wonder what they would have heard if they had listened past the surface.

Introduction

1 This exchange appears on a digitized recording of the *World's Famous Supreme Team Show* accessible in many different locations on the internet. Given the complications involved in determining provenance of recordings, as well as the assumptions required to provide complete citations, I reference all recordings of radio broadcasts as MP3s, using the data and metadata available to me on the recordings available. The version referenced here is indexed with the following metadata: World's Famous Supreme Team Show, "Tape 118 Worlds Famous," aired June 1982, downloaded from oldschool-hiphoptapes.com (accessed May 11, 2018).

2 As a historical period, the "golden era" is said to begin the sonic and commercial maturation of the rap album. This places its beginning somewhere between the 1985 release of Stetasonic's *On Fire,* the 1986 release of Boogie Down Productions' *Criminal Minded,* Eric B. and Rakim's 1987 *Paid in Full*, Public Enemy's 1988 *It Takes a Nation of Millions to Hold Us Back*, Ultra-magnetic MCs' *Critical Beatdown* of the same year, and De La Soul's *Three Feet High and Rising*. This, of course, can be debated, and is. The golden era is said to end—on no particular date, with no particular album—in the mid-to-late 1990s.

3 Rodgers, *Age of Fracture*, 221.

4 For one articulation of America's ever-shifting yet durable, deep historical fascination with Black sound, see, Radano, *Lying Up a Nation*, 3–13.

5 I'm thinking here, of the foundational works: Chang, *Can't Stop Won't Stop*; George, *Hip-Hop America*; Rose, *Black Noise*; Keyes, *Rap Music and Street Consciousness*; and Toop, *Rap Attack*.

6 Bessire and Fisher, *Radio Fields*, 3.

7 Razlogova, *Listener's Voice*, 9. See also Simmons, "Dear Radio Broadcaster," 444–59.

8 Fisher and Bessire, *Radio Fields*, 2, 34–35.

9 Russo, *Points on the Dial*, 195.

10　For radio's effect on notions of space, see Bronfman, *Isles of Noise*, 47, 124–26. For how radio reconfigures public and domestic spaces, see Ehrick, *Radio and the Gendered Soundscape*; and Smith, *Vocal Tracks*.

11　McKittrick, *Demonic Grounds*, 145.

12　Ehrick, *Radio and the Gendered Soundscape*, 28–29. Many historians have remarked upon his irony of how little documentation remains of radio operations given the scale of bureaucracy involved in running a station. See Squire, "Communities of the Air," 1–35.

13　Bohlman and McMurray, "Tape," 7.

14　Armstrong, "Cassette Culture with Stretch Armstrong," Medium, accessed February 27, 2021, https://medium.com/cuepoint/cassette-culture-with-stretch-armstrong-73e1a14652ea.

15　Sterne, *MP3*, 16.

16　Sterne, "Preservation Paradox in Digital Audio," 59–63.

17　Sterne, *MP3*, 9.

18　To this point, Lisa Gitelman has recently observed that capital "M" Media such as print, film, and, here, radio, are always supported by "an embarrassment" of ancillary and supplementary "material forms" and practices. Gitelman, *Paper Knowledge*, 6, 19.

19　Kunzel, "Queering Archives," 211.

20　Taylor, *Archive and the Repertoire*, 32–33.

21　Rohy, "In the Queer Archive," 344.

22　Blow, "The Breaks."

23　There's more than enough work here to fill a book in itself. The works that I converse with directly are present in citations throughout. Some works that have been particularly formative but aren't citationally present include Fred Moten's classic theorization of the break in *In the Break*; works by Sylvia Wynter including but not limited to Sylvia Wynter, "Unsettling the Coloniality of Being" and "On How We Mistook the Map," as well as the formidable contributions to her intellectual project in McKittrick, *Sylvia Wynter*; Spillers, *Black, White, and in Color*; Sharpe, *In the Wake*; Glissant, *Poetics of Relations*; and Gilroy, *Black Atlantic*.

24　WHBI's call letters changed to WNWK after a change in ownership in the mid-1980s.

Chapter 1. Deregulating Radio

1　McKee, "Radio Regulation," 5, 35. On the raucous initial reception of "Rapper's Delight," see Charnas, *Big Payback*, 39–40; Arthur and Harrison, "Reading Billboard," 309; George, *Hip Hop America*, 41; Chang, *Can't Stop Won't Stop*, 129; and Rose, *Black Noise*, 56.

2　"Notice of Inquiry and Proposed Rulemaking," FCC 733 FCC 2d 457, September 6, 1979.

3 "Van Deerlin Wins," 26.

4 See, for example, Cosmopolitan Broadcasting Corporation v. Federal Communications Commission, U.S. Court of Appeals for the District of Columbia Circuit – 581 F.2d 917 (D.C. Cir. 1978), in which the FCC sought to revoke Cosmopolitan Broadcasting's license for WHBI 105.9-FM for failing to adequately monitor the station's programming across dozens of broadcast languages; "Rejected WHBI Claims FCC Didn't Dig Deep Enough for Facts," 37; "Foreign-Language Outlet Finds Support for Fight in Court over Lost License," 30.

5 Horwitz, *Irony of Regulatory Reform*, 6.

6 Hall, "Radio Deregulation Big Topic," 1, 19.

7 HR 13015, "Communications Act," Sponsor Lionel van Deerlin, 1978. Shortly followed by HR 3333, "Communications Act of 1979," Sponsor Lionel van Deerlin, 1979.

8 "Van Deerlin Wins," 26.

9 For example, s.622, "Telecommunications Competition and Deregulation Act of 1979," Sponsor Barry Goldwater, 1979.

10 Rodgers, *Age of Fracture*, 41.

11 Hearings on HR 7357, "To Regulate Radio Communication," before the House Committee on the Merchant Marine and Fisheries, 68th Cong., 1st sess., 10, 1924.

12 Hilmes, *Radio Voices*, 10.

13 Hilmes, *Radio Voices*, 10.

14 The power of the FCC to enforce ownership limits was vociferously contested, but ultimately upheld by the Supreme Court in 1956, *U.S. v. Storer Broadcasting*, 351 U.S. 192.

15 McChesney, *Capitalism and the Information Age,* 17.

16 Derthick and Quirk, *Politics of Deregulation,* 5–7.

17 See, Holt, *Empires of Entertainment.*

18 Krasnow, "1976–1986," B-210.

19 Holland, "Washington Roundup," 15.

20 Bowler, "Under Fowler," 15.

21 Barlow, *Voice Over*.

22 James Winston, quoted in Barlow, 261.

23 Clayton, "Black Group Assails Deregulation," 23.

24 *Metro Broadcasting Inc. v. FCC*, 479 U.S. 54 (U.S. SC, 1990).

25 Dowie, "How ABC Spikes the News," 39.

26 Jones, "FCC Raises Limit," 1.

27 J. H. Duncan, "Introduction," A-15.

28 Keith and Krause, *Radio Station*, 27.

29 Unless otherwise indicated, all financial data for the New York market is taken from "New York" in J. H. Duncan, *American Radio, Tenth Anniversary Issue*, n.p.

30 Harrison, "Radio Prices Climb the Charts," 74.

31 Culp, Gammon, and Gammon, "History and Future," 78.

32 Epstein, "Some Thoughts," 56.

33 J. H. Duncan, "Introduction," A-18.

34 Dickstein, "Equity/Venture Buyouts," 70.

35 Barlow, *Voice Over*, 262.

36 "Fowler's Minority Prescription," 30.

37 Brown, "Black Radio," B-80, B-81.

38 Alston, "Black Owned Radio," 21.

39 Mayo quoted in Love, "Urban Contemporary News."

40 Quoted in Wyman, "Hip Hop Comes to Chicago." See also Love, 57.

41 Bronfman, *Isles of Noise*, 156.

Chapter 2. Sounding Black Progress in the Post–Civil Rights Era

1 Whodini, "Magic's Wand," Jive Records, VJ 12008, 1983.

2 Gibbs, "New York Radio," 49.

3 S. Williams, "Vy Higgensen, April 5, 1995."

4 Hannah Ford, "Mr. Magic Interview May, 1988," https://davidlubich.net/2016/01/08/mr-magic/ (accessed May 9, 2018).

5 Ireland, "Wizard of Ooze," 6.

6 "Guest, Percy E. Sutton," *Conversations with Harold Hudson Channer*, Manhattan Neighborhood Network, March 25, 1996. https://www.youtube.com/watch?v=SxXATIV-Eik, (accessed January 5, 2018).

7 "Suave Borough Chief," 42.

8 See, for example, Martin, "Percy E. Sutton."

9 Booker, "Percy Sutton Suing Mississippi," 38.

10 "Sutton Is NAACP President," 1.

11 Dingle, *Black Enterprise Titans,* 199.

12 Zooks, *I See Black People*, 31–32.

13 Pileggi, "Guess Who's Coming to Gracie Mansion," 39.

14 Kimbro and Hill, "Profiting through Self-Reliance," 111; Coombs, "Percy Sutton Has the Last Laugh," 28.

15 "How Harlem Heard the Mayor's Speech," 1.

16 Hamilton, quoted in Iton, *In Search of the Black Fantastic*, 24.

17 Cruse, *Crisis of the Negro Intellectual,* 474.

18 Goodman Jr., "Sutton the Media Man," 45.

19 "Penetrating the Barriers," 87.

20 Fred Ferretti, "The White Captivity of Black Radio," *Columbia Journalism Review*, Summer 1970, 35. A *Black Enterprise* article covering the same story estimated that thirty of America's eight thousand radio stations were Black-owned. "Nation's 100 Top Black Businesses," 34.

21 Barlow, *Voice Over*, 249–50. See also Krebs, "Ownership of WLIB," 83; "WLIB Nears Turnover"; "Black Group Takes Control of WLIB," A1–A2.

22 Krebs, "Ownership of WLIB," 83.

23 Goodman Jr., "Sutton, the Media Man," 45.

24 Krebs, "Ownership of WLIB," 83.

25 "58 Blacks Buying Station," A1, A3.

26 "Prices FMs Are Fetching These Days," *Broadcasting,* October 7, 1974, 52.

27 "58 Blacks Buying Station," A1, A3.

28 "Other (FM) Shoe Drops," 9.

29 Enkelis, Olsen, and Lewenstein, *On Our Own Terms*, 41; Zook, *I See Black People*, 88.

30 She continued, "There were no salaries. Except light and gas, there was not a person being paid. The bank hadn't been talked to. Nobody knew what the heck had been going on. Chemical Bank gave us the loan, but a year or two later, no one had even called the bank, or sent them any money. And the guy at the bank couldn't attack the borough president of Manhattan, Percy Sutton. . . . Because it was like a million and a half we owed at first, and then it was another million. So that was two and a half million dollars. In those days, they just didn't lend that kind of money to black people." Zook, 92–93.

31 Zook, *I See Black People,* 94.

32 Moore, "WBLS' Frankie Crocker," 34.

33 Murray, "Frankie Crocker Finds Being No. 1."

34 Wanda Ramos, interview with the author, February 14, 2018.

35 In characteristic form, Crocker was disqualified as a judge in a national contest for "Best Air Personality" after violating the rules and voting for himself. "I'm the best personality I've heard," he offered in defense. See Hall, "Vox Jox," 30.

36 Ramos, interview with author.

37 There is some discrepancy as to how WBLS arrived at their new format. The dominant account is that Crocker devised—and tightly controlled—the new format based on a mix of intuition and experience. Brunson, however, notes that she contributed to the development of the format through intensive audience profiling and market research. There is likely truth in both accounts, with Crocker supplying the musical vision and Brunson devising strategy. See Enkelis, Olsen, and Lewenstein, *On Our Own Terms*, 45.

38 "Black FM Finds Right Chemistry," 52, 54.

39 "Growth Market in Black Radio," 16–21.

40 "Growth Market in Black Radio," 17.

41 Williams, "Vy Higgensen."

42 Williams, "Vy Higgensen."

43 Williams, "Vy Higgensen."

44 "Black FM Finds Right Chemistry," 52, 54.

45 "Black FM Finds Right Chemistry," 52.

46 Ramos, interview with the author.

47 "Black FM Finds Right Chemistry." See also S. Williams, "Hal Jackson, April 11, 1995."

48 Enkelis, Olsen, Lewenstein, *On Our Own Terms*, 44.

49 S. Williams, "Vy Higgensen, April 5, 1995."

50 "Late News," 3, 26.

51 Brown, "Blacks Complete the Purchase," 81.

52 "Black FM Finds Right Chemistry," 54.

53 Gibbs, "New York Radio and the Big Beat," D20.

54 "Late News," 3, 26.

55 "WBLS Top NY Station," D2.

56 Gibbs, "New York Radio and the Big Beat," 49.

57 Gibbs, "New York Radio and the Big Beat," 49.

58 Gibbs, "New York Radio and the Big Beat," 49.

59 This shift in rhetoric was gradual, and was repeated by representatives of WBLS at all levels in the organization. As early as 1976, Frankie Crocker was quoted telling a reported for the *Amsterdam News*, "[WBLS] is no longer the biggest black station, it's the biggest station . . . period." Policano, "Interview with Frankie Crocker," D2.

60 Kozak, "People's Station," 30.

61 "Channel 4 to Feature WBLS," 56.

62 Hall, "2 Outlets Battling," 36; Hall, "WBLS's FM Challenge," 24.

63 Hall, "Cossman Low Profile," 20.

64 Hall, "Cossman Low Profile," 20.

65 "WKTU Flied Burkhart Disco Flag," 50.

66 Hall, "WKTU's Disco Is NY King," 5, 20.

67 Lawrence, *Love Saves the Day*, 151.

68 While the history of disco is outside the scope of this chapter, useful treatments can be found in Lawrence, *Love Saves the Day*; Echols, *Hot Stuff*; Shapiro, *Turn the Beat Around;* and Jackson, *House on Fire.*

69 "All NY Ears on WBLS," 37.

70 Hall, "NY WKTU Drops," 30.

71 "Radio's Frankie Crocker Fined," 18.

72 Moore, "WBLS' Frankie Crocker," 34.

73 Moore, "Ain't No Stoppin'," 27; "Ain't No Stoppin' WBLS," 25.

74 Speed, "Disco's Challenge for Black Radio," 44.

75 Speed, "Disco's Challenge for Black Radio," 44.

76 Speed, "Disco's Challenge for Black Radio," 44.

77 Ramos, interview with the author, 2017.

78 Hall, "Word 'Disco' Dirty in New York Radio," 24.

79 Perhaps coming full circle, many of the largest contributors to Sutton's campaign were members of ICBC. See, for example, Hunter-Gault, "Sutton Supporters Link Loss to Beame Running Again and Vote Delay," 30.

80 "Sutton Selling Interest in Newspaper," 45.

81 Brown, "Percy Sutton," 8.

82 Carrol, "Sutton Seeks Equal Time Ruling," 24.

83 Pileggi, "Guess Who's Coming," 31.

84 Dingle, *Black Enterprise Titans,* 204–5; "Sutton Decides: Will Run Stations," A1, B6.

85 Enkelis, Olsen, and Lewenstein, *On Our Own Terms*, 44.

86 Dingle, *Black Enterprise Titans,* 204–5.

87 Zook, *I See Black People*, 38.

88 Charnas, "Long Kiss Goodbye."

89 Rodgers, *Age of Fracture*, 116.

90 Neal, "Sold Out on Soul," 125.

91 "Urban Sounds Pull Emotional Reaction," 23. It's worth noting that, at the next year's NAB conference, the trade group convened another panel in hopes of establishing a definition for the format. See "Seek Definition for Urban Contemporary," 23.

92 See, for example, George, "NAB to Spotlight Urban Contemporary," 4.

93 George, "BMA Puts Spotlight," 3, 27.

94 Halpern, "Radio Downplays Blackness," BM-6.

95 Love, "Urban Vs. Neckbone," 43.

96 "Urban Sounds Pull Emotional Reaction," 23.

97 "Urban Sounds Pull Emotional Reaction," 23.

98 Foti, "Urban Programmers Blast Study," 12.

99 Hall, "WBLS-FM Leads NY Mart," 32; "WBLS-FM Hikes Superiority," 21; Callahan, "WBLS-FM in NY No. 1," 18.

100 "Vintage MOR behind Rise of WBLS-FM," 21.

101 George, "WKTU Carves Its Own Niche," 22; Sacks, "Burnout Is Primary Concern," 22.

102 Sacks, "Whither Urban Contemporary?," 15, 90.

103 Sacks, "In WBLS 'Boycott,'" 10.

104 "Percy Sutton Sets the Record Straight," 36.

105 "American Federation of Radio and Television Actors, New York Local Records," box 36, folder 20, through box 38, folder 13, Tamiment Library and Robert F. Wagner Labor Archive, New York University.

106 Taylor, "WBLS," D-8.

107 Iton, *In Search of the Black Fantastic*, 27.

Chapter 3. Commercializing Rap with Mr. Magic's *Rap Attack*

1 Hannah Ford, "Mr. Magic Interview May, 1988," https://davidlubich.net/2016/01/08/mr-magic (accessed May 9, 2018).

2 Charnas, *Big Payback,* 81, 153; Jay Smooth, "Mister Magic & Mister Cee Interview, 1995," http://www.hiphopmusic.com/2009/10/mister_magic_mister_cee_interv.html (accessed September 17, 2018).

3 Jenkins, Mao, and Wilson, *Ego Trip's Book of Rap Lists*, 106–7.

4 "Mister Magic & Mister Cee Interview, 1995."

5 Sacks, "WBLS Gets Mr. Magic 'Rap Attack,'" 16.

6   Charnas, *Big Payback*, 85–86.

7   DJ Premier, quoted in Davey D, "Hip Hop Legends DJ Premier and DJ Nasty Nes Offer Condolences to Hip Hop Radio Pioneer Mr. Magic," http://hiphopandpolitics.com/2009/10/02/hip-hop-legends-dj-premier-dj-nasty-nes-offer-condolances-to-hip-hop-radio-pioneer-mr-magic/ (accessed September 17, 2018).

8   Sacks, "'Magic' Is Missing," 52.

9   Marley Marl, interview with Jeff "Chairman" Mao, for Red Bull Music Academy, http://www.redbullmusicacademy.com/lectures/marley-marl-tokyo-2014 (accessed September 17, 2018).

10 Marley Marl, interview with Jeff "Chairman" Mao.

11 Marley Marl, interview with Jeff "Chairman" Mao.

12 Marley Marl, interview with Jeff "Chairman" Mao.

13 Marley Marl, interview with Jeff "Chairman" Mao.

14 Ford, "Mr. Magic Interview."

15 At the time of writing, this broadcast is currently available on YouTube; I encourage readers to track down and listen to this recording. Mr. Magic and Marley Marl, "Mr. Magic's Rap Attack (1983 Pt. 1) DJ Marley Marl" WBLS-FM 105.9, n.d.; Mr. Magic and Marley Marl, "Mr. Magic's Rap Attack (1983 Pt. 2) DJ Marley Marl" WBLS-FM 105.9, n.d.

16 Hall, "Urban Radio," 1, 10. In the early 1980s, Arbitron implemented a new sampling technique that weighted the diaries of young and minority listeners, traditionally difficult demographics to survey, to adjust for chronically low response rates. See, for example, George, "Arbitron DST Use," 18; and Freeman, "DST Sparks New Orleans Debate," 20.

17 "Radio: Summer Arbitron Results," 15.

18 The lawsuit only grew more contentious when lawyers for AFTRA subpoenaed Inner City Broadcasting Corporation's financial records and internal correspondence, with the prosecution contending in one memo that "WBLS & WLIB are NOT in economic difficulty. It is these Radio Stations that are providing capital for other ventures by [Inner City Broadcasting]." "American Federation of Radio and Television Actors, New York Local Records," box 36, folders 20–21, Tamiment Library and Robert F. Wagner Labor Archive, New York University.

19 Love, "WRKS's Urban Format No. 1," 52.

20 Percy E. Sutton, interview with Sonya D. Williams, April 10, 1995, in *Black Radio: Telling It Like It Was*, DAT 175, Archives of African American Music and Culture, University of Indiana.

21 "Fall '84 Ratings Wars," 52.

22 Bornstein, "Arbitrons," 14. "Vox Jox," 22; Love, "Happy New Year," 54.

23 Jenkins, Mao, and Wilson, *Ego Trips Book of Rap Lists*, 106–7.

24 Mr. Magic and Marley Marl, "Mr. Magic's Rap Attack feat. Roxanne Shanté WHBI 1985," WHBI-FM, 105.9, Newark, n.d.

25 Mr. Magic and Marley Marl, "WHBI Mr. Magic & Marley Marl (1985),"
   WHBI-FM, 105.9, Newark, n.d.
26 Jenkins, Mao, and Wilson, *Ego Trip's Book of Rap Lists*, 107.
27 Charnas, *Big Payback*, 176.
28 Mr. Magic and Marley Marl, "Mr. Magic's Rap Attack (1986) Pt. 1,"
   WBLS-FM 105.9, Newark, n.d.
29 Turner, *Blazing the Trail,* 49, emphasis mine.
30 For summaries of these debates, see Collins Hill, *From Black Power to Hip-Hop*, 3–8; and Rose, *Hip-Hop Wars*, 24–42.
31 For another version of this argument, see Charnas, "Long Kiss Goodnight."
32 George, "Bad Rap for NYC Rap Concert?," 26. The event was still the
   second-highest-grossing concert of 1985. See "Boxscore," 35; and Jefferies,
   "Police Action at Garden," 9, 19.
33 Ravo, "1 Killed, 5 Injured," B-4.
34 Marriott, "One Is Killed and 12 Are Injured," A-1.
35 Rosa and Kriegel, "Concert Tipsters," 17.
36 Tapley, "Does Rap Music Create Violence?," 28.
37 Even as early as 1985 it was possible for one influential New York program
   director to state, "Two years ago, there was more rap music on the radio. We
   have slowed down a bit, and a number of stations around the country seem to
   be doing that." Tony Quartarone, quoted in Love, "Words of Wisdom," 50.
38 George, "Spoken Here," Y-14.
39 Freeman, "At WBLS," 19.
40 Law, "Letter to the Editor," 28.
41 George, "Black on Black Crime," 27.
42 George, "Stop the Violence," 26.
43 Olson, "As Rap Goes Pop," 1.
44 Olson, "As Rap Goes Pop," 68.
45 Stuart, "Rap against Rap," R-8.
46 Stuart, "Rap against Rap," R-21.
47 Olson, "As Rap Goes Pop," 68.
48 Rahsaan, "Guest Commentary," 18.
49 Coleman, "Dance Trax," 27.
50 Nas, "Halftime."
51 Notorious B.I.G., "Juicy."
52 Quasimoto, "Rappcats."

Chapter 4. Programming the Street at WRKS

1 Advertisement for RKO Radio, "WRKS Is New York," 99.
2 "Programmers Discuss 'KISS of Success,'" 20.
3 Chin, "Top 40 Explosion," 21.

4 George, "Club Play Open's Gwen Guthrie's 'Padlock,'" 58.

5 Chuck Chillout, interview with the author, December 14, 2014. Unless otherwise noted, material for this section is drawn from this interview.

6 Here, it doesn't make sense to adjudicate whether or not claims to "street knowledge" were issued in good faith (who can say?) or whether or not major labels held more sway over which records entered daytime rotation than programmers publicly admitted (they probably did) nor does it make sense to mount a critique of what could be considered authentically "street" (for whom?). This narrative is instead concerned with how different individuals at KISS positioned hip-hop to represent their understandings of "the street." Those varying definitions produced something of a consensus over time. By suspending present definitions of the street, we begin to see how KISS's street-oriented urban contemporary format shaped the genre as we know it today.

7 Breithaupt and Breithaupt, *Precious and Few*, 3.

8 Hall, "Heads Roll," 4.

9 Hall, "NY WXLO-FM Turns from Teens," 22.

10 Grein, "Radio Needs Flexible AOR/Crossover Format," 54.

11 Brenner, "Burkhardt to Advise RKO," 24.

12 RKO General, Inc. v. FCC, 670 F.2d 215—Court of Appeals, Dist. of Columbia Circuit 1981.

13 "RKO Decision is Formally Promulgated," 34.

14 "RKO Decision is Formally Promulgated," 34. For a more detailed account of the FCC's charges against RKO, see, RKO General Inc. v. FCC, 670 F.2d 215.

15 This equates to a fine of roughly $1,200,000,000 at the time of writing.

16 "FCC Lifts Three RKO Licenses," 27.

17 "FCC Lifts Three RKO Licenses," 27.

18 "Jencks Picked to Head 'NewCo,'" 30.

19 "Fates and Fortunes," 107.

20 Advertisement for RKO Radio, "Meet Lee Simonson," 79.

21 "Playback," 5.

22 "Old Medium's Learning New Tricks," 44.

23 "Name Change for WXLO," 29; "Call Letters," 110.

24 Duncan, "Ethnic and Street Music," 54.

25 "RPC V," 33.

26 "Vox Jox," 29.

27 "Editorial: Enough," 114.

28 Bornstein, "Mayo Named VP/GM," 12.

29 Bornstein, "Mayo Named VP/GM," 12.

30 Speed, "WGCI/Chicago," 58.

31 Penchasky, "Chicago WGCI-FM," 29.

32 Speed, "WGCI/Chicago," 58.

33 "RKO Names Mayo PD," 1.

34 "WRKS Shows Growth," 20.

35 "WRKS Shows Growth," 20.

36 See, for example, advertisement for the Research Group, "It surprised me . . . ," 2.

37 Foti, "Urban Programmers Blast Study," 12.

38 "Research Put in Perspective," 49.

39 Levitt, "Marketing Success," 3–9.

40 Some media scholars refer to this phenomenon as the "audience commodity," referring to the fact that groups of listeners can be identified, marketed, and sold, just as any other commodity. See Smythe, "Communications," 1–27.

41 Smith, "Hip-Hop History." http://hiphopandpolitics.com/2013/10/04/hip -hop-history-kool-dj-red-alert-gives-ultimate-interview/ (accessed January 22, 2022).

42 Smith, "Hip-Hop History."

43 Adler, "Interview: Chuck Chillout," Red Bull Music Academy, accessed January 2, 2021, https://daily.redbullmusicacademy.com/2015/05/chuck -chillout-interview.

44 Chillout, interview with the author.

45 Smith, "Hip-Hop History."

46 Smith, "Hip-Hop History."

47 Smith, "Hip-Hop History."

48 "Interview: Chuck Chillout."

49 Red Bull TV, "Revolutions on Air," accessed January 19, 2015, http://www .redbull.tv/film/AP-1K3UG78F11W11/revolutions-on-air.

50 Chuck Chillout, interview with author, December 14, 2014.

51 Smith, "Hip-Hop History."

52 Smith, "Hip Hop History."

53 For a complete treatment of DJ practice and culture in the 1970s, see Lawrence, *Love Saves the Day*.

54 Smith, "Hip-Hop History."

55 Red Alert, "Kool DJ Red Alert Live on KISS FM in NYC—Dec. 1984," accessed May 14, 2019, https://www.youtube.com/watch?v=R1JSAKpraxQ.

56 Red Alert, "DJ Red Alert (1984) (My Xmas Present to You All 3/6)," accessed May 14, 2019, https://www.youtube.com/watch?v=SjELEmZA86A.

57 Chillout, interview with the author.

58 Smith, "Red Alert."

59 Smith, "Red Alert."

60 Chillout, interview with the author.

61 See, for example, Chuck Chillout, "Chuck Chillout on KISS-FM 98.7 (1986)," accessed May 14, 2019, https://www.youtube.com/watch?v =depNm9pj7kE.

62 Chillout, interview with the author.

1 "Dutch," email with the author, July 28, 2016.

2 "DJ Afrika Islam—The Unkut Interview," UnKut, October 15, 2015, http://www.unkut.com/2015/10/afrika-islam-the-unkut-interview/.

3 For a summary of writing on "radiophonic space," see Bessire and Fisher, *Radio Fields,* 5–6.

4 Questions about the history of cassette practice across culture and time have seen renewed relevance in current music scholarship as well as hip-hop journalism. In the introduction of an issue of *Twentieth-Century Music,* Andrea Bohlman and Peter McMurray use the cassette to push back against the privileged position accorded to the phonograph in histories of twentieth-century sound and media, while chapters in a recent collection on technology and memory examine intimate cassette recording and listening practices. See Bohlman and McMurry, "Tape"; Bijsterveld and van Dijck, "Introduction"; Bijsterveld and Jacobs, "Storing Sound Souvenirs"; and Jensen, "Tape Cassettes and Former Selves." Canonical treatments of the cassette medium include Manuel, *Cassette Culture*; and Hirschkind, *Ethical Soundscape.* For its relation to hip-hop history, see Harrison, "Cheaper Than a CD."

5 Chang, *Can't Stop Won't Stop,* 141.

6 Lawrence, *Life and Death,* 338–39.

7 Lawrence, *Life and Death,* 338.

8 "DJ Afrika Islam—The Unkut Interview."

9 Troy L. Smith, "An Interview with Se' Divine The Master Mind of the Legendary Supreme Team Show on Radio Station WHBI," Oldschoolhiphop.com, fall 2007, http://www.oldschoolhiphop.com/interviews/sedevine.htm (accessed May 16, 2017).

10 "DJ Afrika Islam—The Unkut Interview."

11 It became clear throughout the course of writing this chapter that the typically triumphal history of Afrika Bambaataa and the Zulu Nation is more complicated than has previously been captured. Around the time I finished the first drafts of this chapter in 2016, several individuals came forward to accuse Afrika Bambaataa of sexually assaulting them as minors. In the following years, several more individuals have shared similar stories, alleging that Bambaataa groomed and assaulted vulnerable members of the Zulu Nation. In the fall of 2021, a lawsuit was filed against Bambaataa and the Zulu Nation, alleging that Bambaataa sexually abused and trafficked the victim, and that the Zulu Nation failed to take reasonable steps to protect them. Bambaataa and his organization are ubiquitous in the source material for this chapter. By the mid-1980s, his influence was felt far and wide in New York City. Now we must contend with the possibility that he used that same platform to exploit and abuse vulnerable members of his circle. For more on this developing matter, see Jacobs, Kochman, Shapiro, and O'Keefe, "Afrika Bambaataa Sex Accuser"; Wedge, "Afrika Bambaataa Al-

legedly Molested"; Kreps, "Afrika Bambaataa Sued"; Complaint, John Doe v. Lance Taylor, Zulu Nation, Universal Zulu Nation, and XYZ Corp. (Supreme Court of the State of New York County of Bronx) (No. 70331/2021E).

12 For more on the history of the Zulu Nation, see Chang, *Can't Stop Won't Stop*, 89–109; Ahearn and Fricke, *Yes Yes Y'All*, especially chapter 4.

13 Hager, "Afrika Bambaataa's Hip-Hop," 21.

14 Lawrence, *Life and Death*, 158.

15 Islam quoted in Lawrence, 182.

16 "1981–6th Annual Zulu Nation Celebration—Live @ The Bronx River Centre New York," https://www.mixcloud.com/abstraktsoundz/1981-6th -annual-zulu-nation-celebration-live-the-bronx-river-centre-new-york/ (accessed October 2, 2021).

17 "DJ Afrika Islam—The Unkut Interview."

18 Islam quoted in Lawrence, *Life and Death*, 284–85.

19 "DJ Afrika Islam—The Unkut Interview."

20 Frere-Jones, "RIP Mr. Magic."

21 DJ Afrika Islam, "Tape 1_9 DJ Grazzhoppa Collection," *Zulu Beats*, WHBI-FM 105.9, Newark, https://old-school-hiphop-tapes.blogspot.com/ (accessed July 16, 2014).

22 DJ Afrika Islam, "April 21st 1983 Part 1," *Zulu Beats,* WHBI-FM 105.9, Newark, https://old-school-hiphop-tapes.blogspot.com/ (accessed November 16, 2016).

23 Warner, *Publics and Counterpublics*, 10.

24 For example, Alexander Russo argues for approaches to radio broadcasts that hear the production of "space, place, and identity" within "the form and content of sound texts." In his study of broadcast localism during the golden age of America radio, this focus allows him to locate in broadcasts the sonic features of regional identity that advertisers and networks employed to attract recalcitrant audiences. Elena Razlogova's account of listener letter-writing campaigns shows how mid-century radio networks tailored their programming to the ethical and sonic expectations of listeners, inflecting the sounds of broadcasts with the values of an American "moral economy." And Christine Ehrick hears the sound of women's voices on Uruguayan and Argentinian radio as a mediatization of a feminist intellectual counterpublic, addressing and interpellating a modern, cosmopolitan female listener. See Russo, *Points on the Dial*, 151–53; Razlogova, *Listener's Voice*; and Ehrick, *Radio and the Gendered Soundscape*.

25 Fisher, "The Voice and Its Doubles," 29.

26 Here I'm reprising a line of inquiry opened by Benedict Anderson in his germinal *Imagined Communities*. For a more recent take, see Lacey, *Listening Publics*, 7.

27 DJ Afrika Islam, "July 7th 1983 Part 1," *Zulu Beats,* 105.9 WHBI-FM, Newark, July 7, 1983, https://old-school-hiphop-tapes.blogspot.com/ (accessed October 2, 2016).

28 Fisher, *Voice and Its Doubles,* 53, 66.

29 Teddy Tedd, conversation with the author, May 10, 2017.

30 Ettleson, "Zulu Nation Radio."

31 DJ Afrika Islam, "Tape 5-9 DJ Grazzhoppa Collection," *Zulu Beats,* WHBI-FM 105.9, Newark, https://old-school-hiphop-tapes.blogspot.com/ (accessed July 16, 2014).

32 DJ Afrika Islam, "Tape 8-9 DJ Grazzhoppa Collection," *Zulu Beats,* WHBI-FM 105.9, Newark, https://old-school-hiphop-tapes.blogspot.com/ (accessed July 16, 2014).

33 DJ Afrika Islam, "Tape 3-9 DJ Grazzhoppa collection," *Zulu Beats,* WHBI-FM 105.9, Newark, https://old-school-hiphop-tapes.blogspot.com/ (accessed July 16, 2014); DJ Afrika Islam, "Tape 7-9 DJ Grazzhoppa collection," *Zulu Beats,* WHBI-FM 105.9, Newark, https://old-school-hiphop-tapes.blogspot.com/ (accessed July 16, 2014).

34 While the dedications to the "Boogie Down" occurred nearly every show, these specific dedications are drawn from DJ Afrika Islam, "Tape 6-9 DJ Grazzhoppa Collection," https://old-school-hiphop-tapes.blogspot.com/ (accessed July 16, 2014).

35 Forman. *'Hood Comes First,* 179.

36 Islam, "Tape 5-9."

37 Ginsburg, "Afterword," 269.

38 Islam, "Tape 2-9."

39 Russo, *Points on the Dial,* 20–30.

40 DJ Afrika Islam, "April 7th, 1983."

41 Chamberlayne, *Kingdom Hall No More,* 48–49.

42 Awesome 2, interview with the author, January 7, 2016.

43 DJ Afrika Islam, "Tape 4-9 DJ Grazzhoppa Collection," *Zulu Beats,* WHBI-FM 105.9, Newark, https://old-school-hiphop-tapes.blogspot.com/ (accessed July 16, 2014).

44 Ettleson, "Zulu Nation Radio."

45 Islam, "Tape 7-9."

46 Islam, "Tape 7-9."

47 DJ Afrika Islam, "July 7th 1983 Part 1," *Zulu Beats,* 105.9 WHBI-FM, Newark, July 7, 1983, https://old-school-hiphop-tapes.blogspot.com/ (accessed October 2, 2016).

48 Islam, "Tape 7-9."

49 Ettleson, "Zulu Nation Radio."

50 Islam, "Tape 7-9."

51 Ettleson, "Zulu Nation Radio."

52 DJ Afrika Islam, "April 13th, 1983." *Zulu Beats,* 105.9 WHBI-FM, Newark, April 13, 1983, https://old-school-hiphop-tapes.blogspot.com/ (accessed October 2, 2016).

53 Islam, "April 7th, 1983."

54 Ettleson, "Zulu Nation Radio."

55 DJ Afrika Islam, "Tape 4-9 DJ Grazzhoppa Collection," *Zulu Beats*, WHBI-FM 105.9, Newark.

56 This section is informed by an email exchange I had with Dutch in July 2016.

57 "Dutch," email with the author, July 28, 2016.

58 Larkin, *Signal and Noise*, 50.

59 Chuck Chillout, interview with the author, December 14, 2014.

60 Teddy Tedd, interview with the author, January 7, 2016.

61 Keeling, "Looking for M—," 565–82.

62 Chenier, "Privacy Anxieties," 131.

63 Thi Nguyen, "Minor Threats," 13.

64 Iton, *In Search of the Black Fantastic*, 149.

65 Scholars have recently taken up such questions; see, for example, Browne, *Dark Matters*; and Wagner, *Disturbing the Peace*, 2009.

Chapter 6. Listening to the Labor of *The Awesome 2 Show*

1 The previous example is excerpted from DJ Afrika Islam, "Tape 2-9 DJ Grazzhoppa Collection," WHBI-FM 105.9, Newark.

2 Allen, "Hip Hop Radio: Power to the People," 36.

3 For a polemical take on the end of hip-hop as an organic culture, see Tate, "Hiphop Turns 30." https://www.villagevoice.com/2004/12/28/hiphop-turns-30/, accessed January 23, 2022.

4 This chapter is assembled from three formal interviews with the Awesome 2 (January 7, 2016; May 19, 2016; and August 9, 2016), each totaling a little over an hour; numerous shorter conversations and email exchanges spanning the fall of 2015 to the spring of 2021; and around eleven hours of extant MP3 recordings of *The Awesome 2 Show*. I have cited the date and year of the extant recordings of broadcasts to the best of my ability.

5 For longer examinations of the relationship between Black radio and independent labels, see Roberts, "Papa's Got a Brand New Bag." See also Stahl, *Unfree Masters*.

6 See Rock Master Scott and the Dynamic 3, "It's Life (You Gotta Think Twice)," Reality Records, IR1374, 1983; Tranquilizing Preview/Tranquilizing Three, "Vote Like You Party/A Fact of Life." Apexton Records, AP-116, 1983.

7 Portes and Haller, "Informal Economy," 404.

8 Before long, the most famous rap acts entertained offers for corporate sponsorship. The most famous example from this period is Run-DMC's long-standing relationship with Adidas, culminating in the 1987 track "My Adidas." For a treatment of this relationship, see Taylor, *Sounds of Capitalism*, 196–97.

9 Tsing, *Mushroom*, 65.

10 It's worth noting that what the Awesome 2 refer to as "flow" is surprisingly consonant with Raymond Williams's exploration of the concept, especially with regards to the way formal features of television programming harness the inherently linear structure of broadcasting. See Williams, *Television*.

11 This, adding to Kodwo Eshun's observation that "to scratch is to think with vinyl. The DJ is a tactilist who goes on a journey of the hands, opening up a new field of objective thought: fingertip perception. The distributed brain of the hand emerges with its own point of touch, a manual memory of terror wrists and scizzorhands." Quoted in Eshun, *More Brilliant Than the Sun*, 24.

12 See, for example, C. H. Smith, "I Don't Like to Dream," 69–79.

13 For help thinking through hip-hop entrepreneurship, see Basu and Werbner, "Bootstrap Capitalism and the Culture Industries," 239.

14 The reporting on the Latin Quarter is characteristic of a trend in *New York Times* reporting in the 1980s, stoking the flames of radicalized fear, See Iverem, "Violence Plagues New Latin Quarter," 23; and "3 Shot and 5 Arrested Near the Latin Quarter," 6.

15 In addition to arising in the course of our interview, a version of this story appears in Philip Mlynar's Red Bull Music Academy interview with the Awesome 2, http://daily.redbullmusicacademy.com/2014/08/awesome-two-interview (accessed September 17, 2018).

Epilogue

1 Dreyfuss, "Harlem's Ardent Voice," 18.

2 Dreyfuss, "Harlem's Ardent Voice," 18.

3 Marriott, "Harlem Pastor to Campaign," 24.

4 Olmstead, "From a Powerful Pulpit," 23.

5 Levy, "Harlem Protest of Rap Lyrics," 39; "Anti-Rap Rally Crushes Explicit Music," https://www.upi.com/Archives/1993/06/05/Anti-rap-rally-crushes-explicit-music-with-steamroller/2283739252800/ (accessed January 23, 2022).

6 Levy, "Harlem Protest of Rap Lyrics," 39.

7 Levy, "Harlem Protest of Rap Lyrics," 39.

8 "Stations Crack Down on Rappers."

9 Puig and Steve, "Top-Rated Station Bans 3"; Armstrong, "Backlash Is Brewing."

10 Myers, "WBLS-FM," 52.

11 See Baldwin, "Black Empires, White Desires," 138; Gladney, "Black Arts and the Hip-Hop Movement"; Smitherman, "Chains Remain the Same."

12 Charnas, "Long Kiss Goodnight."

13 Tricia Rose, *Black Noise*; and Rose, *Hip-Hop Wars*.

14 Tate, "Hip-Hop Turns 30," https://www.villagevoice.com/2004/12/28
    /hiphop-turns-30/ (accessed January 23, 2022).

15 Charnas, "Long Kiss Goodnight."

16 DJ Red Alert, "Kool DJ Red Alert Live on KISS-FM in NYC—Dec. 1984,"
    YouTube https://www.youtube.com/watch?v=R1JSAKpraxQ (accessed
    January 23, 2022).

17 There are more promising lines of inquiry than ever. A few I find particu-
    larly heartening include Stoever, "Crate Digging Begins at Home"; Cod-
    dington, "Check Out the Hook"; and Cheng, "Black Noise, White Ears."

18 Black Moon, "Black Smif-N-Wessun."

Audiovisual Media

Black Moon. "Black Smif-N-Wessun." *Enta Da Stage*. Nervous Records, 1993.

Blow, Kurtis. "The Breaks." Mercury MDS-4010, 1980, 12-inch single.

DJ Afrika Islam. "April 21st 1983 Part 1." *Zulu Beats,* WHBI-FM 105.9, Newark, https://old-school-hiphop-tapes.blogspot.com/Newark (accessed November 16, 2016).

DJ Afrika Islam. "July 7th 1983 Part 1." *Zulu Beats,* 105.9 WHBI-FM, Newark, July 7, 1983, https://old-school-hiphop-tapes.blogspot.com/ (accessed October 2, 2016).

DJ Afrika Islam. "Tape 1_9 dj Grazzhoppa Collection." *Zulu Beats*, WHBI-FM, 105.9. https://old-school-hiphop-tapes.blogspot.com/Newark (accessed July 16, 2014).

DJ Afrika Islam. "Tape 2_9 dj Grazzhoppa Collection." *Zulu Beats*, WHBI-FM, 105.9. https://old-school-hiphop-tapes.blogspot.com/Newark (accessed July 16, 2014).

DJ Afrika Islam. "Tape 3_9 dj Grazzhoppa Collection." *Zulu Beats*, WHBI-FM, 105.9. https://old-school-hiphop-tapes.blogspot.com/Newark (accessed July 16, 2014).

DJ Afrika Islam. "Tape 4_9 dj Grazzhoppa Collection." *Zulu Beats*, WHBI-FM, 105.9. https://old-school-hiphop-tapes.blogspot.com /Newark (accessed July 16, 2014).

DJ Afrika Islam. "Tape 5_9 dj Grazzhoppa Collection." *Zulu Beats*, WHBI-FM, 105.9. https://old-school-hiphop-tapes.blogspot.com/Newark (accessed July 16, 2014).

DJ Afrika Islam. "Tape 6_9 dj Grazzhoppa Collection." *Zulu Beats*, WHBI-FM, 105.9. https://old-school-hiphop-tapes.blogspot.com /Newark (accessed July 16, 2014).

DJ Afrika Islam. "Tape 7_9 dj Grazzhoppa Collection." *Zulu Beats*, WHBI-FM, 105.9. https://old-school-hiphop-tapes.blogspot.com/Newark (accessed July 16, 2014).

DJ Afrika Islam. "Tape 8_9 dj Grazzhoppa Collection." *Zulu Beats*, WHBI-FM, 105.9. https://old-school-hiphop-tapes.blogspot.com/Newark (accessed July 16, 2014).

DJ Afrika Islam. "Tape 9_9 dj Grazzhoppa Collection." *Zulu Beats*, WHBI-FM, 105.9. https://old-school-hiphop-tapes.blogspot.com/Newark (accessed July 16, 2014).

Mr. Magic and Marley Marl. "Mr. Magic's Rap Attack (1983 Pt. 1) DJ Marley Marl." WBLS-FM 105.9, n.d. https://www.youtube.com/watch?v=Nc6eJ5rdD9Q (accessed January 27, 2022).

Mr. Magic and Marley Marl. "Mr. Magic's Rap Attack (1983 Pt. 2) DJ Marley Marl." WBLS-FM 105.9, n.d. https://www.youtube.com/watch?v=4c-3oeBP59E (accessed January 27, 2022).

Mr. Magic and Marley Marl. "Mr. Magic's Rap Attack feat. Roxanne Shanté WHBI 1985." WHBI-FM, 105.9, Newark, n.d. https://www.youtube.com/watch?v=uuB61T6oQ-s (accessed January 27, 2022).

Mr. Magic and Marley Marl. "Mr. Magic's Rap Attack (1986) Pt. 1." WBLS-FM 105.9, Newark, n.d. https://www.youtube.com/watch?v=ySl1dRul-kE (accessed January 27, 2022).

Mr. Magic and Marley Marl. "WHBI Mr. Magic & Marley Marl (1985)." WHBI-FM, 105.9, Newark. https://www.youtube.com/watch?v=RCNB_CcPpzA (accessed January 27, 2022).

Nas. "Halftime." *Illmatic*. Columbia Records, 1994.

"1981–6th Annual Zulu Nation Celebration—Live @ The Bronx River Centre New York." https://www.mixcloud.com/abstraktsoundz/1981-6th-annual-zulu-nation-celebration-live-the-bronx-river-centre-new-york/ (accessed October 2, 2021).

Notorious B.I.G. "Juicy." *Ready to Die*. Bad Boy Entertainment, 1994.

Quasimoto. "Rappcats." *The Further Adventures of Lord Quas*, Stones Throw Records, 2005.

"Revolutions on Air." Red Bull TV. http://www.redbull.tv/film/AP-1K3UG78F11W11/revolutions-on-air (accessed January 19, 2015).

Rock Master Scott and the Dynamic 3. "It's Life (You Gotta Think Twice)." Reality Records, IR1374, 1983.

Tranquilizing Preview/Tranquilizing Three. "Vote Like You Party/A Fact of Life." Apexton Records, AP-116, 1983.

Williams, Sonja. "Hal Jackson, April 11, 1995." In *Black Radio: Telling It Like It Was*, DAT 114, Archive of African American Culture, Indiana University Bloomington.

Williams, Sonja. "Vy Higgensen, April 5, 1995." In *Black Radio: Telling It Like It Was*, DAT 105, Archive of African American Culture, Indiana University Bloomington.

"Actions." *Broadcasting*, July 29, 1974, 21.

Adler, Bill. "Interview: Chuck Chillout." Red Bull Music Academy, https://daily.redbullmusicacademy.com/2015/05/chuck-chillout-interview (accessed January 2, 2021).

"Ain't No Stoppin' WBLS/FM." *New York Amsterdam News*, September 8, 1979, 25.

Allen, Harry. "Hip-Hop Nation: Power to the People." *Village Voice*, January 19, 1988. https://www.villagevoice.com/2019/04/03/hiphop-nation-power-to-the-people/ (accessed January 23, 2022).

"All NY Ears on WBLS/FM 'Disco and More.'" *New York Amsterdam News*, June 21, 1980, 37.

Alston, Roland. "Black Owned Radio: Taking to the Airwaves in a Hurry." *Black Enterprise*, July 1978, 21.

"Anti-Rap Rally Crushes Explicit Music with Steamroller." United Press International, June 5, 1993. https://www.upi.com/Archives/1993/06/05/Anti-rap-rally-crushes-explicit-music-with-steamroller/2283739252800/ (accessed January 23, 2022).

"Approved." *Broadcasting*, July 3, 1972, 23.

"ARBreakouts." *Radio and Records*, June 20, 1975, 6.

Armstrong, Scott. "Backlash Is Brewing over 'Gangsta Rap' Lyrics as Public Says 'Enough.'" *Christian Science Monitor*, December 13, 1993. https://www.csmonitor.com/1993/1213/13012.html.

Armstrong, Stretch. "Cassette Culture with Stretch Armstrong." Medium. Accessed February 27, 2021. https://medium.com/cuepoint/cassette-culture-with-stretch-armstrong-73e1a14652ea.

Autodidact 17. "Reflections on Hip-Hop's Mr. Magic." *New York Amsterdam News*, March 30, 2017. http://amsterdamnews.com/news/2017/mar/30/reflections-hip-hop-pioneer-mr-magic/.

"Bartell Co. Absorbs MacFadden Affiliate." *Radio-Television Daily*, February 13, 1962, 6.

"Black FM Finds Right Chemistry for Success in New York." *Broadcasting*, March 5, 1973, 52, 54.

"Black Group Takes Control of WLIB." *New York Amsterdam News*, October 13, 1983, A1–2.

"Black Group to Buy WLIB (AM) New York." *Broadcasting*, July 19, 1971, 61.

"Black Radio: Top 82 of '82." *Radio and Records*, December 18, 1982, 53.

Booker, James. "Percy Sutton Suing Mississippi for Million: 'Riders' Fight Back." *New York Amsterdam News*, June 17, 1961, 1, 38.

Bornstein, Rollye. "Arbitrons: Most Formats Healthy." *Billboard*, October 13, 1984, 14.

Bornstein, Rollye. "Mayo Named VP/GM." *Billboard*, June 16, 1984, 12.

"Borough President: Sutton." *New York Times*, October 22, 1966, 25.

Bowler, Peter J. "Under Fowler, FCC Treated TV as Commerce." *New York Times,* January 17, 1987, 15.

"Boxscore: Top Concert Grosses." *Billboard*, January 18, 1986, 35.

Brenner, Jerry. "Burkhardt to Advise RKO." *Billboard*, August 30, 1980, 24.

Brown, Amos. "Black Radio: Adapting to a Changing World." In J. H. Duncan, *American Radio, Tenth Anniversary Issue, 1976–1986*, B-79–B-85.

Brown, Les. "Blacks Complete the Purchase of Black-Oriented FM Station." *New York Times,* October 8, 1974, 81.

Brown, Mary R. "Percy Sutton: Running Hard to Be New York's Next Mayor." *New York Amsterdam News*, September 24, 1977, 8.

Bruno, Vito. "Rap: A Positive Force for Social Change: Corralling the Violence." *Billboard*, November 8, 1986, 9.

"Burke New York Survey Released." *Radio and Records,* January 19, 1979, 4.

Callahan, Jean. "WBLS-FM in NY No. 1." *Billboard*, May 10, 1980, 18.

"Call Letters." *Broadcasting*, June 8, 1981, 110.

Carroll, Maurice. "Sutton Seeks Equal Time Ruling." *New York Times*, May 6, 1977, 24.

Carroll, Maurice. "If You're Thinking of Living In: The Upper West Side." *New York Times*, November 20, 1983, 8–9.

"Channel 4 to Feature WBLS." *New York Amsterdam News*, August 29, 1981, 56.

Chin, Brian. "Top 40 Explosion Changing New York 'Street' Sounds." *Billboard,* November 10, 1984, 21.

Clayton, Rose. "Black Group Assails Deregulation, Media Coalition Fears Loss of Platform to Air Views." *Billboard*, May 9, 1981, 23.

"Columbia Records Bio of Public Enemy." September 1, 1991. Box 8, folder 30, collection no. 8092, Adler Hip-Hop Archive, Cornell University.

Complaint, John Doe v. Lance Taylor, Zulu Nation, Universal Zulu Nation, and XYZ Corp. Supreme Court of the State of New York County of Bronx (No. 70331/2021E).

Coombs, Orde. "Percy Sutton Has the Last Laugh." *New York Magazine*, August 17, 1981, 28.

Cosmopolitan Broadcasting Corporation v. Federal Communications Commission. U.S. Court of Appeals for the District of Columbia Circuit - 581 F.2d 917 (D.C. Cir. 1978).

Culp, Craig, Dan Gammon, and Tom Gammon. "The History and Future of Selling Radio Stations." In J. H. Duncan, *American Radio, Tenth Anniversary Issue, 1976–1986*, B-33–B-43.

Cutchin, Rusty. "And the Beat Goes On: Mr. Magic Goes National." *Cash Box*, June 22, 1985, 29.

Davey D. "Hip Hop Legends DJ Premier and DJ Nasty Nes Offer Condolences to Hip Hop Radio Pioneer Mr. Magic." Hip-Hop and Politics, October 10, 2009. http://hiphopandpolitics.com/2009/10/02/hip-hop-legends-dj-premier-dj -nasty-nes-offer-condolances-to-hip-hop-radio-pioneer-mr-magic/.

Dickstein, Barry. "Equity/Venture Financing." In J. H. Duncan, *American Radio, Tenth Anniversary Issue, 1976–1986*, B-25–B-29.

"DJ Afrika Islam—The Unkut Interview." UnKut, October 15, 2015. http://www.unkut.com/2015/10/afrika-islam-the-unkut-interview/.

Dowie, Matt. "How ABC Spikes the News." *Mother Jones Magazine*, November–December 1985, 39.

Dreyfuss, Joel. "Harlem's Ardent Voice." *New York Times*, January 20, 1991, 18.

Duncan, James H., ed. *American Radio, Tenth Anniversary Issue, 1976–1986: A Prose and Statistical History*. Kalamazoo, MI: Duncan's American Radio, 1986.

Duncan, James H. "Introduction." In J. H. Duncan, *American Radio, Tenth Anniversary Issue, 1976–1986*, A-1.

Duncan, Pearl. "New York Ethnic and Street Music." *Record World*, September 29, 1979, 54.

Epstein, Jeff. "Some Thoughts on Radio's Move to Wall Street." In J. H. Duncan, *American Radio, Tenth Anniversary Issue, 1976–1986*, B-11–B-16.

Ettleson, Robbie. "Zulu Nation Radio: A Tribute." Red Bull Music Academy. Accessed May 16, 2017. http://daily.redbullmusicacademy.com/2015/09/zulu-nation-radio-feature.

"Fall '84 Ratings Wars." *Radio and Records*, November 16, 1984, 52.

"Fates and Fortunes." *Broadcasting*, September 15, 1980, 109.

"FCC Finale: Taking Action on HVN, FM Subcarriers, Daytimers." *Broadcasting*, August 9, 1982, 26–27.

"FCC Lifts Three RKO Licenses, 13 More in Jeopardy." *Broadcasting*, January 28, 1987, 27.

"58 Blacks Buying Station, WBLS-FM." *New York Amsterdam News*, October 13, 1973, a1, a3.

Ford, Hannah. "Mr. Magic Interview May, 1988." https://davidlubich.net/2016/01/08/mr-magic (accessed May 9, 2018).

"Foreign-Language Outlet Finds Support for Fight in Court over Lost License." *Broadcasting*, November 29, 1976, 30.

"For the Record." *Broadcasting*, April 15, 1963, 86.

"For the Record." *Broadcasting*, August 28, 1972, 41.

Foti, Laura. "Urban Programmers Blast Study: 'Street Ears,' Not Research, Called Key to Success." *Billboard*, September 10, 1983, 12.

"Fowler's Minority Prescription." *Radio and Records*, October 18, 1985, 30.

Freeman, Kim. "At WBLS, Kirkland Looks For New Black Talent." *Billboard*, October 10, 1987, 19.

Freeman, Kim. "Featured Programming." *Billboard,* July 13, 1985, 19.

Freeman, Kim. "New Rap Show in Gotham: 'Jive 106' Debuts on WNWK." *Billboard*, July 6, 1985, 16.

Freeman, Kim. "Radio: Featured Programming." *Billboard*, June 15, 1985, 23.

Freeman, Kim. "Vox Jox." *Billboard,* June 29, 1985, 16.

Freeman, Wanda. "DST Sparks New Orleans Debate." *Billboard*, September 4, 1982, 20.

Frere-Jones, Sasha. "RIP Mr. Magic." *New Yorker*, October 2, 2009. https://www.newyorker.com/culture/sasha-frere-jones/r-i-p-mr-magic.

Hunter-Gault, Charlayne. "Sutton Supporters Link Loss to Beame Running Again and Vote Delay." *New York Times,* September 9, 1977, 30.

Gent, George. "Unit Formed by Sutton and Jones Buys WLIB-AM." *New York Times*, July 15, 1971, 63.

George, Nelson. "Arbitron DST Use Aids WBLX Ratings." *Billboard*, August 21, 1982, 18.

George, Nelson. "Bad Rap for NYC Rap Concert? Arrests May Have been Unrelated." *Billboard*, August 9, 1986.

George, Nelson. "BMA Puts Spotlight on Format Direction." *Billboard*, June 19, 1982, 3, 27.

George, Nelson. "Club Play Opens Gwen Guthrie's 'Padlock.'" *Billboard*, August 17, 1985, 58.

George, Nelson. "NAB to Spotlight Urban Contemporary." *Billboard*, September 4, 1982, 4.

George, Nelson. "Spoken Here: 1987, The Year in Music and Video." *Billboard,* December 26, 1987, y-14.

George, Nelson. "WKTU Carves Its Own Niche, NY Leader Takes 'Offbeat' Slant on Urban Format." *Billboard*, October 23, 1982, 22.

Gibbs, Vernon. "Indie Labels: Players with the Rap Attack Making the Most Impact—and It's Not Just for the Money." *Billboard*, June 18, 1988, B-7, B-18.

Gibbs, Vernon. "New York Radio and the Big Beat: Part II." *New York Amsterdam News*, July 23, 1975, D20.

Gibbs, Vernon. "New York Radio and the Big Beat, Part III." *New York Amsterdam News*, July 30, 1975, 49.

Goodman, George, Jr. "Sutton the Media Man, Stirring Controversy." *New York Times*, October 11, 1972, 45.

Gould, Jack. "Methods of Covering King Slaying Vary Widely: Most Outlets Break in with Special Reports, Negro Radio Stations in City Call for Calm." *New York Times*, April 6, 1968, 79.

Gould, Jack. "Radio-TV: Broadcasters Catch Mood of a Nation." *New York Times*, April 8, 1968, 95.

Grein, Paul. "'Disco Still Picking the Top R&B Hits'—Zager." *Billboard*, August 16, 1980, 54.

Grein, Paul. "Radio Needs Flexible AOR/Crossover Format." *Billboard,* August 16, 1980, 54.

"Growth Market in Black Radio." *Broadcasting,* January 24, 1972, 16–21.

Hall, Claude. "Vox Jox." *Billboard*, August 10, 1974, 30.

Hall, Doug. "Cossman Low Profile Fades with Disco Rage." *Billboard*, December 23, 1978, 20.

Hall, Doug. "Heads Roll as Disco Sound Dominates N.Y." *Billboard,* July 7, 1979, 4.

Hall, Doug. "NY WKTU Drops, But Still Dominates." *Billboard*, March 17, 1979, 30.

Hall, Doug. "NY WXLO-FM Turns from Teens to Adult Contemporary." *Billboard*, June 7, 1980, 22.

Hall, Doug. "Radio Deregulation Big Topic at NRBA Parley." *Billboard,* September 30, 1978, 1, 19.

Hall, Doug. "R&B Programming Hides Extinct Disco." *Billboard*, July 18, 1980, 25.

Hall, Doug. "2 Outlets Battling for 'Mellow Rock' Listeners. At WKTU, More Hits Are Added." *Billboard,* June 3, 1978, 36.

Hall, Doug. "Urban Radio: Up or Down in Gotham." *Billboard*, January 15, 1983, 1, 10.

Hall, Doug. "WBLS's FM Challenge." *Billboard*, June 24, 1978, 24.

Hall, Doug. "WKTU's Disco Format Hottest in New York." *Billboard*, September 16, 1978, 1, 20.

Hall, Doug. "WKTU's Disco Is NY King, Mediatrend Supports WKTU-FM at Crest." *Billboard*, December 23, 1978, 5, 20.

Hall, Doug. "WBLS- FM Leads NY Mart." *Billboard*, March 29, 1980, 32.

Hall, Doug. "Word 'Disco' Dirty in New York Radio." *Billboard,* December 8, 1987, 24.

Halpern, Donna L. "Radio Downplays Blackness: Urban Image Blends Audiences." *Billboard*, June 5, 1982, BM-6.

Harrison, Susan. "Radio Prices Climb the Charts." In J. H. Duncan, *American Radio, Tenth Anniversary Edition, 1976–1986*, B-29–B-33.

Holland, Bill. "Washington Roundup: Fowler Stumps for Deregulation." *Billboard*, November 6, 1982, 15.

"How Harlem Heard the Mayor's Speech." *New York Amsterdam News*, August 1, 1964, 1.

Ireland, Doug. "The Wizard of Ooze." *New York Magazine*, January, 31, 1977, 6.

"It's Traditional R&B Getting More Airplay." *Billboard,* February 9, 1980, 1, 20.

"It surprised me . . ." *Broadcasting*, August 30, 1982, 2.

Iverem, Esther. "Violence Plagues New Latin Quarter." *New York Times,* September 7, 1987, 23.

Jacobs, Shayna, Ben Kochman, Michael O'Keefe, and Rich Shapiro. "Afrika Bambaataa Sex Abuse Accuser Ronald Savage Details Years of Torment Following Hip-Hop Icon's Molestation: 'He Damaged Me.'" *New York Daily News*, April 9, 2016, https://www.nydailynews.com/news/national/afrika-bambaataa-sex-abuse-accuser-ronald-savage-speaks-article-1.2594599 (accessed January 31, 2022).

Jefferies, Ira. "Police Action at Garden Frightens Concert Goers." *New York Amsterdam News*, August 9, 1985.

"Jencks Picked to Head 'NewCo.'" *Broadcasting*, August 18, 1980, 30.

Joe, Radcliffe. "Disco Thriving in Heart of America." *Billboard*, August 30, 1980, 15.

Jones, Alex S. "FCC Raises Limit on Total Stations Under One Owner." *New York Times*, July 27, 1984, 1.

Kimbro, Dennis, and Napoleon Hill. "Profiting through Self-Reliance." *Black Enterprise*, November 1992, 111.

Knowles, Clayton. "Sutton Elected Manhattan Borough President; Will Serve Until Dec. 31–He Is Nominated for 3-Year Term Starting Then." *New York Times*, September 14, 1966, 40.

Kozak, Roman. "A People's Station—Not Black, New York WBLS- FM Exec Says." *Billboard*, March 11, 1978, 30.

Krasnow, Erwin. "1976–1986, A Turbulent Decade for Communications Lawyers or Radio Lawyering and Other Oxymorons." In J. H. Duncan, *American Radio, Tenth Anniversary Issue, 1976–1986*, B-210–B-214.

Krebs, Albin. "Ownership of WLIB Is Passing into Blacks' Hands." *New York Times*, June 27, 1972, 83.

Kreps, Daniel. "Afrika Bambaataa Sued for Sexual Abuse, Sex Trafficking." *Rolling Stone*, September 10, 2021, https://www.rollingstone.com/music/music-news/afrika-bambaataa-accused-sexual-abuse-sex-trafficking-new-lawsuit-1222888/ (accessed January 31, 2022).

"Late News: Pulses." *Radio and Records*, December 13, 1974, 3, 26.

Law, Bob. "Letter to the Editor: Sir-Mix-A-Lot." *Cash Box*, February 2, 1987, 38.

Levy, Clifford J. "Harlem Protest of Rap Lyrics Draws Debate and Steamroller." *New York Times*, June 6, 1993, 39.

Lewis, Donald J. "A Foreign Air." *New York Magazine*, February 7, 1983, 9.

Love, Walt. "Happy New Year: Year-End Action Wrap-Up." *Radio and Records*, January 6, 54.

Love, Walt. "KSOL's Urban Contemporary Approach." *Radio and Records*, July 23, 1982, 26.

Love, Walt. "Urban Contemporary News." *Radio and Records*, January 9, 1987, 53.

Love, Walt. "Urban Radio News." *Radio and Records*, June 23, 1989, 57.

Love, Walt. "'Urban vs. Neckbone': The Changing Sound of Black Radio." *Radio and Records*, April 29, 1983, 43.

Love, Walt. "WGCI Takes Over Chicago. Barry Mayo Claims That Black Music Has Vast General Market Appeal and His Ratings Back Him Up." *Radio and Records*, February 20, 1981, 3, 58.

Love, Walt. "Words of Wisdom: Oral History, 1985." *Radio and Records*, December 20, 1985, 50.

Love, Walt. "WRKS's Urban Format No. 1 in the Big Apple." *Radio and Records*, May 11, 1984, 52.

Lyhall, Sarah. "11 Youths Wounded in and near 2 Nightspots." *New York Times*, December 27, 1988, B-3.

Magid, Beverly. "Listening Post." *Record World*, January 20, 1973, 14.

"Majors Emulate Indies." *Billboard*, August 11, 1984, D-14.

Marriott, Michel. "Harlem Pastor to Campaign against Rap Lyrics." *New York Times,* May 8, 1993, 24.

Marriott, Michel. "One Is Killed and 12 Are Injured as LI Rap Concert Turns Violent." *New York Times*, September 12, 1988, A-1.

Martin, Douglas. "Percy E. Sutton, Political Trailblazer, Dies at 89." *New York Times*, December 27, 2009, 1.

McKee, Clarence. "Radio Regulation: Don't Count Your Chickens." *Broadcast Programming and Production*, September 1979, 5, 35.

"Meet Lee Simonson." *Broadcasting*, September 9, 1980, 79.

Moore, Marie. "Ain't No Stoppin' McFadden and Whitehead." *New York Amsterdam News*, August 4, 1979, 27.

Moore, Marie. "Frankie: Glad to Be Back." *New York Amsterdam News*, January 27, 1979, 21.

Moore, Marie. "WBLS's Frankie Crocker: Radio Industry's Enigma." *New York Amsterdam News*, May 29, 1982, 34.

Murray, James P. "Frankie Crocker Finds Being No. 1 in New York Means Some Listen, Others Turn You Off." *New York Amsterdam News*, December 14, 1974, D1.

Murray, James P. "Lampell Wants to Reach the People." *New York Amsterdam News*, June 10, 1972, D1.

"Mutual Eyeing New York Buy." *Broadcasting*, May 6, 1974, 10.

Myers, Steven Lee. "WBLS-FM to Stop Playing Violent Songs." *New York Times*, December 5, 1993, 52.

"Name Change for WXLO; to be WRKS." *Billboard,* June 6, 1981, 29.

"The Nation's 100 Top Black Businesses." *Black Enterprise*, June 1973, 29–35.

"NBN In on, Mutual Out of WLIB Buy." *Broadcasting,* June 10, 1974, 7.

"NY WABC-AM Spurts Ahead of WBLS-FM in Arbitron Book." *Billboard*, September 16, 1978, 1, 20.

"The Old Medium's Learning New Tricks." *Broadcasting*, August 30, 1982, 44.

Olmstead, Larry. "From a Powerful Pulpit, a Moral Warrior Takes Aim." *New York Times,* June 5, 1993, 23.

Olson, Yvonne. "As Rap Goes Pop, Some Say Black Radio Is Missing Out." *Billboard*, June 18, 1988, 1.

"On New York's WLIB: Guzman Makes Music Part of Talk Show Mix." *Billboard*, August 14, 1982, 53.

"The Other (FM) Shoe Drops." *Broadcasting*, October 21, 1974, 9.

Palmer, Robert. "Rap Music, Despite Adult Fire, Broadens Its Teen-Age Base." *New York Times*, September 21, 1986, 23.

Penchasky, Alan. "Chicago WGCI-FM Killing Disco Format." *Billboard*, April 4, 1980, 29.

"Penetrating the Barriers of Harlem's Ghetto." *Broadcasting,* May 22, 1967, 87.

"Percy Sutton Sets the Record Straight." *New York Amsterdam News*, June 20, 1981, 36.

Pileggi, Nicholas. "Guess Who's Coming to Gracie Mansion." *New York Magazine*, May 27, 1974, 39.

"Playback: Switching." *Broadcasting*, October 20, 1980, 45.

Policano, Chris. "An Interview with Frankie Crocker." *New York Amsterdam News*, March 13, 1976, D2.

Prescott, Pat. "Radio: A Business of Idea, A Conversation with Emmis/New York's Barry Mayo." *Radio and Records*, January 21, 2005, 53.

"The Prices FMs Are Fetching These Days." *Broadcasting,* October 7, 1974, 52.

"Programmers Discuss 'KISS of Success.'" *Billboard*, September 4, 1984, 20.

"Public Enemy: A Body Block on 'Buppies.'" 1987. Box 8, folder 30, collection no. 8092, Adler Hip-Hop Archive, Cornell University.

Puig, Claudia, and Steve Hochmann. "Top-Rated Station Bans 3 Derogatory Words in Rap." *Los Angeles Times*, December 9, 1993. https://www.latimes.com/archives/la-xpm-1993-12-09-mn-65503-story.html.

"Radio's Frankie Crocker Fined." *Billboard*, July 8, 1978, 18.

"Radio: Summer Arbitron Results." *Billboard*, October 15, 1983, 15.

Rahsaan, Anthony. "Guest Commentary: Rap Music and Stereotypes." *Cash Box*, July 2, 1988, 18.

Ravo, Nick. "1 Killed, 5 Injured, and 16 Arrested at Rap Concert." *New York Times*, November 26, 1987, B-4.

"Rejected WHBI Claims FCC Didn't Dig Deep Enough for Facts." *Broadcasting,* July, 19, 1976, 37.

"RKO Decision is Formally Promulgated." *Broadcasting*, June 9, 1980, 30, 34.

RKO General, Inc. v. FCC, 670 F.2d 215—Court of Appeals, Dist. of Columbia Circuit 1981.

"RKO Names Mayo PD." *Radio and Records,* September 17, 1982, 1.

Robinson, Marjorie. "The World of Frankie Crocker Just Simply Can't Believe It!" *New York Amsterdam News*, August 14, 1976, A3.

Rogers, Charles. "Krushing Rap's Bad Rep Groove." *New York Amsterdam News*, January 4, 1986, 22.

Rosa, Jerry, and Mark Kriegel. "Concert Tipsters Lead Cops to 9 Nailed in Rap Rampage." *New York Daily News*, September 19, 1988, 17.

"RPC V: Format by Format." *Broadcasting*, September 6, 1982, 33.

Sacks, Leo. "Burnout Is Primary Concern for Urban Contemporary Formats." *Billboard,* July 17, 1982, 22.

Sacks, Leo. "In WBLS 'Boycott': Demand Crocker's Ouster; Sutton Defends Playlist." *Billboard*, July 4, 1981, 10.

Sacks, Leo. "The 'Magic' Is Missing from Two NY Stations." *Billboard*, December 18, 1982, 52.

Sacks, Leo. "WBLS Gets Mr. Magic *Rap Attack*." *Billboard*, July 31, 1982, 16.

Sacks, Leo. "Whither Urban Contemporary? New York Ratings Point to Volatility of Format." *Billboard*, January 29, 1983, 15, 90.

"Seek Definition for Urban Contemporary." *Billboard*, August 29, 1981, 23.

Smith, Troy L. "An Interview with Se'Divine The Master Mind of the Legendary Supreme Team Show on Radio Station WHBI." OldSchoolHipHop .com, fall 2007. http://www.oldschoolhiphop.com/interviews/sedevine .htm (accessed May 16, 2017).

Smith, Troy L. "Hip-Hop History: Kool DJ Red Alert Gives the Ultimate Interview." http://hiphopandpolitics.com/2013/10/04/hip-hop-history -kool-dj-red-alert-gives-ultimate-interview/ (accessed January 22, 2022).

Smooth, Jay. "Mister Magic & Mister Cee Interview, 1995." Hiphopmusic .com. http://www.hiphopmusic.com/2009/10/mister_magic_mister_cee _interv.html (accessed September 17, 2018).

Speed, Bill. "Disco's Challenge for Black Radio, Parts I and II." *Radio and Records*, December 8, 1978, 44.

Speed, Bill. "WGCI/Chicago—Taking the Urban Contemporary Lead." *Radio and Records,* February 20, 1981, 58.

"Stations Crack Down on Rappers." *Journal Times*, December 10, 1993. https://journaltimes.com/news/national/stations-crack-down-on -rappers/article_8e30146d-2824-512e-8f4c-51dfeff11eab.html.

Stuart, Dan. "The Rap against Rap at Black Radio: Professional Suicide or Cultural Smokescreen?" *Billboard*, December 24, 1988, R-8.

"Suave Borough Chief: Percy Ellis Sutton." *New York Times,* September 20, 1966, 42.

"Sutton Decides: Will Run Stations." *New York Amsterdam News*, January 14, 1978, A-1, B-6.

"Sutton Is NAACP President." *New York Amsterdam News*, December 24, 1960, 1.

"Sutton Selling Interest in Newspaper." *New York Times*, November 13, 1975, 45.

Tannenbaum, Frederic D. "Monday Memo: Financing Broadcast and Cable Properties in the Wake of Deregulation." *Broadcasting*, March 11, 1985, 22.

Tapley, Mel. "Does Rap Music Create Violence or Is It Just a Bad Rap?" *New York Amsterdam News*, October 15, 1988, 28.

Tate, Greg. "Hiphop Turns 30." *Village Voice*, December 28, 2004. https:// www.villagevoice.com/2004/12/28/hiphop-turns-30/.

Taylor, Cassandra. "WBLS: The Successful Voice with Mass Appeal Broadcasting." *New York Amsterdam News*, August 13, 1977, D-8.

"3 Shot and 5 Arrested near the Latin Quarter." *New York Times*, August 17, 1987, 6.

"Urban Sounds Pull Emotional Reaction." *Billboard*, October 18, 1980, 23.

"Van Deerlin Wins NRBA Audience with Talk of Total Deregulation." *Broadcasting,* October 17, 1977, 26.

"Vintage MOR Behind Rise of WBLS-FM." *Billboard*, January 12, 1980, 21.

"Vox Jox." *Billboard*, January 21, 1984, 22.

"Washington Watch—WHBI Bids Open." *Broadcasting*, February 22, 1982, 68.

"Wave of the Future? Urban Contemporary Format Growth Sparking New Concerns." *Billboard*, January 9, 1982, 15.

Wedge, David. "Afrika Bambaataa Allegedly Molested Young Men For Decades. Why Are the Accusations Only Coming out Now?" *Vice*, October 10, 2016. https://www.vice.com/en/article/8xx5yp/afrika-bambaataa-sexual-abuse-zulu-nation-ron-savage-hassan-campbell (accessed January 31, 2022).

"WBLS-FM Hikes Superiority In NY; LA KMET-FM Tumbles." *Billboard*, July 19, 1980, 21.

"WBLS(FM) Sale in Jeopardy." *Broadcasting*, August 12, 1974, 8.

"WBLS Top NY Station." *New York Amsterdam News*, July 23, 1975, D2.

"WKTU Flied Burkhart Disco Flag." *Billboard*, August 26, 1978, 50.

"WLIB Nears Turnover to Black Group." *New York Amsterdam News*, May 6, 1972, A9.

"WLIB Sold: Sutton-Jones Group Expands." *New York Amsterdam News*, July 17, 1971, A1, D11.

"WRKS Is New York." *Broadcasting,* November 16, 1981, 99.

"WRKS Shows Growth in Gotham's 3-Way Urban Contemporary Race." *Billboard*, November 28, 1981, 20.

Wyman, Bill. "Hip Hop Comes to Chicago." *Chicago Reader*, September, 1, 1994. https://chicagoreader.com/music/hip-hop-comes-to-fm/ (accessed January 23, 2022).

Books and Journals

Adorno, Theodore W. *Current of Music*. New York: Polity, 2009.

Ahearn, Charlie, and Jim Fricke. *Yes Yes Y'All: The Experience Music Project Oral History of Hip-Hop's First Decade*. New York: Da Capo, 2002.

Ahmed, Sarah. *The Cultural Politics of Emotion*. London: Routledge, 2004.

Althusser, Louis. *On The Reproduction of Capitalism: Ideology and Ideological State Apparatuses*. London: Verso, [1971] 2001.

Anderson, Benedict. *Imagined Communities: Reflections on the Origins of Nationalism*. London: Verso, 1991.

Appadurai, Arjun. "Archive and Aspiration." In *Information Is Alive*, edited by Joke Brouwer and Arjen Mulder, 14–25. Rotterdam: v2_Publishing/ NAI, 2003.

Arthur, Craig, and Anthony Kwame Harrison. "Reading Billboard 1979– 1989: Exploring Rap Music's Emergence through the Music Industry's Most Influential Trade Publication." *Popular Music and Society* 34, no. 3: 309–27.

Austin, Joe. *Taking the Train: How Graffiti Art Became an Urban Crisis in New York City*. New York: Columbia University Press, 2002.

Avery, Robert K., and Robert Pepper. "An Institutional History of Public Broadcasting." *Journal of Communication* 30, no. 3 (September 1980): 126–38.

Avery, Robert K., and Alan G. Stavitsky. "The FCC and the Public Interest: A Selective Critique of U.S. Telecommunications Policy-Making." In *Public Broadcasting and the Public Interest*, edited by Michael P. McCauley, B. Lee Artz, DeeDee Hallock, Paul E. Peterson, 52–61. Armonk, NY: M. E. Sharpe, 2003.

Baker, Edwin C. *Media, Markets, and Democracy*. Cambridge: Cambridge University Press, 2002.

Baldwin, Davarian L. "Black Empires, White Desires: The Spatial Politics of Identity in the Age of Hip-Hop." In *That's the Joint: The Hip-Hop Studies Readers*, edited by Murray Forman and Marc Anthony Neal, 159–76. New York: Routledge.

Ball, Jared. *I Mix What I Like: A Mixtape Manifesto*. New York: AK, 2011.

Barlow, William. *Voice Over: The Making of Black Radio*. Philadelphia: Temple University Press, 1998.

Basu, Dapinnita, and Pnina Werbner. "Bootstrap Capitalism and the Culture Industries: A Critique of Invidious Comparisons in the Study of Ethnic Entrepreneurship." *Ethnic and Racial Studies* 24, no. 2 (March 2001): 236–62.

Bessire, Lucas, and Daniel Fisher. "The Anthropology of Radio Fields." *Annual Review of Anthropology*, no. 42 (July 2013): 364.

Bessire, Lucas, and Daniel Fisher. "Introduction: Radio Fields." In Bessire and Fisher, *Radio Fields*, 1–47.

Bessire, Lucas, and Daniel Fisher, eds. *Radio Fields: Wireless Sound in the Twenty-First Century*. New York: New York University Press, 2012.

Bijsterveld, Karin, and José van Dijck. "Introduction." In Bijsterveld and Dijck, *Sound Souvenirs*, 11–24.

Bijsterveld, Karin, and José van Dijck, eds. *Sound Souvenirs: Audio Technologies, Memory, and Cultural Practices*. Amsterdam: Amsterdam University Press, 2009.

Bijsterveld, Karin, and Annelies Jacobs. "Storing Sound Souvenirs: The Multi-Sited Domestication of the Tape Recorder." In Bijsterveld and van Dijck, *Sound Souvenirs*, 25–42.

205

Bohlman, Andrea F., and Peter McMurry. "Tape: Or, Rewinding the Phonographic Regime." *Twentieth-Century Music* 14, no. 1 (2017): 3–24.

Bolter, Jay David, and Richard Grusin. *Remediation: Understanding New Media*. Cambridge, MA: MIT Press, 1998.

Bordin, Elisa. "Expanding Lines: Negotiating Space, Body, and Language Limits in Train Graffiti." *Rhizomes*, no. 25 (2013). http://www.rhizomes.net/issue25/bordin.html (accessed November 16, 2021).

Brackett, David. *Categorizing Sound: Genre and Twentieth-Century Popular Music*. Berkeley: University of California Press, 2016.

Breithaupt, Don, and Jeff Breithaupt. *Precious and Few: Pop Music of the Early '70s*. New York: St. Martin's, 1996.

Bronfman, Alejandra. *Isles of Noise: Sonic Media in the Caribbean*. Chapel Hill: University of North Carolina Press, 2016.

Browne, Simone. *Dark Matters: On the Surveillance of Blackness*. Durham, NC: Duke University Press, 2015

Butler, Judith. *Excitable Speech: A Politics of the Performative*. New York: Routledge, 1997.

Butler, Judith. *Precarious Life: The Power of Mourning and Violence*. New York: Verso, 2004.

Cantor, Louis. *Wheelin' on Beale: How WDIA-Memphis Became the Nation's First All-Black Radio Station and Created the Sound that Changed America*. New York: Pharos, 1992.

Chamberlayne, Daniel J. *Kingdom Hall No More*. Authorhouse, 2008.

Chang, Jeff. *Can't Stop Won't Stop: A History of the Hip-Hop Generation*. New York: St. Martin's, 2005.

Charnas, Dan. *The Big Payback: The History of the Hip-Hop Business*. New York: Penguin, 2010.

Charnas, Dan. "Long Kiss Goodbye: How Fear of a Black Planet Killed a Black Radio Station." News One, May 12, 2002. https://newsone.com/2005493/long-kiss-goodbye-charnas-987-kiss-fm-wbls/.

Cheng, William. "Black Noise, White Ears: Resilience, Rap, and the Killing of Jordan Davis." *Current Musicology* 102 (April 2018): 115–89.

Chenier, Elise. "Privacy Anxieties: Ethics versus Activism in Archiving Lesbian Oral History Online." *Radical History Review*, no. 122 (May 2015): 129–41.

Chignell, Hugh. *Key Terms in Radio Studies*. New York: SAGE, 2009.

Coddington, Amy. "'Check Out the Hook While My DJ Revolves It': How the Music Industry Made Rap into Pop in the Late 1980s." In *The Oxford Handbook of Hip Hop Studies*, forthcoming. New York: Oxford University Press, 2018.

Coleman, Brian. *Check the Technique: Liner Notes for Hip-Hop Junkies*. New York: Villard, 2007.

Cruse, Harold. *The Crisis of the Negro Intellectual: A Historical Analysis of the Failure of Black Leadership*. New York: New York Review of Books, 2005.

Denning, Michael. "Wageless Life." *New Left Review*, no. 66 (December 2010): 79–97.

D'Errico, Michael A. "Behind the Beat: Technical and Practical Aspects of Instrumental Hip-Hop Composition." Master's thesis, Tufts University, 2011.

Derthick, Martha, and Paul J. Quirk. *The Politics of Deregulation*. Washington, DC: Brookings Institution.

Dingle, Derek T. *Black Enterprise Titans of the BE 100s: Black CEOs Who Redefined and Conquered American Business*. New York: John Wiley & Sons, 1999.

Douglass, Susan. *Listening In: Radio in the American Imagination*. Minneapolis: University of Minnesota Press, 2004.

Echols, Alice. *Hot Stuff: Disco and the Remaking of American Culture*. New York: W. W. Norton, 2010.

Ehrick, Christine. *Radio and the Gendered Soundscape: Women and Broadcasting in Argentina and Uruguay, 1930–1950*. New York: Cambridge University Press, 2015.

Ely, Melvin Patrick. *The Adventures of Amos 'n' Andy: A Social History of an American Phenomenon*. Charlottesville: University of Virginia Press, 1991.

Enkelis, Liane, Karen Olsen, and Marion Lewenstein. *On Our Own Terms: Portraits of Women Business Leaders*. San Francisco: Berrett Koehler, 1995.

Eshun, Kodwo. *More Brilliant Than the Sun: Adventures in Sonic Fiction*. London: Quartet, 1998.

Faier, Lieba, and Lisa Rofel. "Ethnographies of Encounter." *Annual Review of Anthropology* 43 (October 2014): 363–77.

Fanon, Franz. *A Dying Colonialism*. New York: Monthly Review, 1965.

Ferretti, Fred. "The White Captivity of Black Radio." *Columbia Journalism Review* 9, no. 2 (Summer 1970): 35–39.

Fisher, Daniel. "Experiencing Self-Abstraction: Studio Production and Vocal Consciousness." In *Phenomenology in Anthropology*, edited by Kalpana Ram, Christopher Houston, and Michael Jackson, 153–74. Bloomington: Indiana University Press, 2015.

Fisher, Daniel. *The Voice and Its Doubles: Music and Media in Northern Australia*. Durham, NC: Duke University Press, 2016

Forman, Murray. *The 'Hood Comes First: Race, Space, and Place in Rap and Hip-Hop*. Middletown, CT: Wesleyan University Press, 2002.

Fraser, Colin, and Sonia Restrepo Estrada. *Community Radio Handbook*. Bangkok: Unesco, 2001.

George, Nelson. *Hip-Hop America*. New York: Viking, 1998.

Gershon, Ilana. "Neoliberal Agency." *Current Anthropology* 52, no. 4 (August 2011): 537–55.

Gibson-Graham, J. K. *The End of Capitalism (As We Knew It): A Feminist Critique of Political Economy*. Minneapolis: University of Minnesota Press, 2006.

Gilroy, Paul. *The Black Atlantic: Modernity and Double Consciousness*. Cambridge, MA: Harvard University Press, 1993.

Ginsburg, Faye. "Radio Fields: An Afterword." In Bessire and Fisher, *Radio Fields*, 268–78.

Gitelman, Lisa. *Always Already New: Media, History, and the Data of Culture*. Cambridge, MA: MIT Press, 2006.

Gitelman, Lisa. *Paper Knowledge: Towards a Media History of Documents*. Durham, NC: Duke University Press, 2014.

Gladney, Marvin J. "Black Arts and the Hip-Hop Movement." *African American Review* 29, no. 2 (Summer 1995): 291–301.

Glissant, Édouard. *Poetics of Relations*. Translated by Betsy Wing. Ann Arbor: University of Michigan Press, 1997.

Gold, Steven J. "A Critical Race Theory Approach to Black American Entrepreneurship." *Ethnic and Racial Studies* 39, no. 9 (2016): 1679–718.

Graeber, David. *Towards an Anthropological Theory of Value: The False Coin of Our Own Dreams*. New York: Palgrave Macmillan, 2001.

Hager, Steve. "Afrika Bambaataa's Hip-Hop." In *And It Don't Stop: The Best American Hip-Hop Journalism of the Last 25 Years*, edited by Raquel Cepeda, 12–26. New York: Farrar, Straus and Giroux, 2004.

Haraway, Donna. *When Species Meet*. Minneapolis: University of Minnesota Press, 2007.

Harrison, Anthony Kwame. "Black College Radio on Predominantly White Campuses: A 'Hip-Hop Era' Student-Authored Inclusion Initiative." *Africology: The Journal of Pan African Studies* 9, no. 8 (October 2016): 135–54.

Harrison, Anthony Kwame. "'Cheaper than a CD, Plus We Really Mean It': Bay Area Underground Hip-Hop Tapes as Subcultural Artefacts." *Popular Music* 25, no. 2 (2006): 283–301.

Hartley, John. "Radiocracy: Sound and Citizenship." *International Journal of Cultural Studies* 3, no. 2 (2000): 153–59.

Hartman, Saidiya. "Venus in Two Acts." *Small Axe* 12, no. 2 (2008): 1–14.

Heller, Michael C. *Loft Jazz: Improvising New York in the 1970s*. Berkeley: University of California Press, 2016.

Hendy, David. *Radio in the Global Age*. London: Polity, 2000.

Hill, Patricia Collins. *From Black Power to Hip-Hop: Racism, Nationalism, and Feminism*. Philadelphia: Temple University Press, 2006.

Hilmes, Michele. *Radio Voices: American Broadcasting, 1922–1952*. Minneapolis: University of Minnesota Press, 1997.

Hirschkind, Charles. *The Ethical Soundscape: Cassette Sermons and Islamic Counterpublics*. New York: Columbia University Press, 2006.

Hobson, Janell, and Dianne Bartlow. "Representin': Women, Hip-Hop, and Popular Music." *Meridians: Feminism, Race, Transnationalism* 8, no. 1 (2007): 1–14.

Holmes Smith, Christopher. "'I Don't Like to Dream about Getting Paid': Representations of Social Mobility and the Emergence of the Hip-Hop Mogul." *Social Text 77* 21, no. 4 (Winter 2003): 69–79.

Holt, Jennifer. *Empires of Entertainment: Media Industries and the Politics of Deregulation, 1980–1996*. New Brunswick, NJ: Rutgers University Press, 2011.

Horwitz, Robert. *The Irony of Regulatory Reform*. New York: Oxford University Press, 1989.

Huff, W. A. *Regulating the Future: Broadcasting Technology and Governmental Control*. Westport, CT: Greenwood, 2001.

Iton, Richard. *In Search of the Black Fantastic: Politics and Popular Culture in the Post–Civil Rights Era*. New York: Oxford University Press, 2008.

Jackson, Hal, with James Haskins, Kuwana M. Haulsey, and Mel Watkins. *The House That Jack Built*. Phoenix, AZ: Colossus, 2001.

Jackson, John A. *Beyond the Hustle: Seventies Social Dancing, Discotheque Culture and the Emergence of the Contemporary Club Dancer*. Urbana: University of Illinois Press, 2009.

Jackson, John A. *A House on Fire: The Rise and Fall of Philadelphia Soul*. New York: Oxford University Press, 2004.

Jaji, Tsitsi Ella. *Africa in Stereo: Modernism, Music, and Pan-African Solidarity*. New York: Oxford University Press, 2015.

Jaker, Bill, Frank Sulek, and Peter Kanze. *The Airwaves of New York: Illustrated Histories of 156 AM Stations in the Metropolitan Area, 1921–1996*. Jefferson, NC: McFarland, 1998.

Jenkins, Sacha, Jeff Mao, and Elliot Wilson. *Ego Trip's Book of Rap Lists*. New York: Griffin, 1999.

Jensen, Bas. "Tape Cassettes and Former Selves: How Mix Tapes Mediate Memories." In Bijsterveld and van Dijck, *Sound Souvenirs*, 43–54.

Kahn, Douglass, and Gregory Whitehead. *Wireless Imagination: Sound, Radio, and the Avante-Garde*. Cambridge, MA: MIT Press, 1992.

Kaplan, Danny. "Editing the Nation: How Radio Engineers Encode Israeli National Imaginaries." In Bessire and Fisher, *Radio Fields*, 89–107.

Katz, Mark. *Groove Music: The Art and Culture of the Hip-Hop DJ*. New York: Oxford University Press, 2012.

Keeling, Kara. "Looking for M—: Queer Temporality, Black Political Possibility, and Poetry from the Future." *GLQ: A Journal of Gay and Lesbian Studies* 15, no. 4 (2009): 565–82.

Keith, Michael C., and Joseph M. Krause. *The Radio Station*. 2nd ed. Boston: Focal, 1989.

Kelley, Norman, ed. *Rhythm and Business: The Political Economy of Black Music*. New York: Akashic, 2005.

Keyes, Cheryl. *Rap Music and Street Consciousness*. Urbana: University of Illinois Press, 2002.

Klineberg, Eric. *Fighting for Air: The Battle to Control America's Media*. New York: Metropolitan Media, 2007.

Kohn, Eduardo. *How Forests Think: Towards an Anthropology Beyond the Human*. Berkeley: University of California Press, 2013.

Kosnick, Kira. "'Foreign Voices': Multicultural Broadcasting and Immigrant Representations at Germany's Radio MultiKulti." In Bessire and Fisher, *Radio Fields*, 179–96.

Krattenmaker, Thomas G., and Lucas A. Powe Jr. *Regulating Broadcast Programming*. Cambridge, MA: MIT Press, 1994.

Krims, Adam. *Rap Music and the Politics of Identity*. Cambridge: University of Cambridge Press, 2000.

Kunzel, Regina. "Queering Archives: A Roundtable Discussion." *Radial History Review,* no. 122 (May 2015): 211–31.

Labelle, Brandon. *Acoustic Territories: Sound Culture and Everyday Life*. New York: Bloomsbury, 2010.

Labelle, Brandon. "Transmission Culture." In *Re-Inventing Radio: Aspects of Radio as Art*, edited by Heidi Grundman, Elisabeth Zimmerman, Reinhard Braun, Dieter Daniels, Andreas Hirsch, and Anne Thurmann-Jajes, 63–86. Frankfurt: Revolver: 2008.

Lacey, Kate. *Listening Publics: The Politics and Experience of Listening in the Media Age*. Cambridge: Polity, 2013.

Larkin, Brian. *Signal and Noise: Media, Infrastructure, and Urban Culture in Nigeria*. Durham, NC: Duke University Press, 2008.

Lawrence, Tim. *Life and Death on the New York Dance Floor, 1979–1983*. Durham, NC: Duke University Press, 2016.

Lawrence, Tim. *Love Saves the Day: A History of American Dance Music Culture, 1970–1979*. Durham, NC: Duke University Press, 2003.

Levitt, Theodore. "Marketing Success Through Differentiation—Of Anything." *Harvard Business Review*, January 1980. Accessed January 22, 2022. https://hbr.org/1980/01/marketing-success-through-differentiation-of-anything.

Liu, Alan. "Imagining the New Media Encounter." In *A Companion to Digital Literary Studies*, edited by Ray Siemens and Susan Schreibman, 3–25. Malden, MA: Blackwell, 2007.

Manuel, Peter. *Cassette Culture: Popular Music and Technology in North India*. Chicago: University of Chicago Press, 1993.

McChesney, Robert W. *Capitalism and the Information Age: The Political Economy of the Global Communication Revolution*. New York: Monthly Review, 1998.

McKittrick, Kathleen. *Demonic Grounds: Black Women and the Cartographies of Struggle*. Minneapolis: University of Minnesota Press, 2006.

McKittrick, Kathleen, ed. *Sylvia Wynter: On Being Human as Praxis*. Durham, NC: Duke University Press, 2014.

Miller, Paul, ed. *Sound Unbound: Sampling Digital Music and Culture*. Cambridge, MA: MIT Press, 2008.

Mitchell, W. J. T., and Mark B. N. Hansen, eds. *Critical Terms for Media Studies*. Chicago: University of Chicago Press, 2010.

Montano, Ed. "'How do you know he's not playing Pac-Man while he's supposed to be DJing?': Technology, Formats, and the Digital Future of DJ Culture." *Popular Music* 29, no. 3 (2010): 397–416.

Moten, Fred. *In the Break: The Aesthetics of the Black Radical Tradition*. Minneapolis: University of Minnesota Press, 2003.

Neal, Mark Anthony. "Sold Out on Soul: The Corporate Annexation of Popular Music." *Popular Music and Society* 21, no. 3 (July 2008): 117–31.

Negus, Keith. "The Music Business and Rap: Between the Street and the Executive Suite." *Cultural Studies* 13, no. 3 (1999): 488–508.

Neilson, Brett, and Ned Rossiter. "From Precarity to Precariousness and Back Again." *Fibreculture Journal,* no. 5 (2005): http://journal.fibreculture .org/issue5/neilson_rossiter.html (accessed November 16, 2021).

Neilson, Brett, and Ned Rossiter. "Precarity as a Political Concept, or Fordism as Exception." *Theory, Culture, Society* 25, nos. 7–8 (2008): 51–72.

Newman, Mark Allen. "Entrepreneurs of Profits and Pride: From Black Appeal to Soul Radio." PhD diss., University of California, Los Angeles, 1986.

Nguyen, Mimi Thi. "Minor Threats: On Being in the Archive." *Radical History Review*, no. 122 (May 2015): 11–24.

Ogg, Alex. *The Men behind Def Jam: The Radical Rise of Russell Simmons and Rick Rubin*. New York: Omnibus, 2002.

Ouellette, Laurie. "'Take Responsibility for Yourself': *Judge Judy* and the Neoliberal Citizen." In *Reality TV: Remaking Television Culture*, edited by Susan Murray and Laurie Ouellette, 231–50. New York: New York University Press, 2004.

Piekut, Benjamin. *Experimentalism Otherwise: The New York Avant-Garde and Its Limits*. Berkeley: University of California Press, 2011.

Portes, Alejandro, and William Haller. "The Informal Economy." In *The Handbook of Economic Sociology*, edited by Neil J. Smelser and Richard Swedberg, 403–25. Princeton, NJ: Princeton University Press, 2005.

Radano, Ronald. *Lying Up a Nation: Race and Black Music.* Chicago: University of Chicago Press, 2003.

Razlogova, Elena. *The Listener's Voice: Early Radio and the American Public*. Philadelphia: University of Pennsylvania Press, 2012.

Roberts, Michael. "Papa's Got a Brand New Bag: Big Music's Post-Fordist Regime and the Role of Independent Music Labels." In *Rhythm and Business: The Political Economy of Black Music*, edited by Norman Kelley, 24–46. New York: Akashic Books, 2005.

Rodgers, Daniel T. *Age of Fracture*. Cambridge, MA: Belknap Press of Harvard University, 2011.

Rodriguez, Jos Manuel Ramos. "Indigenous Radio Stations in Mexico: A Catalyst for Social Cohesion and Cultural Strength." *Radio Journal: International Studies in Radio and Audio Media* 3, no. 3 (2005): 155–69.

Rohy, Valery. "In the Queer Archive: Fun Home." *GLQ* 16, no. 3 (2010): 341–61.

Rose, Tricia. *Hip-Hop Wars: What We Talk About When We Talk About Hip-Hop—and Why It Matters*. New York: Civitas, 2008.

Rose, Tricia. *Rap Music and Black Culture in Contemporary America*. Middletown, CT: Wesleyan University Press, 1994.

Russo, Alexander. *Points on the Dial: Golden Age Radio beyond the Networks*. Durham, NC: Duke University Press, 2010.

Russo, Alexander. "Tick Tock Goes the Musical Clock: Time Discipline and Early Morning Musical Programs." In *Radio's New Wave: Global Sounds in the Digital Era*, edited by Jason Loviglio and Michelle Hilmes, 194–208. New York: Routledge, 2013.

Saucier, Khalil, and Tyrone P. Woods. "Hip-Hop Studies in Black." *Journal of Popular Music Studies* 36, nos. 2–3 (2014): 268–94.

Schloss, Joseph. *Making Beats: The Art of Sample-Based Hip-Hop*. Middletown, CT: Wesleyan University Press, 2004.

Schulz, Dorothea. "Reconsidering Muslim Authority: Female 'Preachers' and the Ambiguities of Radio-Mediated Sermonizing in Mali." In Bessire and Fisher, *Radio Fields*, 108–23.

Shapiro, Peter. *Turn the Beat Around: The Secret History of Disco*. New York: Faber & Faber, 2005.

Sharpe, Christina. *In the Wake: On Blackness and Being*. Durham, NC: Duke University Press, 2016.

Simmons, Charlene. "Dear Radio Broadcaster: Fan Mail as a Form of Perceived Interactivity." *Journal of Broadcasting and Electronic Media* 53, no. 3 (September 2009): 444–59.

Smith, Christopher Holmes. "'I Don't Like to Dream About Getting Paid': Representations of Social Mobility and the Emergence of the Hip-Hop Mogul." *Social Text 77* 21, no. 4 (Winter 2003): 69–97.

Smith, Jacob. *Vocal Tracks: Performance and Sound Media*. Berkeley: University of California Press, 2008.

Smith, Reed W. "Charles Ferris: Jimmy Carter's FCC Innovator." *Journal of Radio and Auditory Media* 21, no. 1 (2014): 149–62.

Smitherman, Geneva. "'The Chains Remain the Same': Communicative Practice in the Hip-Hop Nation." *Journal of Black Studies* 28, no. 1 (September 1997): 3–25.

Smythe, Dallas W. "Communications: Blindspot of Western Marxism." *Canadian Journal of Political and Social Theory* 1, no. 3 (1977): 1–27.

Spillers, Hortense. *Black, White, and in Color: Essays on American Literature and Culture*. Chicago: University of Chicago Press, 2003.

Squire, Susan M. "Communities of the Air: Introducing the Radio World." In *Communities of the Air: Radio Century Radio Culture,* edited by Susan M. Squire, 1–38. Durham, NC: Duke University Press, 2001.

Stahl, Matt. *Unfree Masters: Popular Music and the Politics of Work*. Durham, NC: Duke University Press, 2012.

Sterne, Jonathan. *MP3: The Meaning of a Format*. Durham, NC: Duke University Press, 2012.

Sterne, Jonathan. "Preservation Paradox in Digital Audio." In Bijsterveld and van Dijck, *Sound Souvenirs*, 55–68.

Stewart, Kathleen. *Ordinary Affects*. Durham, NC: Duke University Press, 2007.

Stoever, Jennifer Lynn. "Crate Digging Begins at Home: Black and Latinx Women Collecting and Selecting Records in the 1960s and 1970s Bronx." In *The Oxford Handbook of Hip Hop Music*, online ed., edited by Justin D. Burton and Jason Lee Oakes. Oxford: Oxford University Press, 2018. DOI: 10.1093/oxfordhb/9780190281090.013.1.

Stoever, Jennifer Lynn. *The Sonic Color Line: Race and the Cultural Politics of Listening*. New York: New York University Press, 2016.

Taylor, Charles. "Modern Social Imaginaries." *Public Culture* 14, no. 1 (Winter 2002): 91–124.

Taylor, Diana. *The Archive and the Repertoire: Performing Cultural Memory in the Americas*. Durham, NC: Duke University Press, 2003.

Taylor, Timothy D. *The Sounds of Capitalism: Advertising, Music, and the Conquest of Culture*. Chicago: University of Chicago Press, 2012.

Toop, David. *The Rap Attack: African Jive to New York Hip-Hop*. Boston: South End, 1984.

Tsing, Anna. *Friction: An Ethnography of Global Connection*. Princeton, NJ: Princeton University Press, 2005.

Tsing, Anna. *The Mushroom at the End of the World: On the Possibility of Life in Capitalist Ruins*. Princeton, NJ: Princeton University Press, 2015.

Tsing, Anna. "Supply Chains and the Human Condition." *Rethinking Marxism: A Journal of Economics, Culture, and Society* 21, no. 2 (2009): 148–76.

Tsing, Anna. "Worlding the Matsutake Diaspora: Or, Can Actor-Network Theory Experiment with Holism?" In *Experiments in Holism: Theory and Practice in Contemporary Anthropology*, edited by Ton Otto and Nils Bubandt, 47–66. Malden, MA: Wiley and Blackwell, 2010.

Turner, Victor. *Blazing the Trail: Way Marks in the Exploration of Symbols*. Edited by Edith Turner. Tucson: University of Arizona Press, 1992.

Van Maas, Sander. "Scenes of Devastation: Interpellation, Finite and Infinite." In *Thresholds of Listening: Sound, Technics, Space*, edited by Sander van Mass, 51–69. New York: Fordham University Press, 2015.

Vogl, Joseph. *The Specter of Capital*. Stanford, CA: Stanford University Press, 2015.

Wagner, Bryan. *Disturbing the Peace: Black Culture and Police Power after Slavery*. Cambridge, MA: Harvard University Press, 2009.

Ward, Brian. *Radio and the Struggle for Civil Rights in the South*. Gainesville: University of Florida Press, 2004.

Warner, Michael. *Publics and Counterpublics*. New York: Zone, 2005.

Weheliye, Alexander G. *Phonographies: Grooves in Sonic Afro-Modernity*. Durham, NC: Duke University Press, 2005.

Williams, Justin. *Rhymin' and Stealin': Musical Borrowing in Hip-Hop*. Ann Arbor: University of Michigan Press, 2013.

Williams, Raymond. *Television: Technology and Cultural Form*. London: Routledge, 1974.

Woods, Tyron P. "Hip-Hop and the 'Post-Racial' Legal Unconscious." *Journal of Race, Gender, and Poverty*, no. 35 (2009): 35–49.

Wynter, Sylvia. "On How We Mistook the Map for the Territory and Re-Imprisoned Ourselves in Our Unbearable Wrongness of Being, of Désêtre: Black Studies toward the Human Project." In *Not Only the Master's Tools: African-American Studies in Theory and Practice*, edited by Lewis R. Gordon and Jane Anna Gordon, 107–69. New York: Routledge, 2006.

Wynter, Sylvia. "Unsettling the Coloniality of Being/Power/Truth/Freedom: Towards the Human, After Man, Its Overrepresentation—An Argument." *CR: The New Centennial Review* 3, no. 3 (2003): 257–337.

Zooks, Kristal Brent. *I See Black People: The Rise and Fall of African American Owned Television and Radio*. New York: Nation, 2008.

216